Transforming HR

Creating Value through People

Transforming HR
Creating Value through People

Martin Reddington
Mark Williamson
Mark Withers

ELSEVIER
BUTTERWORTH
HEINEMANN

AMSTERDAM BOSTON HEIDELBERG LONDON NEW YORK OXFORD
PARIS SAN DIEGO SAN FRANCISCO SINGAPORE SYDNEY TOKYO

Elsevier Butterworth-Heinemann
Linacre House, Jordan Hill, Oxford OX2 8DP
30 Corporate Drive, Burlington, MA 01803

First published 2005

British Library Cataloguing in Publication Data
A catalogue record for this book is available from the British Library

Library of Congress Cataloguing in Publication Data
A catalogue record for this book is available from the Library of Congress

ISBN 0 7506 6447 9

For information on all Elsevier Butterworth-Heinemann
publications visit our website at www.bh.com

Typeset by Charon Tec Pvt. Ltd, Chennai, India
www.charontec.com
Printed and bound in Great Britain

Contents

Foreword

Contemporary organisations face constant pressure to enhance levels of service and productivity whilst also improving levels of cost efficiency. The volatility of the external environment and the rapid pace of technological change increasingly demand innovative means of improving business performance and securing competitive advantage. People are increasingly recognised as the prime source of competitive advantage and the need for effective people management is therefore more important than ever before. The responsibility for effective people management is shared between senior managers, HR professionals and line managers but the challenges facing today's organisations provide an ideal opportunity for the HR function to demonstrate its ability to contribute to organisational performance at a strategic level. To take advantage of this opportunity it is necessary not only to recognise the changes that are required but also to identify the steps to ensure that they can be implemented effectively.

Whilst much has been written about strategic HR management and its contribution to organisational performance, real life examples of what works and what doesn't remain thin on the ground. We recognise that HR professionals and senior managers alike face a sometimes overwhelming pressure to follow trends or apply quick-fixes to a wide range of people management challenges and it can be difficult to get impartial advice about what to change and how to change it in order to create lasting results. We have therefore developed this series to bridge the gap between theory and implementation by providing workable solutions to complex people management issues and by sharing organisational experiences. The books within this series draw on live examples of strategic HR in practice and offer practical insights, tools and frameworks that will help to transform the individual and functional delivery of HR within a variety of organisational contexts.

Taking its rightful place in this series, ***Transforming HR*** shows how HR can be at the leading edge of organisational transformation. Drawing on their extensive practitioner and consultancy experience, the authors have created a vision of the new world of HR in which the benefits to the business are obvious. HR is under significant pressure to transform its service delivery model and provide measurable value, both in terms of service quality and cost effectiveness. This book outlines how investing in HR transformation and the technologies to support more effective people management in organisations pays significant ongoing dividends. The authors are aware that demonstrating an appropriate return on investment can be difficult, especially when competing priorities for scarce resources can mean that obtaining funding for worthwhile projects often puts HR at the back of the queue. Readers are guided through the process of how to build a compelling case for organisational change as well as a step-by-step approach to implementing the HR value model. Effective change management is the foundation for more effective delivery and the authors demonstrate how to drive out the benefits of transformation. The authors outline not only the process of change, including stakeholder engagement, but how HR roles can be reconfigured to add more strategic value. The book is eminently readable, practical and contains contributions from a number of leading practitioners in a range of sectors. For HR professionals seeking to bring about significant and effective change in their own service delivery we can think of few better models to follow than the approach mapped out in this book.

Julie Beardwell
Principal Lecturer in Human Resource Management and Strategy
De Montfort University

Linda Holbeche
Director of Research
Roffey Park Institute

Preface

This book has been written in response to the considerable demand by HR practitioners for robust practical advice in changing the way human resource management is undertaken in organisations – HR transformation. Our conversations with HR practitioners have lifted up three substantive needs. Firstly, to walk through the process of change from "starting out", right through to "evaluating the outcomes" of efforts. Secondly, to suggest ways to ensure HR transformation is joined up – that technology and process change is fully integrated with change around capabilities, culture and structure. Thirdly, to address critical questions which are reflected in our chapter headings.

The contents draw on our experiences, and the experiences of a number of leading HR practitioners, of implementing HR transformation for a wide range of organisations. So the material we present, and the principles we advance, are our experience of what works, underpinned as necessary by academic argument but not stifled by it. The contents have been tried and tested and have proved to have been helpful at the cutting edge of organisational change.

Our sincere thanks go to Linda Holbeche, Director of Research at the Roffey Park Institute, Horsham, UK. Linda has been a great sponsor, encourager and mentor to us throughout. She commissioned the initial masterclass that provided the catalyst for us to capture our experiences about HR transformation and to articulate them more coherently. We are grateful for the subsequent opportunity to publish our masterclass as one of Roffey Park's guides. We would also like to thank the CEO of Roffey Park, John Gilkes, and all the members of the marketing and desktop publishing teams for their help and support.

We would also like to thank our clients, without whom there would be no book. We are particularly indebted to all of the senior practitioners who have allowed us to interview them on their experiences of HR transformation, and who have shared with us in such a candid way the highs and lows of their transformation journey. We give full and proper acknowledgment to their contribution in the section "Contributing Senior Practitioners".

Special thanks must go to Matthew Tickle of Partners for Change. Matthew has travelled each step of the way with us in helping us to prepare and write this book, drawing on his previous publishing experience to guide us through some complex and difficult challenges at different stages of the journey of composition. Laura Perkins, who provided invaluable help with general administrative support, ably assisted him.

We would also like to thank all those who have been kind enough to review drafts and help us make our points more clearly. In particular, we would like to thank Olivia Warburton.

Finally, we would like to thank our respective families, who have been great supporters and encouragers.

Martin Reddington
Mark Williamson
Mark Withers

The Authors

Martin Reddington

MBA; BSc (Hons); DMS; MCMI; MIPR; MIEE

A graduate of Aston University, Martin obtained his MBA at Roffey Park in 1999. He spent the early part of his career working in the nuclear power industry in various engineering capacities before moving into corporate strategy and public affairs. He later moved into the telecommunications sector with NYNEX plc, which was merged into Cable & Wireless Communications in 1997. Martin managed the brand launch of the new company and then global communications for Cable & Wireless plc as part of its millennium readiness programme.

In January 2000, he was appointed Programme Director of e-HR Transformation at Cable & Wireless. This global programme received prestigious acclaim at the National Business Awards and Human Resources Excellence Awards in 2002.

After leaving Cable & Wireless in October 2002, Martin blends academic research with consultancy. His doctorate in Business Administration at Bournemouth University is examining the perceptions that managers have towards e-HR and how these perceptions can affect future HR-led investment decisions.

Martin frequently runs workshops and masterclasses on e-HR transformation. He passionately advocates the need for HR to measure its effectiveness within the business and to include in these measures accurate and meaningful perception analysis from its principal customers.

Mark Williamson MBA, BEng (Hons)

Mark is a Director of Partners for Change, a management consultancy that focuses on enabling organisations to realise maximum value and benefit from business change, especially where technology is a major driver of that change. Mark led the team from Partners for Change that supported Martin Reddington and the e-HR programme team at Cable & Wireless – a project for which Partners for Change was recognised by a Guardian/Management Consultancies Association Best Management Practice Award in 2002.

In his work with clients, Mark specialises in business performance improvement through business change management and implementation; business and information strategy planning; and evidence-based planning and action. He has spearheaded Partners for Change's work in HR transformation with its focus on business and HR strategy alignment, programme definition and mobilisation, business case development, HR process definition and change management within HR and across the line functions. He is especially interested and adept in building the linkages between the technical design and technology elements of HR transformation programmes with the business processes and the benefits that ensue.

During his career Mark has undertaken assignments in a wide variety of industries and business functional areas, giving him a very broad base of project and programme experience particularly in HR and e-HR transformation. Mark's recent HR clients have included: AstraZeneca, Amersham, Barclays, Inland Revenue, Novartis and Cable & Wireless.

Before joining Partners for Change, Mark spent 3 years with CTG, an international professional services company, and prior to that 6 years with Rolls Royce in a number of line roles. During his early career, Mark laid the foundations for his subsequent consulting career and interests by gaining a thorough grounding in business analysis and programme management, through experience in the UK, mainland Europe and the USA. Following his first degree in Engineering from Sheffield University in 1987, Mark was awarded his MBA from Warwick Business School in 2000.

Mark Withers Chartered Fellow, CIPD; MSc; BSc (Econ)

Mark is Managing Director of Mightywaters Consulting Limited, a management consultancy that specialises in strategic HR and organisational development. He has over 20 years' experience of working in the field of human relations and organisational behaviour and throughout his career he has been closely involved in a wide range of large-scale business transformations.

His early career was spent in line HR roles with Shell and a Whitbread/Allied Domecq joint venture, where he also gained early top team experience as a member of the business's Executive Committee. In 1990 he joined Price Waterhouse Management Consultants (PwC), working in the areas of HR consulting and strategic change.

At PwC Mark worked with a wide range of private and public sector organisations both in the UK and, internationally, in Hungary, Switzerland, the Caribbean, Poland and the USA. He has also delivered a number of global change projects for large organisations.

Since forming Mightywaters Consulting in 1998, Mark has worked mainly with senior business and HR teams to support business change and transformation. His clients include National Grid Transco plc, Cable & Wireless plc, BT, NCH, Barclaycard, The British Museum and AWG plc.

Mark is passionate about the need to create working environments where people are valued and are able to make purposeful contributions to the success of their organisation. He is equally passionate about the contribution HR professionals can make in nurturing and developing these high performance cultures.

Mark holds an undergraduate degree from the London School of Economics and a Masters in Organisational Behaviour from London University (Birkbeck College). He is a Chartered Fellow of the CIPD and has written and spoken on organisational change internationally.

Contributing Senior Practitioners

Steve Ashby began his varied HR career in New Zealand and Australia with a variety of national and international businesses. He has worked in the heavy industry, horticulture, manufacturing, packaging, brewing and food-related sectors. He joined ESS Support Services Worldwide, a division of the Compass group, in 2002 as International HR Director. ESS provides a full range of remote site support services for clients in the defence, oil and gas and mining sectors as well as facilities management services in urban environments.

Steve's primary task is mobilising then supporting newly won contracts across Africa, the Middle East (most recently in Iraq and Kuwait), Europe, Eurasia and South East Asia. He is developing innovative approaches to the recruitment and selection of top-grade talent for positions in those countries. He is particularly interested in developing e-HR as a means of transforming bureaucratic HR processes into tools managers want to use.

Steve is passionate about the commercial value high-quality HR can add to an organisation and believes that any HR function that cannot show significant demonstrable value to the business should be disbanded immediately.

Philip Barr has held a range of senior HR roles, most recently as HR Director for Cable & Wireless's UK, US and European businesses. A graduate of the University of Cambridge, he has worked in a variety of HR roles for 20 years. Before joining Cable & Wireless, he was an HR Director for Barclays Bank, Retail Banking. Previously he held HR Director and other senior HR roles in Barclaycard, The Boots Company and Unilever. He has a strong interest in learning and development and holds a Masters qualification in neuro-linguistic-programming.

Richard Brady is the Managing Director of Mentis Consulting Limited, a team of corporate psychologists and HR specialists that helps organisations to attract, develop and retain talented people.

Richard graduated in 1989 with an honours degree in Psychology from the University of Birmingham. He has a Masters degree in Occupational Psychology from the University of London.

Since 1997 he has worked primarily with large international companies, government departments and agencies helping to design and deliver innovative and effective approaches to selecting and developing people, executive selection programmes, 360-degree feedback systems, coaching, and employee feedback mechanisms. He has a special interest in the psychological aspects of performance management and organisational development, and he has project-managed some substantial organisation change projects.

Janice Cook is the Director of Human Resources at NCH, the children's charity. Her career began by working for a national government organisation. She then moved into the private sector, then local government, and has spent the last 5 years in NCH, one of the UK's largest not-for-profit organisations working with children. Janice is a Chartered Fellow of the Chartered Institute of Personnel and Development. She has recently spent 3 years as a Trustee of the Multiple Sclerosis Society and 3 years as Vice Chair. Her sister, who sadly passed away in 2001, had struggled against Multiple Sclerosis for 20 years. She co-edited a book called "The Learning Organization in the Public Services" (Cook *et al.*, 1996, Gower).

Helen Corey is the Head of Consumer Finance Strategic Initiatives for MBNA Europe, where she is responsible for leveraging existing and current financial products. Helen is a recognised expert in HR and information technology. For over a decade, through senior executive and consulting roles, she has created, designed, implemented and managed HR information systems. Helen's passion for organisational information has allowed her to champion and enhance HR transformation for companies such as Cisco Systems, Rhone-Poulenc Rorer, Dun & Bradstreet, Donaldson, Lufkin & Jenrette, Swiss Bank, Bell Atlantic and First USA.

Andrew Field is the HR Operations Manager with the London Stock Exchange (LSE). His main role is to introduce e-enabled technology to support all aspects of HR services to the business. Key drivers are the quality and speed of services, along with the reduction of administration costs to the business. Previously, Andrew worked for Cable & Wireless as a project manager on their global e-HR SAP rollout. Andrew is an experienced manager, having worked in various HR roles for both the London Underground and Cable & Wireless before joining the LSE. Andrew's main career interests lie within the application of technology to HR services, change management and developing HR to become a more business-focused organisation.

Claudia Hall joined Nextel in September 2001 as the Vice-President of Recruiting. In this role, Claudia established a centralised recruiting organisation designed to strengthen the company's ability to attract and retain employees while at the same time driving down recruitment costs.

She has a degree from Hood College Frederick, Maryland and studied at the University of Strasbourg, France. She is fluent in French.

Claudia has over 20 years' experience in the recruiting industry, both in executive search and on the corporate side. Prior to Nextel, Claudia was the Director of Recruiting for Cable & Wireless in the US, where she set up a nationwide recruiting organisation, which she then modelled for global rollout in the UK, Ireland, seven countries in mainland Europe and Japan. At Wang Global in Boston she was the Director of Recruiting responsible for developing and running a nationwide recruiting organisation supporting all government and private sector business. During her 10 years at Unisys she ran nationwide recruitment programs for DoD and Federal businesses.

Randall C. Harris is the Senior Vice-President of Human Resources for Nextel Communications. His responsibilities include general oversight and management of Nextel's corporate-wide HR activities.

Prior to joining Nextel in 1999, Randall was Senior Vice-President and Chief Human Resources Officer at Sodexho Marriott Services, a $4.5 billion company providing contract management/outsourcing solutions to corporations and healthcare and education clients. He has also held senior management positions at Sprint, First Data Corporation, Avanti Communications and Dun & Bradstreet.

Randall received a Bachelor of Science degree from the US Naval Academy in 1973 and a Masters Degree in Human Resource Management from the American University in 1985.

Maggie Hurt is the HR Director for National Grid Transco. She has a BSc Honours degree in Behavioural Science and a Masters Degree in Personnel Management. She has over 28 years' experience of HR in blue-chip companies and in a variety of sectors. Her working life started with Thorn EMI, learning the basic HR role in the domestic appliance field. She then moved on to Lucas Industries, working in the automotive, aerospace and electronic sectors in a variety of senior HR roles, culminating in international assignments, including 3 years based in Paris. During this time, Lucas went through two major mergers with US companies, so she is well used to the change agenda. She joined National Grid in January 2001 and was an active force in the merger with Transco in 2002. She is passionate about the role HR can play in securing a better bottom line and enabling an excellent working environment in all aspects ... provided that there is the right calibre of HR partnering.

Vance Kearney is Vice-President for Human Resources Oracle Corporation Europe, having joined Oracle in 1991 as Director of Human Resources. Prior to this, he was with Data General Corporation UK Limited as their Director of Human Resources.

He has an honours degree in Business Studies.

Vance has overall responsibility for all aspects of HR and staff policies, including salaries, pay and benefits, employment terms and conditions, management and personal development, recruitment and resourcing strategies and business organisation.

Vance is the spokesperson on all matters employment-related, and has a special interest in HR systems and technology as it relates to HR and the management of people.

Kath Lowey began her career with Marconi, then the Plessey Telecomms Company, in 1980 in the services business providing support to field based operations. Two years later she transferred to Headquarters HR in Liverpool, taking up a role supporting employee relations and remuneration activities, and was later promoted to remuneration and administration manager for the Customer Services Division. Kath progressed in HR general management, undertaking several HR Director roles within different parts of the Marconi business and heading the HR Shared Service function globally, before taking up her current role as Head of HR for the Northern Europe business in 2003.

Miles Warner began his career with Schlumberger in 1985, and held a succession of international engineering and managerial posts before becoming the Personnel Director for Schlumberger Wireline and Testing in 1997. Between 2000 and 2002, he was Personnel Director for WesternGeco, with primary responsibility for the merger of two international geophysics companies into a new organisation. In his current role as HR Services Director, he has responsibility for developing the HR services business within SchlumbergerSema. Miles has a particular interest in the field of HR transformation from a human science perspective, and has actively championed the enhancement of the HR role both within and outside his organisation.

Tony Williams is Head of HR Shared Services for the Royal Bank of Scotland Group, supporting over 200,000 employees, pensioners and former employees of the Group. He is responsible for a wide selection of transactional and professional HR services as well as more specialised functions including HR information strategy, corporate governance, business restructuring, change management and acquisitions.

He is a qualified banker, has an MBA in Financial Services and has been with the RBS group for 6 years.

In 2003, he collected the HR Excellence Award for "M&A contribution" presented by HR Excellence Magazine, and in 2004 he collected the "outstanding contribution to shared services thought leader" award presented by the European Shared Services Network. He is an active member of the Shared Services & Business Process Outsourcing Advisory Board (SPBOA) and the Conference Board of the European Council on Shared Services.

His book with Peter Reilly, *How to Get the Best Out of HR – The Shared Services Option*, was published in February 2003.

Introduction

For many functions, HR transformation is currently one of their critical deliverables. As with all change, there are huge possibilities and exciting opportunities that lie at the end of the implementation journey. However, the obstacles stand in the way of effective implementation are considerable, and many HR functions lose their way or find that they have failed to deliver the outcomes that were initially anticipated.

One of the key themes of this book is that the advances around e-HR provide organisations with great opportunities to re-think the way HR management is undertaken in organisations and yet technology-driven change is often disconnected from other changes that are needed around capabilities, culture and structure. To transform HR effectively, change needs to be integrated. There needs to be an investment in e-HR, absolutely, but technology is not the end in itself. Technology is only a tool – an enabler – that supports more effective ways of working and of managing the human capital component of business organisations. Before any technology can be effectively deployed, the fundamental approaches to people management must be transformed. In most cases, this involves transforming the way HR management is done in organisations and the repositioning of the HR function: its ways of working, as well as the ways in which the HR function interacts with the wider organisation and external providers.

So What is Different About This Book?

Businesses do not have time to waste. The velocity of change is increasing and businesses need to find new ways to compete effectively. These new market realities require new organisational capabilities to ensure that customer, investor and employee expectations are met. There has never been a greater need, nor has there been a bigger opportunity, for those engaged in the field of people and organisations to make a strong contribution.

This book will help organisations to adapt quickly and build new organisational capabilities. It is about building organisations so that they compete effectively in their chosen markets; delivering value to customers, superior performance and opportunity to employees.

So what has this got to do with transforming HR? It is our contention that value-adding HR will have a critical influence on the ability of the business to respond quickly to change in its competitive environment. Why? Because the change agenda – the development of organisational capability – is the domain where HR professionals *should* be deploying their knowledge and expertise. If done well, the questions being asked about the value of HR professionals in organisations will be answered with interest! To make this contribution, the HR function must use e-HR and the opportunities presented by different service delivery models to get the administration right and transactional costs under control. Through partnership with line management, it needs to acquire and deploy new capabilities to help organisations to change and ultimately transform.

There is no guarantee of a place for HR professionals in future organisations. HR management will be undertaken for sure. But whether there is a HR function, as such, will depend on whether it can transform sufficiently to demonstrate that it is creating value through people. Our view is that HR transformation needs to integrate technology, process, structure and people/cultural aspects of change and that HR professionals need to develop and deploy the capabilities to achieve this.

So why should you invest a few hours in reading this book? We offer you four good reasons:

1. It is a "how to" book. We do not claim to have a magic wand. But we offer approaches that we have seen work and that will help you to make decisions that are right for your business.
2. We offer approaches that also deliver quickly. We present the content of this book because we are assured of its effective application across a wide variety of organisations.
3. This book helps you to build your HR tool kit. The approaches we present in this book to help you transform HR can also be deployed by HR professionals to change their businesses.

4. We include practitioner perspectives from a number of leading HR professionals who are on the transformation journey and are able to "tell it as it is".

Whilst this book is highly practical in its focus, the approach used to effect HR transformation is underpinned by a small number of robust change management tools and techniques. These tools and frameworks are presented in *Chapter 1: Getting Started* and form an important backdrop to the remaining content. It is recommended that you take time to familiarise yourself with this material.

The remainder of the book is structured as follows:

Chapter 2: Envisioning the New World of HR sets out a process and practical tools that will help you to get stakeholder agreement on how HR is currently being delivered in your business and the future HR delivery model you want to create. This work is an important initial phase of the transformation journey and frames how HR will deliver value in the future.

Chapter 3: Service Delivery Approaches tackles and addresses issues around the use of external suppliers and, in particular, the issues you need to take into account in deciding whether to outsource or not. The outsourcing debate is explained and practical tests offered to help you with your decisions.

Chapter 4: Making the Business Case for Transformation naturally follows on from the envisioning work and service delivery approaches. It explores the key considerations in developing the business case for HR transformation and, in particular, the case for capital investment in e-HR and HR transformation. In addition to defining benefits and costs (the so-called "hard" elements of the case), the approaches to building business commitment are also explored (the so-called "softer" elements of the case). Taken together, these hard and soft elements build commitment and credibility and establish the foundations for transformation.

Chapter 5: Stakeholder Engagement and Programme Management provides practical tools that enable you to understand who your key stakeholders are and their likely reactions to your HR transformation proposals. We also present ways to move stakeholder opinion away from resistance to commitment. In addition, we consider how programme management approaches can be used to engage purposefully with stakeholders through ongoing communication and the use of governance structures. We also explore issues and risks around e-HR-led HR transformation.

Chapter 6: Implementation: Structure, Culture and Capability focuses on the organisation, roles and capabilities in the newly transformed HR function. In particular, we explore the capabilities needed in the new business partner role and the ways to build these capabilities. We also consider the impact of HR transformation on the role of line manager.

Chapter 7: Implementation: Process and Technology sets out the main considerations in delivering the process and technology aspects of HR transformation, including the impact of e-HR on employees and managers. In addition, we explore how to track key benefits areas and how to measure and evaluate implementation effectiveness.

Chapter 8: Taking Stock and Moving Forward explores ways to review progress in HR transformation and sets out our thoughts on future directions for HR in organisations.

Chapter 9: Summary of Key Points and Actions is the final chapter and collates the key actions and themes captured from the preceding chapters.

The content of this book is aimed at organisations that may be at different stages of the HR transformation journey. Why not check for yourself? If you can relate to any of the statements below, then we confidently predict that this book is going to be of value to you and your organisation:

- We are starting to think about the use of e-HR in my organisation.
- We know we need to implement e-HR, but have not yet developed a clear vision and/or business case.
- We have different stakeholder views about what HR transformation should mean for our organisation.
- We have not really thought about the impact of e-HR on the way HR is done in the organisation and/or its impact on what the HR function does.
- We need to think about the benefits of outsourcing parts of HR.
- We have not really defined the benefits of HR transformation.
- We need to have an effective way of delivering HR transformation.
- We are in the process of e-HR-led HR transformation, but are stuck.
- We have made some progress in HR transformation, but believe that there are still improvements that can be made.

■ We believe we have completed our HR transformation and are beginning to consider what is next.

Overall, the book is seeking to educate and inform HR practitioners and line managers about the challenges and opportunities presented by HR transformation, and to stimulate debate and discussion about the possible evolutionary next steps for the HR profession.

1

Getting Started

This chapter sets out the foundation approaches we use when supporting HR transformation. We strongly recommend that you take time to engage with and understand these approaches, as they will be referenced throughout the book. The point of this chapter is to equip you with the tools to address the following questions:

- How do I make HR transformation changes stick?
- How do I frame a transformation project?
- What can I do to bring people on board with the proposed changes?

These are the classic organisational development (OD) questions, and although given within the context of HR transformation, the approaches we discuss are applicable equally to any other large business change.

Chapter Structure

Key Themes

- Effective business change benefits from the use of tried and tested OD tools and approaches.
- HR professionals often fail to influence as effectively as they could because they lack a strong theoretical base.
- To develop a stronger theoretical base, HR professionals need to focus on the development of three mindsets: "systems mindset", "process consulting mindset" and "project mindset".
- Systems thinking sees HR transformation within the context of the wider organisational (and extra-organisational) system and integrates more effectively different facets of HR transformation.
- Process consulting focuses on the steps needed to effect change so that at each stage of the transformation journey there is constant learning and engagement with reality.
- A project mindset shapes HR transformation using the principles and practices of project and programme management.

1.1 Context

This book is not a theoretical text. It is intended to be practical, and is something that HR practitioners will actually find useful.

It may therefore appear odd that we start by making a case for theory. We know from our dealings with HR professionals at all organisational levels that HR folk are the "doers". They want to know about what works, and what they can use. They are pragmatic.

We agree with a bias for action – up to a point. We believe that to be an effective doer, to make interventions that work, to be pragmatic, you need to know *why* things done in this or that way work better. That is where theory comes in. Theory helps to explain why things happen. Good theory is the product of observable and generalised patterns. It is the product of shared knowledge and shared experience. Without theory, HR practices and interventions are little more than isolated acts. We need a reference point to inform our actions. It is our contention that one of the reasons that HR has not been as influential in businesses as it should have been is the result of a real and lasting lack of engagement with our theoretical base.

It is not as if the theoretical base does not exist. HR professionals can draw from a strong theoretical hinterland: psychology, sociology, economics, business management, political science, law and so on. Each of these areas enables us to observe and analyse the role of people in organisations from different perspectives and make powerful contributions to complex business issues.

Based on our collective experiences of architecting and implementing transformations of the HR function, we intend to show in this book how a small number of theoretical models, frameworks and tools can help to bring about more effective change and transformation. The point of this chapter is to set out these approaches, with the remainder of the book focused strongly on practical application. Having made a case for theory, this book does not attempt to give an exhaustive overview of prevailing theoretical models, but rather dwells on a few of the practices that have worked for us in the real world of organisations.

We have chosen the approaches in this chapter is because of the following:

- They are actually *helpful* – enabling us to shape HR transformation in a way that accelerates the pace of change, maximises buy-in and delivers anticipated benefits.
- They are *tried and tested* – enabling us not only to learn from other organisations but to deploy these models and frameworks in a way that gives structure and focus to workshops and other interventions.
- They need to become *part of the HR professional's tool kit* – enabling HR professionals to take into their organisations a theoretical body of knowledge that will support their clients in bringing about effective organisational change.

1.2 The OD Role of HR

What does the term "organisational development", or OD, mean for you?

It may mean nothing. Alternatively, it may conjure up one of a number of meanings, ranging from the soft and fluffy side of people management epitomised by the 1960s OD movement to organisational redesign, to organisational therapy and the psychological aspects of organisational life such as group effectiveness and individual motivation, to more recent incarnations such as resprayed management/leadership development and talent management. Our work with a wide range of organisations suggests that this spectrum of understanding about OD is currently prevalent in people's thinking.

In this book we use the term "OD" in a very specific way. Although our view of OD in many ways reflects aspects of each of the above, it is essentially a broader interpretation. For us, OD is about the effective management of change – intervening in the organisational system in ways that will help it to adapt and thrive in response to changes in the external environment.

For HR there are some profound implications. Clearly, senior line management have a key role in executing business change, including the people and organisational aspects of change. However, if we accept that HR has a strong theoretical base in the domains of people and organisation, then there is a case for a strong functional/professional contribution in the area of business change.

This means not only operating within the traditional HR skill areas – managing headcount reductions, appointing to new structures, skilling people to perform new roles, managing employee relations, etc. – but also being able to deploy broader OD skills with clients. This means being able to contribute in shaping the business change in the first place; construct a change programme, facilitate workshops, deploy change management tools and techniques throughout, support individuals as they adjust psychologically to change, and so on. We do not stop doing the traditional HR work. But the OD areas outlined above is the stuff that gets noticed and adds value. Why? Because OD puts HR professionals at the heart of business change, and being smart at adapting to change in the external environment is what makes for successful businesses.

Whilst this is not a particularly new challenge for the HR function, developments in technology now leave HR with no excuses for remaining in the transactional/operational zones. If the internal HR function is to exist at all, it needs to be able to make its contribution at the heart of business primarily as a strategic partner and change agent.

This book is about HR seizing the opportunities it now has and, enabled by technology, executing its own transformation. In Chapter 6 we discuss in greater detail the role of the HR professional in a transformed function and the capabilities they need to acquire. At the heart of this transformed role is the contribution HR professionals must make to the development of their organisations.

1.3 Three Mindsets

To become effective in the area of OD, HR professionals need to develop three mindsets:

- *Systems mindset*: A recognition and understanding that all organisations are open systems. They are systems in that they maintain their existence, and function as a whole, through the interaction of different parts. We discuss these parts in greater detail in Section 1.4. Organisations are "open systems" in that they can influence and be influenced by the external environment.
- *Process consulting mindset*: An appreciation that, as HR professionals, it is our role to help our internal clients, deal with reality and find solutions that will work for them. This does not mean abandoning our expertise, but it does mean that we need to deploy our expertise in a way that leaves ownership of the problem and solution with our internal clients/customers.
- *Project mindset*: An adoption of the principles and approaches of project management to organise and shape the work more effectively so that activity and effort are focused on the work that will add most value.

The models and frameworks that underpin these mindsets are explored below. What we hope will become clear as you read this book is that these mindsets are not only key to effective transformation of the HR function, but critical to HR's transformed role; expressing the key capabilities that HR professionals need to develop to engage purposefully with their organisational clients.

As Figure 1.1 illustrates, at the heart of these three mindsets exists contingent thinking.

Contingent thinking forces us to take account of the unique situation and context within which we are trying to solve business problems. It forces us to think through scenarios based on cause and effect: "*If* we do this, *then* the consequences are likely to be these ..." What is also important is that contingent thinking moves us away from attempts to

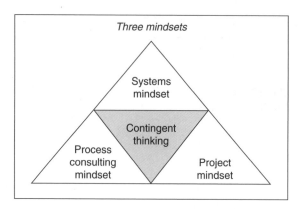

Figure 1.1 Three mindsets

adopt without adapting acknowledged "best practices". We must learn from others, yes. But we must work out for ourselves the solutions that will best serve our business and help us in sustaining competitive advantage.

1.4 Systems Mindset

We defined what we mean by a systems mindset in Section 1.3. A systems mindset embraces the core change management tools and frameworks that have helped us in supporting HR transformation. A systems mindset reflects that in any change programme, and HR transformation is no different, we cannot ever be in total control of change. So there is recognition that sometimes we do things intentionally in organisations that actually lead to the outcome we intended; sometimes we do things intentionally that result in outcomes we had not intended; that we make unintentional actions that may help or hinder us and there are also outcomes we never see.

What this means is that however intentional we are with our interventions in the organisational system, we cannot assume that the outcome will be what we intended, and nor can we assume that what we see is the only outcome. This means that we need to obtain feedback and take stock as we move through a change process. This approach is explored further in Section 1.5. What systems thinking does is to give us tools that will enable us to make more powerful and purposeful intentional interventions in order to steer the change process more effectively.

Above are the three core change models and frameworks that have helped us to make better intentional interventions. For each we will set out the model or framework and then illustrate how it has been used.

Organisational Levers Model

Figure 1.2 represents visually the organisational levers model.

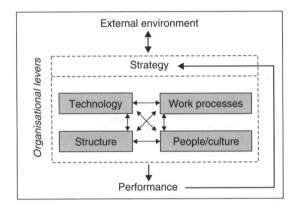

Figure 1.2 Organisational levers

The expression "levers" is used to represent the different parts in an organisational system. A systems approach seeks to integrate change across each of the organisational levers. As the organisation is an open system (as described above), each lever will interact to a greater or lesser degree with the other levers and the external environment.

As organisations are complex systems, what we often face during periods of change are multiple changes, initiated in different areas of the wider organisational system, that can clash and compete as much as reinforce one another.

Let us explore the model further. The main elements of the model are the following:

External environment: In this framework the external environment can be seen in two ways.

Firstly, as the environment external to your organisation as a whole. This external environment includes forces for change that come from government, regulation, societal changes, legislative change, competition, customer requirements, shareholder expectations, products and service provision, etc. These are the forces we need to understand and interpret in order to develop strategy.

Secondly, in the case of HR transformation, the external environment to an HR function can be seen in terms of the above plus the other functions and departments within the organisation but external to the HR function. So, in this instance, competition may be seen as alternative suppliers of HR services, customers will be primarily the internal clients, services will be the things that the HR function actually delivers to clients, etc.

The external environment is clearly a "change lever", as organisations are not insulated from external changes; for example, a change in customer expectations requires the organisation to consider how it will respond.

Internal organisational levers: In this framework there are four internal organisational levers. You might have come across other similar models that may use different terminology. It really does not matter what terminology is used or how many organisational levers are defined. The important point is the principle that the organisation is a system comprised of different parts that interact. We will use the following internal organisational levers:

- *Structure* – which includes consideration of areas such as reporting structure (formal and virtual), job and work group design, sourcing, role expectations/measures, facilities and organisational integrating mechanisms (those things that help people to work together more effectively).
- *Technology* – the technological infrastructure of the organisation.
- *Work processes* – the key work processes, reflecting both the services that are delivered and the channels through which they are delivered.
- *People and culture* – the skills and knowledge, core capabilities, values, style and behaviours.

Performance: Performance is the final lever. Although changes in performance are often driven by the external environment (e.g. shareholder expectations or the realisation that new benchmarks have been set), it is important to recognise performance as a separate driver for change, not least because it has such a high focus in organisational life. We need to know whether we are achieving key performance indicators, being cost efficient, delivering value for money, achieving return on investment, delivering to customer expectations, being competitive against external benchmarks, setting and delivering to agreed service levels. Also, decisions around capital investment should be linked to anticipated benefits. Therefore, in making the case for investment in technology we need to be clear about the performance gains which we expect to bring to the organisation.

Strategy is part of the organisational levers model, but not highlighted as a lever in its own right. Clearly strategy sets direction, but essentially it is the product of considering what we need to do inside the organisation in response to actual or anticipated change in the external environment. As such it is a reference point, a context, for change.

Change may be initiated in any of these organisational levers, and a systems mindset will recognise that there will be an impact on the other levers.

Okay, so that is the theory. But how would this model be applied in practice? Let us take the example of technology-driven change in HR: moving transactional and operational HR activities to an e-HR platform. As we consider the above model, we may easily make the link between *technology* and *work processes*, as many HR processes will become embedded in the new e-HR solutions. But do the other organisational levers come into play?

The *external environment* to the organisation may be driving the case for e-HR transformation through a number of drivers: it is now technologically possible and more affordable; other organisations are adopting e-HR, setting new benchmarks; new outsourcing possibilities are being offered, etc. There may also be drivers for change inside the organisation but external to HR, such as higher client expectations about the services that HR will provide; the desire of managers to have information about their people on demand, and so on. E-HR-driven transformation will affect individual employees and managers in terms of how HR services are delivered and the ownership of the data.

So we can see that there is a clear interaction between the external world and change being driven from the technology lever. But how are the other organisational levers impacted?

Structure may be impacted in a number of ways. The types of roles needed in HR will change and the number of people involved in transactional work/handling enquiries are likely to change. Transactional and enquiry work may be outsourced (resulting in a different organisational sourcing model) or brought into a shared service centre (perhaps even outside the direct reporting lines of the HR function or in multiple centres). What remains in the HR function may be a different type of professional role. The need to integrate the work of HR management may increase as HR delivery channels become broader and outside the HR function's direct reporting lines. What line managers and employees are expected to do may change.

When organisational structures change, the way in which work is organised will also change. This means that organisational boundaries (whether between different roles or between different teams or groups) must be addressed in order to ensure that work is properly integrated. This means considering aspects of organisation that integrate work activity, such as communication processes, cross-organisational teams/committees and other forms of reporting and governance.

Therefore not only structure is impacted, but also there is potential for it to be impacted quite profoundly.

Performance requirements from HR are certain to be affected. There may be fresh challenges around HR costs or ratios, expectations around service levels, delivery of a different kind of professional HR agenda. The way performance is monitored may also change, with clearer metrics and more transparent data.

As a consequence of the above, *people and culture* are impacted. New roles require new capabilities. Clients need to learn new skills. The relationship between HR and the line needs to be recast.

Hopefully, this illustration brings the organisational levers model to life and shows how change in one organisational lever impacts the others. What this model also illustrates is that if change initiatives are contained and not joined up, then the risk of conflict and dissonance between competing changes becomes very high.

In this book we will show how this model has been used practically to support the transformation process: to undertake a gap analysis, to support the envisioning of the new HR, to shape the transformation programme and work streams, and to monitor/mark progress.

Change Cycle Model

This model recognises that intentional change is a cyclical process. Like any model, it seeks to simplify in order to draw out general principles. The change cycle shows that any change tends to go through four main stages:

- developing a clear case for wanting to change,
- planning the change,
- implementing the change,
- reviewing and sustaining the change.

Underpinning each of these stages is the need to secure and sustain commitment to the change. At the heart of the change cycle is the need to realise agreed benefits. The change cycle is shown in Figure 1.3.

In reality, change is not quite as logical and symmetrical as the model suggests. There are often overlaps between the stages and there is a need to rework the content of earlier stages.

Figure 1.3 shows the highest level of the change cycle. The next level of detail (Figure 1.4) shows the main activities that are undertaken in each of the four phases and the most important change tools that support that phase of work.

In applying this model, we have found that each phase represents a "gateway" that, if properly signed off, will enable you to proceed with a high degree of confidence to the next phase of work. If key stakeholders are not committed, or if circumstances change, the chances are that

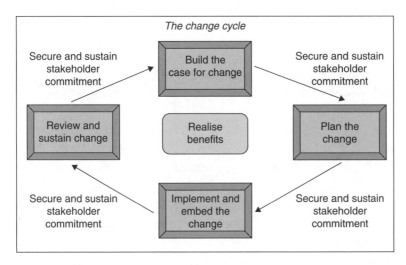

Figure 1.3 Change cycle

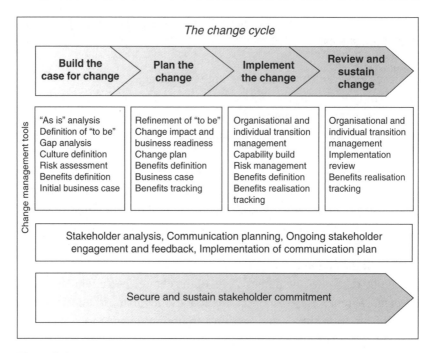

Figure 1.4 Change cycle – key activities and tools

you will need to remake the case for change at some point further down the change process. However painful it might be and however slow it might appear to be, there is little to be gained in trying to shortcut these phases.

Case Study

During one of the HR transformation projects we have supported, a great deal of effort was invested in making a compelling business case for change in HR to the various stakeholder groups. However, due to significant deterioration in the external business environment, what was thought to have been a clear mandate to proceed to the next phase proved not to be the case. The HR transformation team had to remake the case for change on a number of subsequent occasions to prove that the benefits justified the investment and for new stakeholders to satisfy themselves that there was a clear business case for change.

Change Equation Model

This change tool is extremely helpful in ensuring that both the rational and emotional aspects of change have been properly considered. Developed by Beckhard and Harris (1987), the change equation has been repackaged in a number of different ways over the years, and you may well have come across one of its various incarnations.

The change equation proposes that change is most likely to be successful when four conditions exist:

1. there must be dissatisfaction with the way things are
2. there must be a shared sense of how things should be in the future
3. there is agreement and clarity around the appropriate next step (note *not* the whole journey) to take to get from where you are now to where you want to be
4. there must be sufficient will amongst key stakeholders to make the change happen.

These conditions need to outweigh the perceived costs of change – money, time, resources, emotional, political etc.

This is an extremely versatile model, which can be used to support a wide range of interventions: at the early stages of change when there is a need to test commitment; as a means of reviewing progress; as an aid to shape stakeholder communication; as a way to get people talking about change and as a framework for workshop design.

Let us look at one example of how the change equation has been used. In this instance we used the change equation to shape a series of interventions with key stakeholder groups to test whether there was sufficient commitment to the proposed HR transformation process.

Each person was asked to rate, out of 10, each of the dimensions in the equation. So if someone was dissatisfied with the current situation they gave a high rating, and so on. Ratings were then discussed so that different perspectives on the change were gathered and agreement was reached on those areas where further interventions needed to be made, for example, achieve greater clarity on the next steps that need to be taken.

If you only use these three models to develop your transformation effort, we can safely say that their application will significantly increase the probability of your integrating change and delivering target outcomes.

Throughout this book we will refer to these models and give further illustrations of their use in practice to help you make better interventions.

1.5 Process Consulting Mindset

Before describing in greater detail what a process consulting mindset is, it is perhaps fitting to start with a statement of what it is not. The word "process" has been popularised in management literature in the past decade, and has become mainly associated with business process re-engineering/work process redesign. HR work process re-engineering is certainly going to feature as one of the HR transformation work streams. But this is not what we mean by process consulting or the development of a process consulting mindset.

We seem to be restricted in our vocabulary in the world of management, so we need to continue to use the word "process", but in a very different way. If we think about what a process is – a number of steps that lead to an outcome – this may help us to understand better what we mean by process consulting.

A process consulting mindset is about *the way* we bring about change. The approach is about working with clients step by step through a change process. This involves taking account of new realities/information at each step and adjusting tactics accordingly. The change tools/frameworks mentioned in Section 1.4 can help this process. For example, the change equation is a good tool to use with stakeholders to develop a shared view of "where we are now" and the next practical steps that will best ensure progress. This means that those involved in the work of HR transformation (both internal and external consultants) must engage purposefully with their critical stakeholders. HR transformation is a collaborative effort, and when there are questions, concerns or resistance these must be properly dealt with rather than swept under the carpet. There is no place for those involved in leading work streams *doing* change to people.

Looking specifically at HR transformation, the relationship that the HR transformation programme team must establish with its internal clients should have the following goals in mind:

- Engage in actions (with individuals or groups) that are most likely to promote successful change.

- Establish a collaborative relationship.
- Work to solve problems in a way that they stay solved.
- Ensure that attention is given to both technical and relationship issues.
- Develop internal client commitment.
- Think constantly about how you can best deliver value.

To achieve this, it is necessary to work with clients through a change process. The HR transformation programme team brings tools, models, frameworks, technical know-how to the table. But the ownership must remain with the clients.

How is this achieved?

Firstly, by bringing our knowledge and expertise to the table in ways that enable our clients to take decisions, rather than presenting them with a *fait accompli*.

Secondly, by not remaining bound by the original plan. Regardless of how much time we may have invested in agreeing the future vision for HR and developing an implementation plan with our key client stakeholders, the reality of change is that the unexpected happens and we need to make adjustments to reflect whatever new reality we now face. Change is not achieved through a business version equivalent of "painting by numbers".

Thirdly, by focusing on the next practical step within the context of the overall programme goals (building on the change equation, "in the light of what we now know, what is our most purposeful next step to get us from where we are now to where we want to be?").

A process consulting mindset also accepts that resistance to change is natural and seeks to surface it and work with it, even if embracing resistance appears to slow down the programme. A process consulting mindset also recognises that there will be multiple interests and that it is necessary to invest in building a strong coalition (but not absolute consensus) around a change vision.

Features of the process consulting mindset that we will refer to in this book, and which help us to achieve the above, include the following tools:

- The use of a *straw man* to engage people in decision-making: this means making a proposal that is, robust enough to stand with credibility, but not so robust that it cannot be tested and potentially pulled apart and reconstructed. One of the main benefits of using a straw man is to surface opinion and issues so that areas of agreement are identified and disagreements resolved. We have found that the use of the straw man is a very effective way to accelerate decision-making.

- Ensuring key discussions and critical decisions are held in *workshops*. Often preceded by one-to-one meetings, workshops nevertheless have great value (and are time efficient if well structured) in bringing key stakeholders together to work through issues and take decisions. (Although frequently the most convenient way of meeting with stakeholders, a dependency on one-to-one meetings only is unlikely to lead to purposeful dialogue and collaborative working.)
- Adopting a *facilitation* role with key stakeholders: working with groups; being able to present information in ways that will engage key stakeholders; surface issues/resistance and areas of agreement; and mobilise to take the next step.

Let us look at an example of a process consulting approach in practice. We often start work around HR transformation with very different stakeholder perspectives on what HR transformation means. Even within the HR function, there can be considerable distance between people on questions such as: What is e-HR and how should it be deployed in our organisation? What should the HR function focus on? Which HR activities should be in-house or outsourced? What skills and capabilities should HR professionals possess? The approaches we will describe in this book show that investing in a process that engages people in conversations about critical questions concerning HR transformation is fruitful, productive and necessary. The process that is, co-created with clients allows them to work with the current reality. This approach builds checks and balances into the way change is implemented, allowing those leading the transformation to accelerate or slow down to ensure that stakeholders remain committed.

One final word on the development of a process consulting mindset. Whilst we would like to claim authorship of this style of working, we cannot. Our consulting approach has been heavily influenced by the work of Ed Schein (1998) and, if you are not familiar with his work, we commend it to you. You will find details in the references section.

1.6 Project Mindset

HR transformation must be run as a programme (i.e. a collection of projects) if it is to be in any way effective. When you consider the broader organisational system and include the people, culture and structural dimensions of HR transformation, the need for good programme management and project management skills does not need to be spelled out.

Why the focus on developing a project mindset?

If an organisation is serious about HR transformation, there will be an HR transformation programme team. In this team there will need to be some people with high levels of project management/programme management skills. The team as a whole will adopt programme management practices. Chapter 5 explores this in greater detail.

However, the point about the development of a project management mindset is that it needs to extend beyond those people responsible for effecting change in HR. It needs to be embedded as a way of working and thinking across the HR function, not least because of the need for strong input from users throughout the transformation process.

Additionally, we have already made it clear that the tools and models we use to support HR transformation are not just right for HR transformation, but are also right for the way HR professionals will need to work with their clients in the transformed HR function; we are role-modelling practices that the HR function needs to embed as working practices. As a generalisation, we have found that the HR community is not particularly strong in the area of project management.

So, although there is no ambition to turn HR professionals into certified PRINCE 2 programme managers, there is an ambition to develop a way of thinking akin to external consultants, who package work using the principles of project management. We will explore this theme in greater detail in Chapter 6 when we discuss capabilities for HR professionals.

Figure 1.6 presents a very simple framework which has helped to focus the HR community on the key principles of project management without overwhelming people with procedures, paperwork and plans.

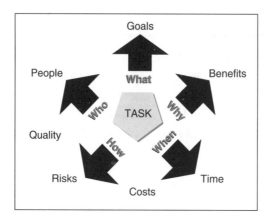

Figure 1.5 A project management mindset – key questions

When we present this framework to clients, there is typically quick intellectual buy-in: it is not difficult to understand! However, the challenge is actually to use the framework so that there is a clear focus on deliverables and what it will take to achieve these.

Within HR functions, we have often met with some initial resistance to a project approach. There is an argument that you cannot do the "day job" using project management principles, as the work of an HR professional is unpredictable and reactive. There is an element of truth in this, and it is not our belief that all HR work can be managed this way. However, we know that a high percentage of HR work can be managed more effectively through the development of a project mindset.

Our observation of the HR community is that some of the reasons why this way of working is often resisted are due to:

- reluctance to be pinned down about deliverables;
- inability to articulate concrete business benefits;
- unwillingness to identify and be held to deadlines (projects have to fit around the day job);
- lack of process consulting skills;
- unwillingness to share resources across HR's organisational silos.

These are generalisations, and we are not saying that this list in its entirety is true of all HR organisations we have worked with. Nor are we saying that all points will be true of your organisation. However, as you reflect on this list, you may find that some of the points resonate with you. As a slightly provocative parting shot on this point, you may want to consider how you would respond if an external consultant made a proposal to you that lacked any project management element – no clear deliverables, no timeline, no milestones, no resource estimates, no project scope, no budget, no sign off/change control, etc. You may also want to think about the impression HR makes with internal clients when there is an absence of these elements in proposed work.

The important points that we hope you take away are that:

1. developing a project mindset is a key to effective delivery of HR transformation and the ongoing work of HR;
2. developing a project mindset will not come easily for most HR communities because people are not used to working this way.

In this book we will show how we have worked with key stakeholder groups to develop a project mindset and blend the three mindsets together so that you deliver HR transformation in a way appropriate to the needs to your organisation. In particular, we will show how a process consulting and project mindset can be combined effectively to give sufficient structure to the change programme, without losing the ability to be flexible and adaptable. With one HR leadership group acting as the group of accountable executives, this balance was achieved through focusing on a 90-day cycle of deliverables and workshops. This 90-day cycle was long enough for the programme work streams to progress deliverables, but not so long that the HR transformation programme could not respond adequately to changes in the current reality.

Summary

In this chapter we have presented a small number of key models and frameworks that underpin our approaches to HR transformation. It is important for HR professionals to engage with these models and frameworks, as they are relevant to all types of business change and not just to HR transformation. We have discussed the importance of OD in a transformed HR and how this OD role is expressed through the development of three mindsets: systems, process consulting and project management.

We will refer to these underlying approaches throughout this practitioner guide, but particularly in Chapters 2, 6 and 7, where we will show how these approaches have been used in practice.

2

Envisioning the New World of HR

This chapter deals with a number of critical questions faced at the early stages, or indeed at the start of any new major phase, of any transformational effort:

- What is our starting point/current reality?
- Why do we need to do things differently?
- What would "different" and "better" look like?
- How do we start the process of moving from where we are to where we want to be?
- Is there sufficient organisational energy to deliver the proposed change?

Chapter Structure

Key Themes
2.1 Context
2.2 Practitioner Perspectives
2.3 Envisioning Tools

2.4 Fast Tracking the Envisioning Process
Summary

Key Themes

- Whilst there are many common factors influencing the direction of HR, there is no "one size fits all" solution to HR transformation; that is, each organisation will need to develop its own unique vision for HR transformation.

■ HR transformation needs to be aligned with the goals and needs of each business.

■ A shared vision for HR needs to be developed quickly amongst critical stakeholders.

■ A range of envisioning tools can be employed effectively to stimulate discussion and conversation, and ensure the speedy development of a shared vision.

■ Envisioning is the springboard to build an effective and robust business case for HR transformation.

2.1 Context

Opportunities and Threats

The proposition that HR needs to focus less effort on transactional/administrative tasks and become more strategic in focus is not new. Over the past couple of decades, much has been written about transition to a strategic HR function (and, to be fair, in some organisations a great deal of progress has been made). Yet in too many organisations the identity of HR remains firmly in the transactional/operations/advisory zones – comfort zones that often suit HR practitioners and line managers alike.

Yet the opportunities for a more strategic and value-adding contribution from HR are probably greater now than ever before.

Here are some reasons why:

■ *Many critical organisational issues are about people/organisational development*
Some examples of these issues are as follows:
   – Developing organisational cultures that will adapt quickly to external change.
   – Raising organisational, team and individual performance year on year.
   – Improving customer service.
   – Delivering operational efficiency.
   – Securing business benefits from capital investment/strategic projects.
   – Attracting and retaining prized staff.

- Reducing overall personnel-related costs/managing workforce costs more effectively.
- Improving management "bench strength".
- Dealing with increased globalisation/scale/complexity in organisational life.
- Increasing organisational flexibility.
- Improving the effectiveness of groups/teams.
- Improving the people management capability of line managers.
- Encouraging innovation.

The list could go on. Hopefully you will recognise the relevance of some of these issues to your business. The door of opportunity stands open for HR to be an active contributor in each of these areas.

■ *Advances in technology*
There are now several major players that offer enterprise-wide technology solutions. This has enabled the HR function to make its business case for technological investment alongside other support functions, such as finance and procurement. Although there is still likely to be debate in each organisation concerning the extent to which e-HR will be adopted, there is now sufficient critical mass to give organisations genuine cost-effective alternatives. Additionally, the core HR Information System (HRIS) backbone offers in-built "best practices" in HR processes and the ability to apply solutions globally. HR not only has the opportunity to utilise technology, but now the means to make a convincing business case for this investment.

■ *New organisational alternatives*
In the past decade, the management consultancy sector has grown rapidly, offering genuine alternatives to the in-house HR function. At the strategic end, consultants are increasingly stepping into the HR strategy and organisational development spaces where the in-house HR function either has insufficient capacity, or lacks sufficient capability to make a full contribution. At the operational level, there are now many sourcing alternatives in the areas of recruitment, training and development, reward, HR policy development, etc. At the transactional/advisory end, there are now serious players offering HR outsourcing – not just from a technological infrastructure/transactional perspective, but increasingly pitching at a full service handling back office recruitment, learning and HR decision support/advisory

functions. The different approaches to sourcing HR services are covered in more detail in Chapter 3.

■ *Research linking developed people management practices and performance*
There is now a growing body of research linking progressive people management practices to superior organisational performance. Research undertaken by Becker and Huselid (1998), for example, found that firms with the greatest intensity of HR practices that reinforce performance had the highest market value per employee. Their thesis is that improving HR practices can impact enterprise market value quite significantly. Their conclusions are hugely challenging for organisational leaders: that the best firms achieve strategic and operational excellence in HR.

■ *Clearer functional view on what a strategic contribution means*
The emergence of the HR management movement and, in recent years, the contributions made by academics (and especially Dave Ulrich, 1997) have helped HR find a greater sense of identity. The HR roles set out by Ulrich (see Figure 2.1) have found resonance within the HR community, and have become the starting point in exploring what business partnership means for HR.

Whilst the above developments suggest that there are some clear opportunities for HR, the challenge for each HR function is to define for itself a way of making a value-adding contribution that is, right for its organisation. In a nutshell, there are no "off-the-shelf" solutions, and unless HR is clear about the way it can add value, the threat is that the business will turn elsewhere for that contribution and the in-house HR function will become insignificant and impotent.

Dave Ulrich, *HR Champions* (1997)

Figure 2.1 HR roles

It is also true that aspiring to be in the top two quadrants of the Ulrich model without delivering effectively in the transactional/administrative area will not give HR business partners sufficient credibility with line managers for there to be a serious conversation around strategy and change.

What We Mean by "HR"

One of the mistakes that can be made when embarking on HR transformation is to limit the scope of change to the domain of the HR function and, as a result, only to effect functional reorganisation. Clearly, the HR function has a strong and important role to play in the delivery of HR into organisations. However, the HR function is not the sole player in delivering HR management.

The channels through which HR is delivered may include employees (through self-service); line managers (through exercising their people management responsibilities); internal HR generalists, specialists and administrators (who may or may not be part of the HR function); external sourcing; external consultants. This means that HR transformation needs to be broad in scope and should embrace both the wider organisation and external providers that sit outside the formal organisational boundaries.

In this book, we also use the term "HR management" as one that embraces the domains of people and organisational development, seeing HR management in its broadest sense.

In envisioning the new world of HR, it is important to consider how HR activities are currently delivered through each of the above channels and then to work through, with key stakeholders, how responsibilities may change. We will address this in greater detail later in the book.

Irresistible Forces

In thinking about the new world of HR, it is important to recognise that there are a number of external forces that will shape the future. So, as part of the envisioning process, these forces need to be accepted as part of the contextual framework within which the new world of HR is envisioned.

In summary, whether we like it or not:

■ Technology will play an increasing role in the delivery of HR services, providing employees and line managers with greater and greater opportunities for self-service.

- HR processes will continue to standardise around technology.
- The HR administrative backbone will increasingly be delivered by centres of expertise (whether in-houseshared service centres or out-sourced service centres).
- The shape of the in-house HR function will continue to change and HR staffing levels will continue to decline, with the headcount profile shifting from administrative/advisory roles to higher value decision support/strategic roles.
- The delivery of HR management in organisations will continue to disperse across each of the delivery channels.
- The need for HR professionals to bring a unique value proposition to internal clients will increase as line managers become more confident with self-service tools and seize opportunities for genuine choice in sourcing professional HR support.
- The outsourcing of transactional, administrative, advisory and specialist HR activity will continue to increase.

In many organisations we have worked with, the HR community has often struggled to accept the reality of these irresistible forces. The adoption of e-HR, for example, triggers a chain reaction of other consequences that have a profound bearing on the way organisations do HR, and on the skills and capabilities needed within the HR function itself.

For some individuals in the HR community, the shift of people resources away from the administrative, advisory and welfare activities is not welcomed, and there may be a sense of deskilling ("technology has taken over the work I used to do") and a depersonalising of service ("there used to be a person on the other end of the phone"). For others in HR, these forces will be welcomed, as the opportunity to recast the role of HR becomes real and imminent.

Many of the implementation challenges associated with HR transformation come from within the function itself. HR folk are no different from (strictly) other employees when it comes to working through the implications of change at a personal level, and we should expect and embrace resistance. We should not assume that change will be warmly welcomed. One of the tests that need to be applied once the vision for HR starts to emerge is how quickly the function can move to the new world given its starting point.

Using the Above Material

As this book has a strong bias towards application, we suggest that you engage people with these irresistible forces to stimulate debate within and outside the HR function. In this way you will be able to:

■ set the context for discussion about the future HR function in your organisation, maybe through a discussion paper or presentation;
■ present the consequences for your organisation of ignoring them/ staying as you are;
■ engender a common framework for thinking prior to an envisioning workshop, where you can follow up a discussion paper or presentation with one-to-one discussion and debate with key stakeholders;
■ confirm the parameters for discussion at any envisioning workshop so that key stakeholders are starting from the same contextual base.

You are unlikely to reach consensus on how to respond to these forces at the first attempt. For example, one organisation we have worked with found it hard to come to terms with the fact that the HR function would need to shrink significantly, losing most of its in-house training and recruitment teams. It took 9 months and some poor business results before the HR leadership team really confronted the headcount issue.

Our intention is that this section will give you material to engage people, start conversations and help shift thinking about how HR can and should contribute to the business.

2.2 Practitioner Perspectives

The previous section paints some broad-brush strokes about the general context within which we need to think about the new world of HR. But how do senior HR practitioners set about envisioning in practice? What really influences the way they think about how HR should make its contribution to their respective businesses?

Our discussions with leading HR practitioners highlighted a number of important themes:

■ *There is no single right answer*
Maggie Hurt puts this point powerfully. "Nothing we do in HR is governed by the laws of physics. It is all a social construct, and therefore

there is no 'have to' other than working within the law. Our job in HR is primarily about providing business solutions and not about compliance. The way we organise needs to be hard wired into the business context. In that sense there is no one right answer – but some answers will be more appropriate than others. I am keen to get across to my team that the value that comes through good HR is not through ticking the box in a work process. It is about ensuring that the output is right. We need to engage our brain – develop 'Thinking HR' at all levels of the function."

■ *Reflect the unique needs of the business*
Steve Ashby illustrates extremely well the need for HR to reflect the unique circumstances of their business. "We are literally a people business. We tend not to own the bricks and mortar of the facilities from which we provide our services. HR is seen as an integral part of our business. At this stage of our evolution we employ around 25,000 people. Our approach to HR has been very pragmatic and very focused on the short-term business needs. That is, largely because 2 years ago we employed a fraction of that number. So the critical HR issues we are addressing concern the creation of world-class capability at country management level. This is driving a heightened focus on the development of core and common processes that can be implemented consistently across the business, e-enabled where we can to achieve efficiencies, accuracy and speed."

■ *HR transformation must benefit the business*
Janice Cook reacts strongly against the allure of fads and fashions. "I am not an advocate of constant restructuring. We need to have a clear vision and goal for HR transformation and ensure we are still on track. Transformation and the substance of transformation must not be about fad or fashion. Constant restructuring is a disease in organisations and is not about change, but about engendering constant uncertainty which people find debilitating." She adds, "We are very business minded in NCH and have a strong business development culture. We actively engage in business strategy and planning. The HR review came from a business decision to review the whole organisational infrastructure in response to rapid growth. Our envisioning of the new world of HR was therefore grounded in a strong business need. The quality of HR service was not an issue. What was an issue was the cost effectiveness of HR and resource utilisation within the context of a growing organisation."

Miles Warner stresses the importance of aligning HR transformation with the business values. "We start with the Schlumberger values, which are built around people, technology and profit. The technology is obviously supported by a very strong R&D programme, and the generation of profit allows much more freedom to develop proprietary applications. The rest is actually taking care of people."

■ *The client must be at the heart of our HR transformation vision*
Maggie Hurt makes the point that we need to be clear about what is important to our clients. "They judge us on getting the basics right, like pay and offer letters – what we might regard as mundane. We then get the attention of our clients and earn the right to contribute at a more strategic level. It is basically about being helpful first, rolling up our sleeves, and ensuring that we keep taking those opportunities that get us to where we really want to be contributing. We need to factor this into our envisioning and our transformation journey. There is no quick fix."

Randy Harris echoes this point: "From what I have seen in my past working in American Express, Dunn and Bradstreet and some more mature companies, I think that before you can move upstream you need to get the basics right. Nobody is going to want to sit down and talk to you about how you are going to enhance and optimise your organisation if you can't pay people. So our priority has been initially on the basics. Then we were able to get into broader organisational issues. We don't want to stay functional. We want to migrate back to a more customer intimate, customer-centric model. But when we start pushing things back into the field and into the other functional parts of the company it will go with some parameters."

■ *HR transformation needs to take account of the broader organisational system*
Janice Cook observes that "two major organisational issues (not specifically related to HR) surfaced during the envisioning phase of work – the need for whole organisational working and the need to invest strongly in our technological infrastructure. Addressing these issues was a precondition for us achieving change in HR. As a consequence, we are now able to implement an HR organisation that has greater resource sharing, and we are now investing heavily in the technological infrastructure so that we can start moving towards a more e-enabled environment."

Miles Warner emphasises the interaction between the way business evolves and the changing role of HR. "The HR function has traditionally had a very key role in Schlumberger. About 7 years ago, a major reorganisation of the business took place that effectively combined six separate businesses into one organisation. HR had a crucial role in cementing that change from a cultural perspective, and in doing so had to shed its administrative workload to concentrate on people issues."

Claudia Hall also makes the link between the broader organisational context and the way HR is done. "Nextel was born through seed funding a few years ago. HR was set up very much the same way Nextel's business was set up – geographically structured, but centrally managed. More recently, about 3½ years ago, the CEO and COO made a commitment to develop a company that was more scaleable from a cost perspective and more easily able to respond to the customer. As a result, we needed to develop one set of processes and procedures and one way of operating nationally. So across the country it didn't matter what geography you were in: you knew as an employee that this was the 'Nextel way'. To play its part, HR envisioned a strategy called 'One HR', which meant bringing all the elements of the HR organisation together (generalist and specialist functions) so that we operate with one face to the customer."

Vance Kearney points to the relationship between technology and organisation. "The whole e-HR thing is interesting because you need highly developed and efficient technology to truly manage the whole circle of transactions. For example, you have payroll, which pays someone's salary. That's fine, but if you have commission then your commission system has to integrate with payroll. You may have flexible benefits, with a web-based interface with employees and a systems interface with payroll. You may also be operating in a number of countries with different rules. And so on. The technology is becoming increasingly complicated and the transactions that managers are now performing, like processing someone's raise or promotion, actually start to hit a lot of downstream systems."

■ *HR organisational design will vary from business to business*
Maggie Hurt argues that "if we are to provide business solutions, then we need to get close to the business. The pivotal HR role for us is therefore the HR business partner. The HR business partner needs to live and

breathe business problems. For the customer, the HR business partner also provides an important one-stop shop. We need some HR specialists. I am not sure if we would move to a situation where all specialist support was provided externally. One of the realities we have to face, whether right or wrong, is that internal specialist opinion does not carry the same weight as an external opinion. Good HR specialists will have worked as HR business partners for some of their career."

Philip Barr underlines the importance of different sourcing solutions in delivering effective HR to the business. "Good HR is about delivering simple processes well. The heart of HR will remain the areas of resourcing, compensation, development, performance and employee relations. HR professionals must have an understanding of organisational development. We need to help our businesses to change quickly. We will need to pull on external support to supplement internal resource. The HR team cannot be self-contained."

Vance Kearney emphasises the role of HR specialists. "We need a much higher calibre of person in HR. In particular, we need specialists, and I think we need to get back to specialisation. For example, we need to provide our managers when they wish to recruit people with expert in-house recruitment consultants." The focus in specialisation stands in contrast to an approach where the HR manager largely performs the people management aspects of a line manager's job. "What we have done is created a dependency on HR to a point where managers are almost not allowed to do anything with people without HR. We have to give responsibility for managing people back to managers, and that includes the ability to make mistakes."

- *HR transformation is a journey and not a destination ... and deciding the next step should not be a long process*

Janice Cook prefers to think about "the continuous development of HR rather than 'transformation' – which can suggest a linear start and end point. Improving the way we do HR is unlikely to end."

Philip Barr stresses the importance of speed. "Envisioning shouldn't take too long. It is important that decisions are taken quickly so that the function is changed in ways that enable people to get on and deliver things. You don't need full business buy-in into the HR vision. You need key senior buy-in. Beyond that you need to cherry-pick your stakeholders."

These practitioner views underline the need to:

- *Develop a systems mindset.* HR transformation is about change, and change cannot be effected in isolation; for example, technology-driven change inevitably impacts structure, processes, capability and culture. Change in HR impacts and is also impacted by change in the wider organisational system.
- *See HR transformation as a process that needs to be worked through step by step.* This process is not predetermined. There is no schematic that sets out in advance every step; that is, a sort of "paint by numbers" approach to change. The steps needed to effect change will be unique to each organisation. When we refer to "transformation", we refer to a significant shift in changing the way HR contributes in organisations. But this will not be an end-game – a final destination. There will always be another step beyond.
- *Focus on the unique circumstances of each business.* Learn from the experiences of others, yes, but do not become obsessed with "me too" external benchmarking. The most powerful results will be driven through a strong identification with the unique circumstances faced by your organisation at this point in its history. This highlights the need for an approach to change that is, highly contingent, with the focus being on shaping HR in ways that will help the business now at this point in time.

So how do you combine the broad trends presented in Section 2.1 with the practitioners' experiences set out above to ensure purposeful envisioning? In our change tool kit we have a number of tools and frameworks which organisations have found helpful in creating an environment for effective envisioning. Five of these tools are now presented in Section 2.3.

2.3 Envisioning Tools

Much of what we have presented so far in this chapter sets the context for envisioning the kind of HR function you need to become. In this section, we want to turn our attention to practical tools and frameworks that will help you work with individuals and groups to envision the new world of HR. If you have not already read Chapter 1, we suggest that you familiarise yourself with the content, as the chapter sets out our underlying approach to transformation and change. Understanding our approach to organisational transformation and change will help you to understand better how to use these tools and frameworks.

In this section, we aim to achieve two objectives:

1. to explain the tools and frameworks themselves;
2. to explain the use of these tools and frameworks in practice.

As with all the tools and frameworks presented, they are there to be tailored. We are great believers in using language and presentational formats that are right for your organisation. With this in mind, we will also show how we have tailored some of the tools and frameworks to respond to different circumstances.

Why use tools and frameworks? We would like to offer you four good reasons:

1. *They are solution neutral*: The tools are there to help you understand where you are now and what you need to become, given your particular business context.
2. *They enable conversations to happen*: Each of the tools and frameworks is designed for use with individuals or groups to stimulate debate and discussion. We believe that developing a shared vision amongst critical stakeholders is the necessary goal of the envisioning process, and this means that there must be a dialogue.
3. *They accelerate the envisioning process*: Having a common tool or framework actually accelerates envisioning because there is a common point of reference. In this way we accept that debate is, to an extent, contained. However, having a common framework within which points of agreement and disagreement can be identified and, where necessary, worked through is hugely beneficial.
4. *They work*: We have used these tools and frameworks in many different environments, and they are extremely powerful in helping groups to engender speed into the envisioning process and create purposeful outcomes.

The five tools and frameworks we present in this section are:

1. business drivers,
2. organisational levers,
3. HR value pyramid,

4. HR functional evolution,

5. visualisation.

Business Drivers Framework

When should we use this framework?

HR transformation and the envisioned new world of HR must be hard wired to the critical business issues. Our starting point is therefore to consider critical business drivers. Why? Without this thought, it will be impossible to:

- make a coherent case for HR transformation;
- identify HR's priorities;
- link the new world of HR to the realities that face your business.

Put another way, identifying your critical business drivers helps the HR function to answer:

- What is wrong with the way things are?
- Where is the focus for the future?
- How will the proposed way of delivering HR help the business to perform more effectively?

What does the framework look like?

Figure 2.2 represents visually the business drivers framework. This framework has been used in the private, public and not-for-profit sectors; hence its broad applicability has been proven.

The framework considers the three main drivers of organisational effectiveness: revenue growth, cost efficiency and brand identity. Each of the drivers is then considered from three perspectives (you may wish to tailor these, but we have found that they tend to work well).

For *revenue growth* we consider:

- *Customers*, who are the recipients of the products/services provided by the organisation (who are they, how do we retain them, how do we attract new customers in existing markets and will we need to move into new markets and attract new types of customer?).
- *Geography* (where do we operate now and where are we likely to operate in the future?).

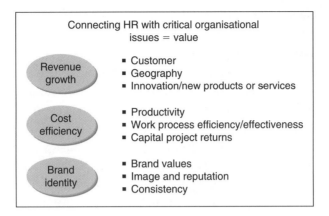

Figure 2.2 Business drivers framework

- *Innovation around new products and services* (what do we need to do differently to compete effectively or satisfy customer requirements?).

For *cost efficiency* we consider:

- *Productivity* (how productive we are compared to relevant benchmarks, where we need to raise performance and productivity and how well we measure and reward productivity).
- *Work process efficiency/effectiveness* (how well key processes work, areas of strength, areas for improvement and future needs).
- *Capital project returns* (identification of key capital projects and track record in delivering anticipated benefits).

For *brand identity* we consider:

- *Brand values* (what do we stand for as an organisation and how well do we demonstrate our values internally and externally?);
- *Image and reputation* (what is our current image and reputation, what might undermine it and how can we protect/enhance it?);
- *Consistency* (to what extent are we acting in a consistent way with our customers and employees and how might future challenges help/hinder our ability to deliver consistently?).

How do I use this framework?

This framework is best used in a workshop setting. We have found it useful in one-to-one discussions to get individual perspectives and stimulate debate, but ultimately there needs to be a sharing of perspectives on critical business drivers, and this is best achieved when people are in the same room and are able to engage with one another.

To have a meaningful discussion about business drivers requires some preparation. You should draw on current knowledge of the business to populate these areas in advance of the workshop or, if you are confident that workshop attendees will have sufficient knowledge, you can populate these areas at the workshop. Where we have doubted that sufficient information will surface at a workshop, we have used a combination of pre-briefing people, inviting a senior internal client to talk about key organisational issues, and allocating pre-work so that participants can research an area.

Once there is a shared understanding of the critical business drivers, this then enables the key HR leaders and stakeholders to address three questions:

1. What are the critical HR priorities that emerge from these business drivers?
2. How well are we currently equipped as an HR function to deliver these priorities?
3. How does the HR function need to change to help the business succeed?

Discussion of these areas will move you a long way towards defining the HR transformation agenda and priorities.

Organisational Levers Model

When should we use this model?

This model is extremely useful when applied to any significant change effort. It is applicable not only to HR transformation, but also to any organisational change. It is a foundation model and helps to explain the impact of change within the context of the broader organisational system.

Its value is to engage key stakeholders in a dialogue concerning "current HR" and "the future world of HR". It is also a powerful way of capturing and presenting the outputs from discussions.

The organisational levers model has already been introduced in Chapter 1. If you have not already familiarised yourself with the model, we strongly suggest that you do so now. We do not intend to repeat the description of the model in this section, but will instead focus in greater detail on its application.

You should note that you might come across other versions of this model with slightly different labels. This does not matter. Taking a systems perspective is the important part of this model, and we would encourage you to use whatever terminology fits best with your business.

How do I use the model?

The examples below show how the organisational levers model has been used in a variety of ways (and alongside the other envisioning tools) to develop a "whole system" approach to HR transformation and build a coalition of support around the new world of HR.

The two main ways in which the organisational levers model has been used to support envisioning are:

1. *As a pre-prepared input to an envisioning workshop*
Prior to an envisioning workshop, a series of one-to-one discussions is held with key stakeholders to discuss "current HR" and "the future world of HR". Interviews are structured using the organisational levers model (although some of the other envisioning tools presented above can also be used if appropriate). The outcome of the interviews is the preparation of a "straw man" set of descriptors relating to "current HR" and "the future world of HR", linked to each of the six organisational levers, namely external forces, performance outcomes, technology, processes, structure and people/culture. These descriptors are displayed in a workshop environment, typically on large sheets of paper; one sheet for each of the six levers.

Participants (hopefully most, if not all, of the key stakeholders you will have interviewed) are asked to challenge any descriptor that they either disagree with or are unclear about. They are also given an opportunity to add anything they believe to be missing from the straw man descriptors.

In debriefing the exercise, focus first on those descriptors where there are most challenges and work through them to seek clarification and gain agreement on the wording. Then follow a similar process with the suggested additions.

The outcome should be agreement of a set of "as is – current HR" and "to be – future world of HR" descriptors. This approach is particularly helpful when working with larger groups, and we have found that in a workshop setting agreement is typically reached within a matter of hours.

2. *Realtime in a workshop*

For smaller groups, you can achieve the above realtime.

Ensure that your room has plenty of wall space and is divided into two areas: "current HR" and "future world of HR". Display the headings of the six organisational levers under each.

Give participants two colours of post-it™ notes. Ask participants to write (on one colour) descriptors that best describe "current HR" for each of the six organisational levers. Repeat the process for "future world of HR" using the other colour. Cluster descriptors where you can. Then work through each of the post-it™ notes to ensure that there is agreement on any new descriptors that have been written (or agree a change to the existing wording).

What might an output look like?

In Appendix 1 we have shown an example from a client exercise. As you will see, the descriptors are succinct, but specific enough to enable the next steps in the process to take place – gap analysis and project planning. Just to illustrate that envisioning is not a one-off exercise, the example shown in the appendix was actually produced one year after the initial envisioning exercise as part of HR transformation review and taking stock.

HR Value Pyramid Model

When should we use this model?

The aim of this tool is two-fold:

1. to engage stakeholders in thinking about where HR adds value;
2. to engage stakeholders in identifying where the balance of effort/ resource in HR is now and where it should be in the future.

The model should clearly be used at the outset of the transformation journey in considering how the function adds value now and where it needs to focus in the future. We have also found the model useful in undertaking quick, high-level reviews during transformation.

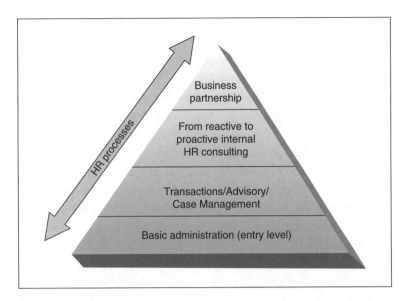

Figure 2.3 HR value pyramid

What does the model look like?

Figure 2.3 represents visually the HR value pyramid. The HR value pyramid has four main propositions:

1. That there is a hierarchy of roles within HR.
2. That basic administration and transactional roles will be most impacted by e-HR (including employee and manager self service) and new organisational arrangements, such as shared service centres and outsourcing.
3. That HR processes impact roles within and outside of the HR function and an important task during the HR transformation process is to determine those activities which can be embedded within e-HR, who is accountable for data entry and where knowledge-based roles need to make their unique contributions.
4. That the HR professionals will acquire widely sought after expertise when they become business partners, proactively engaging with critical organisational issues as part of the management team.

How do I use the model?

This model is helpful in stimulating initial debate with key stakeholders about what they want from HR. On a one-to-one basis, it is a simple model for stakeholders to engage with quickly and can take discussions into a number of interesting areas, such as what service internal clients need from the administrative/transactional side of HR and the nature of business partnership.

In a workshop format, the model has been particularly helpful around sourcing and resourcing discussions; that is, what percentage of HR activity, resource or cost currently sits across the four areas and what percentages should exist in the new world of HR. We have found that this exercise stimulates quality discussion around themes such as cost versus headcount (e.g. you may have fewer people in the administrative/ transactional space, but there are clearly costs associated with e-HR) and cost versus type of resource (e.g. you may have a lower overall headcount in HR, but the people you will have may cost more).

At the early stages of the transformation process there is considerable value in encouraging key stakeholders to play with these ideas and their implications. This helps people to work through for themselves what the new world of HR might look and feel like.

HR Functional Evolution Framework

When should we use this framework?

The aim of this framework is to get people talking about some of the characteristics of the current HR operational model and what the next practical step should be. It is not intended to suggest that HR should move to a transformed state in one step.

What does the framework look like?

Figure 2.4 shows the functional evolution framework. The HR functional evolution framework simplifies for effect. It looks at a theoretical evolution of the HR function through three lenses: traditional, transitional and transformed. The descriptors in each are intended to be caricatures of HR functions and can be tailored to suit your organisational needs. The three main points about the model are as follows:

1. That the model is intended to provoke discussion and debate, hence the descriptors are written provocatively.

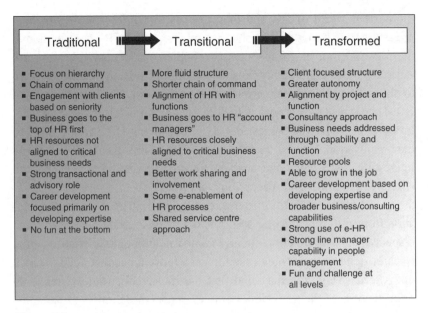

Figure 2.4 HR functional evolution

2. The model shows that HR transformation is a transitional process and that we need to identify and focus on those areas that will have the greatest organisational impact.

3. The model helps people to see possibilities for the future ("there are different approaches to the one we have") and opens up discussion about characteristics of alternative HR delivery models; for example, the term "consultancy approach" can often be bandied about as though there is only one interpretation, and we have found that there is a need to explore quite deeply how far organisations want to adopt an internal consultancy model.

The descriptors are deliberately "high level" and ambiguous, with the intention that groups will be forced to think through meaning and explore the grey areas.

How do I use the framework?

This model can be used on a one-to-one basis or with groups. On a one-to-one basis, first get people to talk about which descriptors best reflect the current world of HR and then discuss those descriptors which, if present, would have the biggest impact in improving HR's contribution to the organisation. In groups, post two copies of the visual on the wall. Allocate six to eight sticky dots of one colour to each person for them to place alongside those descriptors that best describe the current world of HR. Then repeat the exercise with different coloured dots to those descriptors that will have the biggest impact in improving HR's contribution to the organisation. You will find that the spread of dots takes you into some interesting discussions and enables you to reach some conclusions on where you are now and where you want to be.

All HR functions will, of course, engage with e-HR-driven transformation from different starting points of maturity. It could be that in some respects your HR function already identifies with characteristics of the transformed state, in which case focus on those areas that need to catch up. Alternatively, you may find that the most realistic next step is to pitch at some of the transitional descriptors, as these represent the most realistic chance of implementing change – seeing the transformed state as a longer-term goal. In any case, it is likely that you will identify differences of opinion and that you will include descriptors from more than one of the columns.

Visualisation

When should we use this tool?

The other frameworks and models presented in this section are generally aimed at the left side of the brain, which is the logical/rational part of our thinking processes. However, envisioning also needs to tap into the right side of the brain, which is the creative/playful side of our thinking processes. One of the best ways we have found to stimulate a more creative approach to current-state analysis and future-state envisioning is through visualisation.

We could say that you should use this tool with a degree of fear and trepidation – some of your stakeholders may need some encouragement to participate in a visualisation exercise. Do persevere, though, as visualisation usually produces some important and rich insights into the current and future worlds of HR. It is also valuable in engaging at the emotional level around HR.

What do the tools look like and how do I use them?

There are quite a few ways to engage people in visualisation, but the two types of visualisation exercise that we have found to work well are:

1. *Free-form drawing*

A simple exercise to set up, participants are asked to draw a picture (or a number of images) describing (a) the current world of HR and (b) how the future world of HR would look if it was contributing most effectively to the organisation. Remember the focus is on content and not the quality of artwork!

In debriefing the exercise, ask each person in turn to present and talk about their "current HR" picture. Typically there will be a richness of analogy and metaphor. Take time to explore the language and imagery, and do not assume that everyone understands things the same way. Often, metaphors will trigger interesting discussions, either around the original metaphor or through some tangential connections. Record some of the themes that emerge. Then repeat the exercise with the "future world of HR" picture.

2. *Picture cards/collage*

If you are not feeling bold enough to run a free-form drawing exercise, then an alternative approach is to give people images to work with. This is inevitably a more structured approach and less spontaneous. Using the same questions as above, you can introduce images either through giving people some magazines with a good variety of pictures in them and asking them to produce two collages addressing each question, or by giving people a variety of picture stills (we have found that you will need between 50 and 60 pictures) and asking them to identify ones that speak to both questions. As an additional twist to this second exercise, the organisational levers model can be used to give structure to the visual presentation; for example, to pull out pictures that best describe current or future technology, HR people and culture, etc.

The debriefing of the exercise will be the same as for the free-form drawing exercise.

We have used these exercises when working with larger groups (more than 50 people) and with smaller groups (around 12 people).

Case Studies

Organisation 1

Context

A large global telecoms company was in the process of integrating a number of its businesses into a global Internet technology business. An e-HR programme director had been appointed, but there was not yet a proper HR transformation programme team in place or a coherent HR transformation vision.

Process

In the run-up to the launch of the new global business, a series of one-to-one interviews were held with the newly appointed HR leadership team and senior business stakeholders. The organisational levers model was the primary tool used during these interviews, which enabled us to prepare a straw man view of the "as is – current HR" and a straw man view of the "to be – future world of HR".

A workshop was held with all the HR leadership team present, and in working through the process outlined above an HR vision was agreed around the organisational levers model. Additionally, an HR transformation governance structure was agreed based on this work, which ensured that the HR transformation programme team was not solely focused on e-HR, but embraced transformation of the whole function.

Organisation 2

Context

A major energy utility had recently made a major acquisition in the USA, and the group-wide HR leadership team met to think through the implications for the HR function and to identify critical issues that needed to be worked on collaboratively.

Process

The team worked through a process using three of the tools set out above:

1. Identification of critical business issues and the HR implications of these.

2. Use of the visualisation technique mentioned earlier to encourage dialogue about the HR function.
3. Use of the organisational levers model to develop a more structured view of the current and envisioned HR world.

This workshop identified a number of critical HR issues that needed to be progressed and also set the framework for the HR transformation agenda that has been implemented.

2.4 Fast Tracking the Envisioning Process

When we discuss with clients the need for envisioning at the start of the HR transformation process, any resistance usually falls into one or other of these two reactions:

The first, and most worrying, reaction is that there is no need to envision because "we all know what HR transformation is all about". This is worrying because in our experience we have yet to be involved in any major change programme (HR or other business changes) where there is common and absolute agreement on the nature, purpose and vision of the change. It may be that individuals know what they want to achieve. But unless the organisation has a highly autocratic culture, there will be a need to engage with others to build a shared vision and a coalition of support for change. If you find yourself identifying with this reaction, we would encourage you to let go and to recognise that there is nothing to be gained in pressing on regardless – even if it does mean that the vision for HR transformation becomes a shared rather than a single vision and involves some degree of compromise.

The second reaction is that the envisioning process will take too long and end up in navel gazing, without much action. This is always possible, of course, but with good process and facilitation skills a momentum can be gathered. Momentum building is extremely important from the outset, as envisioning can lead to prevarication. We have yet to be involved in an HR transformation programme that has dwelt too long on envisioning.

Indeed, using the tools set out above, the envisioning process does not need to be either a confrontational or long drawn out affair. A good example is how a large global business was able to reach a high level of agreement on "current HR" and the "new, envisioned world of HR" within a 4-week period. (Figure 2.5 illustrates this "fast track" process.) This is not to say that no further work on the HR transformation vision was needed. But, applying the 80/20 rule, there can be sufficient definition to take the next practical steps in the transformation process; that is, to build a case for change.

We believe that if there is good cooperation from key stakeholders, a robust HR transformation vision can be reached within a few weeks, culminating in a stakeholder workshop.

Who should be involved?

This will vary between organisations, but as a minimum we recommend that this initial phase includes:

- the senior HR leadership team;
- key people within the broader HR community;

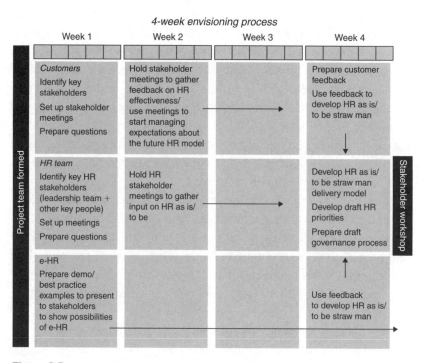

Figure 2.5 Fast-track envisioning process: example

■ critical business stakeholders;
■ a sample of line managers.

Most of these key stakeholders can be involved initially through one-to-one interviews (drawing on the tools presented in this chapter), although in some instances we have used a short HR effectiveness questionnaire with line managers.

The outputs from these interviews will be used to prepare a number of inputs to the envisioning workshop (which should include the senior HR leadership team and, if possible, some senior business stakeholders). These inputs may include:

■ a summary of customer feedback;
■ a straw man "as is – current HR" and "to be – new world HR";
■ draft HR priorities;
■ draft governance process to oversee HR transformation.

Once there is broad agreement around the "as is – current HR" and the "to be – future world of HR", there are three final outputs that flow from this early envisioning work:

1. *Gap analysis*
The "gap" is the distance that needs to be travelled between where you are now and where you want to be.

Having established your "as is" and "to be", you are then able to do a reality check to test whether this gap can be closed within the time and resource constraints of your organisation. Part of this assessment will be your gut feeling about the readiness of the organisation to make the proposed change happen. Other tools that will support this assessment will be the change equation and a more structured look at business impact and change readiness.

The change equation is detailed in Chapter 1, and is not repeated in this chapter. The way in which you can use the change equation with your key stakeholders is as follows:

■ Ask your stakeholders to rate the elements of the change equation from their point of view (and how they might judge the reactions of key decision makers outside of HR). These reactions could be: dissatisfaction with the way we currently do HR; level of clarity about what

HR should be; level of clarity about the next practical steps, and their will to make the change happen (high, medium and low will be sufficient).

- Then ask your stakeholders to identify the main costs, for example financial, resources, time, etc.
- Then ask them to weigh both sides – in their judgement, where is the balance? Is the new world of HR that they have envisioned likely to get the support needed to make it happen?

If the assessment is favourable, then moving to the next task is straightforward. If the assessment is not favourable, then you need to look at:

- Increasing levels of dissatisfaction with the way things are, that is, helping people to realise that what they are currently doing is not what the organisation needs from them and will be of little market value.
- How you might modify your "to be" vision so that the gap that needs to be closed is smaller.
- How you might reduce the perceived costs of making the change – either through reworking what has to be done or by looking for greater organisational benefits.

2. *Building the case for change*

Having completed your gap analysis, you are in a position to put together a compelling case for change. Building a business case is explored in greater detail in Chapter 4. There is also another "case for change" that needs to be made to a range of stakeholder groups. This case for change will be less detailed, broader brush. But it will incorporate all the key outputs that have been developed as part of the envisioning process. Figure 2.6 summarises its key elements.

3. *Planning and keeping on track*

The final outputs from this envisioning process are the next practical steps; in other words the pathway from where we are today to where we want to be.

The programme/project management aspects of this are explored in greater depth in Chapter 5. At this stage, the senior HR leadership group will be in a position to do the following things:

- Set up a process of 90-day milestones to show how the function will bridge the gap from current to future HR.

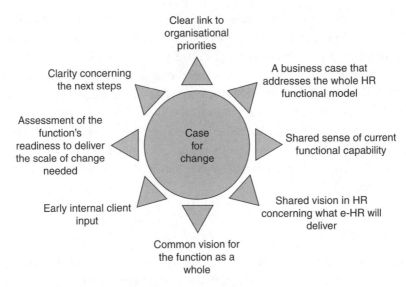

Figure 2.6 Building the case for change: key elements

- Commission (or establish and commission) the HR transformation programme team to initiate work streams/projects around these key 90-day deliverables.
- Establish appropriate levels of reporting between 90-day milestones.

Figure 2.7 shows an example of a high-level 90-day milestone developed by one organisation we have worked with. What this high-level plan does

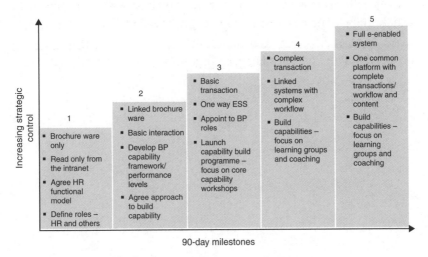

Figure 2.7 90-day milestones: key steps to HR transformation

is to give the senior HR leadership group a sense of focus and enable issues around pacing and resource allocation to be aired in an environment where all have committed to delivery timescales.

The final word in this section is that the most powerful way of ensuring senior HR leadership group focus on HR transformation is to organise 90-day workshops around milestones so that there is a strong focus on reviewing deliverables, assessing progress and mobilising for the next 90 days. This reflects strongly the process consulting approach outlined in Chapter 1 and integrates with the need for strong programme management.

Summary

The whole point of HR transformation is to make it happen; in other words to implement it effectively and reap the benefits. The whole point of envisioning the new world of HR is to give focus and momentum to HR transformation.

Drawing on tried and tested organisational development tools, we have been able to help organisations develop and mobilise quickly around a vision for the new world of HR. In this chapter we have set out the main drivers that suggest that HR needs to be done differently and some practical tools that help the process of envisioning.

What we have also shown is that envisioning is not an "airy fairy" activity. HR vision needs to be hard wired into business reality and goals, and the point of envisioning is to get to grips with reality, enabling HR to make its most effective contribution within the constraints of the business and making changes happen purposefully and quickly.

3

Service Delivery Approaches

This chapter deals with a number of considerations that arise from the envisioning work described in Chapter 2. These considerations concern the means by which the different kinds of HR services can be delivered into the business. The choices made will have a major bearing on likely costs, benefits and timescales of the transformation journey and therefore warrant appropriate attention.

Chapter Structure

Key Themes

- When designing the service delivery strategy, a number of factors need to be borne in mind.
- The elements of e-HR, shared services and outsourcing can all play a part – how do you choose?
- If your organisation does want to move to outsourcing, what are the key considerations to make it work effectively?

3.1 Context

Your transformation solution will encompass considerations concerning the way in which HR services are sourced and delivered. As mentioned in the previous chapters, the pace of change in HR has accelerated in recent years and in many organisations the pendulum has swung between downsizing and recruitment programmes, and recruitment and retention difficulties. Organisations have increasingly paid attention to the customer, to the need for quality and cost improvement, to produce new products that lead to sustainable business growth and brand image. The importance of these factors and their connection to HR services was surfaced in the business drivers framework described in Chapter 2.

The HR function has sought to respond to and support this kind of organisational change, at the same time as finding its own role and contribution under scrutiny. Consequently, HR has had to examine itself, its role and its value in the light of the perceptions of it within the organisation, and this has led to changes in the way HR delivers its services. The organisational levers model described in Chapter 1 provides a useful framework for understanding the connectedness between HR and the organisation and the primary reasons that shape HR service delivery.

With increased devolution of people responsibilities to the line and administrative work outsourced or automated out, if HR cannot demonstrate its worth, then managers will wonder what the point is in continuing with the HR function. Hence the need for HR to envision its future role and take decisive steps to demonstrate it has a worthwhile contribution to make, or it will find itself merely a contract manager of activities done by others. It is in this context that the different types of service delivery approaches are explored.

Shared services

This refers to a service delivery approach where there are three key dimensions:

- The nature of the service provided is determined primarily by the customer.

- There is common provision of services.
- These services are available to a number of users.

In many cases this results in activities being transferred from operating units to the shared services centre – sometimes described as "internal outsourcing".

Some organisations may use the concept of shared services deliberately to centralise for reasons of cost cutting, without having much regard for the customer. However, the attraction of shared services, in its pure form, is both the shift to reflect customer choice in line with business trends and the efficiency benefits that can be derived from concentrating dispersed services.

e-HR

People mean different things by the term "e-HR". The more visionary, advanced interpretations describe a fully integrated, organisation-wide electronic network of HR-related data, information, services, databases, tools, applications and transactions that are generally accessible at any time by employees, managers and HR professionals. More basic, aspirational interpretations suggest that an organisation's implementation of a new software package for payroll, or the posting of company policies on an Intranet, signals its adoption of e-HR.

For the purposes of this book, we define e-HR as:

The application of conventional, web and voice technologies to
improve HR administration, transactions and process performance.

(IES Report 398, 2003)

Typically, the term e-HR is used to describe technology's role in enabling the transformation of solely HR activity. Instead of a centralised personnel team handling everyday tasks such as approving pay rises, sorting out training and checking holiday entitlements, these can be handled by the employees themselves or their line manager.

Crucially, the adoption of e-HR seeks to minimise or eliminate intervention from HR staff, allowing managers and employees to perform HR tasks directly with the use of self-service tools. This can contrast with the shared service centre environment, where the service would normally be expected to be delivered by a customer service operative or other category of HR staff.

Outsourcing

Outsourcing, as the name implies, involves the adoption of a third party provider that delivers HR services into the organisation on the basis of a commercial contract. Of all the approaches, outsourcing is given most coverage in this chapter, because it is currently the subject of intense interest and the market is a significant one. The value of the US out-sourcing market in 2002 was $340 billion. The total value of the UK market from FTSE 100 companies alone in 2001 was £22.9 billion (and is still growing rapidly), with about one-third being invested in business process outsourcing, including HR.

3.2 Practitioner Perspectives

It is self-evident that the overall HR service delivery model for an organisation may be an amalgam of the different approaches described in the context setting part of this chapter. It is certainly the case that each presents its own challenges and opportunities, and the practitioner perspectives that follow illuminate some of the more important ones. They also provide an appropriate link to the remaining parts of this chapter.

Beware the dangers of outsourcing

Miles Warner draws attention to some potential dangers of outsourcing. "My gut feeling is that I think outsourcing overall is quite dangerous, because it is in many cases cost driven, and if it's cost driven why should another organisation be able to take some cost out which you can't? So that's the first question I think you have to answer. The second is around whether you outsource a process or simply a task or action."

"Everyone is essentially doing the same common tasks of running payroll, administering a pension plan or similar. I think what you can outsource is lots of tasks and actions, but you need to keep the infra-structure in the company, the actual process, internal, and if another company can make a saving on that and still provide the same sort of service, then you should be able to make a saving on it by doing it in a slightly different way."

"So I think people are trying to get rid of too much, and that can be detrimental to the company. You've got to decide how much you can get rid of. But you've got to draw the line a little bit closer to the task end rather than the policy and practice end. I think in the long run we're going to end up with organisations that are still focused on their core business, but in fact you can have other companies that are providing common tasks, tasks that are common across a group of companies themselves, in a more efficient way just through economy of scale."

Where to "draw the line"

In this example, Randy Harris talks about the deployment of different sourcing strategies at Nextel and explains where he would draw the line in terms of outsourcing HR services. "Two years ago, on one day, we turned over six call centres and about 5000 people to IBM and Teletek, so we turned over the transactional component of customer service. Same day, 2 years ago, we turned over about 700 people to EDS to do our IT operations support, so as a company, not just within HR, but as a company, we will look and say, "If there are things out there that somebody else can do for us, that is, either better, faster or economically more desirable, we should consider it."

"If I translate that down into HR, I'm going to talk about outsourcing and insourcing because we made a decision to build a shared services centre inside our company for things like payroll, benefits administration, billing, collections, a lot of the transactions, even property taxes – things that are transactional in nature. We have built inside our company a shared services centre, but as I look at it from my perspective, it's another form of outsourcing for HR. I'm outsourcing something outside HR, but it happens to be inside Nextel. It could just as easily have gone to an outsource provider, but the implications to HR stay the same. We're taking a lot of our function and putting it into this shared services environment. This is to eliminate the transactions completely if we can, minimise them at best, at least optimise whatever transactional work and administrative work needs to be done, and that's what we're doing with PeopleSoft and the next step of shared services, to get it out of HR completely. There's really very little benefit that an HR function can provide in adding another step in processing transactions or administration. So any of those things that are transactionally oriented, I'm in the game either to provide as an opportunity to our own internal shared services function or to look outside."

"As another example, even though we outsourced the transactional piece of our call centers to IBM and Teletech, we still have about 3,000 people who do strategic field care for us. This is critical to our customer service strategy and not something we will likely outsource. However, we remain open to considering other functions/processes that can be done better or more efficiently as outsourcing opportunities."

"If I turn to training, we have some 225–250 people in the Nextel University. There are some programmes that we will develop internally and deliver internally, there are some programmes that we do in sales training that we customise, but logic would suggest that I could tap into a 'Thomson Learning' or somebody like that – and we do – to pick up both content, development as well as delivery on high volume, repetitive activities. At the same time, am I going to turn over leadership development, succession planning, and next generation leadership of the company? I may go outside for coaching, I may go outside for a curriculum like we have in Georgetown University and some of the other schools, but that is, an area where I draw the line. That's the heart and soul of our company, and I'm hesitant to turn that over to some-body else. I will leverage resources externally, but not turn it over to them."

Don't do shared services in isolation

In this example, Tony Williams talks about the emphasis on delivering an internal shared services operation at the Royal Bank of Scotland.

"RBS does outsource a number of services, but its primary effort has been in respect of the development of an in-house shared services operation. From my perspective as Head of Shared Services, it is very clear that you don't do shared services in isolation when changing your HR function. Shared services is a fundamental enabler of something much bigger and much more worthy, which is fundamentally changing what you do with the HR function."

"If I allow myself reflection on what might have been outsourced, I do sometimes wonder, if we had outsourced the system management, whether we could have got into some other things quicker. I think we could have probably done some of the e-HR things quicker if we had outsourced our HR technology. Currently, our group technology function supports our in-house management of the PeopleSoft database and PeopleSoft products."

Don't get obsessed with the sourcing debate

Vance Kearney expresses the view that whatever the sourcing strategy is, the main objective is the displacement of transactions away from HR, to allow more value-added specialist services to be deployed.

"Continuing the theme of going back to specialisms, I would see managers either doing transactions themselves or having them done by somebody who doesn't work for the company – whether that's the provider of the benefit or some outsourced HR service, it doesn't matter to me. The in-house HR function is really about specialist expertise and advice not transactions.

"But I think that the change is happening – whether it's because of an in-house shared service centre, e-HR automation or outsourcing – the change is that transactions are going out of HR."

"It doesn't even have to be called outsourcing, as in the case of Oracle providing medical insurance for our staff. We don't do any administration on it, we never outsourced it because we never in-sourced it, we buy medical insurance and we have a health intermediary who handles the claims and deals with the employees, and if our employees are dissatisfied with the service, we change the service provider from time to time and that's it. That doesn't fit into outsourcing: it's what we've always done. We bought in the administration of many of our benefits, and I think that all that's happening is either the system does it, or it's done via self-service, or it's done via a shared service centre, or it's done via an outsourcer. So the debate about whether something is automated or whether it's outsourced or whether it's a bought-in service is frankly not very interesting."

Be wary of treating services as non-core

Richard Brady draws attention to the need to be careful about dismissing services as non-core and therefore suitable for outsourcing. "The move towards the enablement of the human resource business-partnering model has led to the mindset that 'if it's non-core we can look towards outsourcing it'. It is important to decide carefully what is non-core. It may be the customers regard sound, accurate and timely advice around their benefits entitlements and choices as being fundamental. For example, as an expatriate I want to know what's available to me and I want it to be accurate and I actually want to go and speak to a trusted advisor about that. At the top of the pyramid of HR enablement are the things that are possibly the higher added value, and some organisations tend to outsource the consulting advice. So HR has become leaner, and the role is changing in larger organisations to managing the quality of service provided externally, and it relies on an additional relationship now in order to deliver for the internal client base."

The service delivery approach should support the business model

Kath Lowey explains why Marconi withdrew from a major outsource of HR services and how she views the different options for the future.

"I think at the moment I'm comfortable with keeping most of our services in-house because of the speed with which we've changed ourselves. We did consider a major outsource of our services, but the plan was scrapped for a number of reasons, not least the rapidly diminishing scale of our operations caused by the downsizing activities. There was also a sense that the Marconi board didn't want us to go anywhere; they felt like they were losing us, even though, at times, we can be subject to criticism like other support functions."

"I think for me the key is finding a way to change the organisation and the business model to deliver what we need to, and then to put in the system that will underpin that new model. We are currently assessing the feasibility of different routes to doing this, such as a transactional service centre for HR on a European basis. Could we do that ourselves or would we need external help? I still have doubts about whether we would have enough costs to make it a viable option for an outsource provider unless we could demonstrate a future sustained growth and a footprint in Europe in a technology organisation, or we could look more radically and think on a regional basis or even on a European basis – we have IT, we have finance, we have HR, we have facilities management, that's a lot of back office support type activity. Could we house them together and move that forward based on technology, call centres, etc.? I think that's a possibility."

"But for HR globally as we stand today, we haven't got enough that would be attractive unless somebody wanted to use us as a footprint in those territories. My plan has been that we will outsource or partner where that makes commercial sense and service sense."

"Payroll is another issue. Should I look at payroll, do I need my own payroll department? We've only got five people; we've got a huge amount of intelligence from the past. Can I get that service better elsewhere? We outsourced training administration, but then we brought it back in-house and it's working well. So my plan is: I will always look, but I don't know whether I would look at the moment as a complete entity, because I don't think Marconi would stomach that and I don't think we've got enough people and costs to take out or enough projected growth to make it attractive to a provider. Or do we look at something more radical around integrating other functions with the aim to fulfilling the objective of back office to front?"

The tension between controlling costs and maintaining the human interaction

Maggie Hurt currently runs a shared services centre and talks about the tension between controlling costs and retaining the human touch. "We may well evolve to an outsourced model. But what we have tried to achieve with our current operational model is to build knowledge across a wide range of HR areas, for example, from organisational development to pensions."

"We have an in-house shared service centre. Our current challenge is to be as efficient as external outsourcers. We can't afford to get HR administration wrong. When National Grid and Transco merged, there were different approaches to shared services, and a decision was made to keep responsibility for transactional HR out of the HR function. This has not worked well, and transactional HR has now been absorbed back into functional ownership. Why? Our clients didn't see any difference between transactional HR and any other way we supported them. They expected us to sort out any problems with transactional HR activities. Yet we had no direct accountability for the quality of service provided by the shared service centre, and you can't manage these things by SLA or contract. Fundamentally it is back to the same point: for the client the attitude is, 'If you can't get my salary right, why should I trust you with other issues?' "

"Whilst we may, for economies of scale, cluster transactional activity into a shared service centre, we must never lose sight of the fact that we are dealing with individuals and that we need to treat people as individuals. These interactions with our clients are not transactions. We are providing a service. I really don't want to lose the intimacy between what we do in HR and our clients. Our work is about people, not processes, and we need to ensure that whatever decisions are taken in the future regarding outsourcing we do not lose sight of this fact."

The "fog" that surrounds the debate about outsourced cost savings

Philip Barr cautions against outsourcing on cost grounds, and argues that the in-house option can give better overall control of costs and service quality. "Much of the time a decision to outsource is done for the wrong reasons and the benefits are marginal. There needs to be a clear and unambiguous case for outsourcing which takes the longer term into account as well as the short term. Whilst the costs of in-house shared service centres may be higher than an outsourced option (and there is much fog around the realities of these costs), my experience is that the in-sourced option gives you better overall control over service and costs."

Getting your own house in order

Janice Cook stresses the importance of getting your own house in order before embarking on outsourcing. "We are still open-minded about outsourcing. Our priority currently is to get our own house in order. If we did explore the outsourcing option, we would need to identify a partner that shared our values and was able to support 600 sites across four nations. We are not yet confident that this organisation exists."

Only outsource transactions

Andy Field takes the view that once you have e-HR it is time to move transactions out of HR. "Unless it's payroll on its own, my view is that you should never outsource HR as a single entity. If you outsource, then it should be transactions only, and that's irrelevant of departmental/functional boundaries. The reason I say this is that we are now seeing HR splitting into two – professional service delivery/transactions; and also business partners. You cannot put barriers between HR systems and then finance, procurement, payroll: their processes flow right through, across the organisation and then externally (e.g. suppliers) as well. This creates conflicts with KPIs and also between companies, although I do see that you can do something like payroll individually if you really need to.

Look at the transaction irrelevant of where it is. In the future people will manage transactions irrelevant of where they sit. End-to-end processes are easier to manage now if we wanted, but many companies are not set up to do that at the moment."

"In summary, once you are e-enabled, outsource the transactions."

Outsourcing as a way of providing added value in recruitment

Claudia Hall explains how outsourcing may help control variable costs in recruitment. "From my perspective in recruiting, I am investigating the potential of outsourcing to provide added value to my function. Whilst we have scaled recruitment costs beautifully through the company, the pace and variability of the hiring cycle places enormous strains on the recruitment team members and raises important management issues around cost and service quality. At the moment, I have scaled my organisation from an employee basis to the minimum and I try to absorb variability by use of contractors. But how do I keep the contractors? How do I say, 'Go and take a couple of months off because hiring levels are low right now, and come back and work with us in January when things pick up,' when there's no guarantee? And if they did not come back that means I would need all new people, and it would take thirty to sixty days to train them and to get them up to the level they needed to be, from a performance perspective."

"So I started thinking about outsourcing as a means to develop more of a cost-effective variable workforce. If I can outsource recruiting to an organisation, they can maintain the variable workforce, they can maintain the staffing levels that I need, maintain the level of service that I need, and maintain the pipeline. The big issue for us is maintaining pipeline because people don't want to wait thirty days to hire, they want people now, so it's a question of maintaining a continual pipeline of candidates to reduce time-to-fill, making sure that we have a diverse pool of candidates at all times so that we can make our diversity numbers and at the same time being scaleable to cost. I am looking to outsourcing to help me with that."

These practitioner views underline the need to:

- *Understand the impact of your service delivery approaches within the context of your own business environment.* Whatever the mix of shared services/e-HR or outsourced services, it is important that HR understands the impact of this mix in terms of cost, perceived quality of services and the ability to adapt the elements to meet future needs. A cautionary note was sounded about pursuing one delivery approach, such as shared services, in isolation.

- *Manage the inherent tensions between cost savings and human interaction.* The potential danger of over-stretching on the cost-saving aspects, to the detriment of the "human side" of HR, must be borne in mind. Customer intimacy, a key driver of the perception of service quality, can be compromised if a transactional mentality, driven by cost reduction targets, dominates the service delivery philosophy.

- *Be clear about the relative merits of outsourcing, compared with in-house delivery options.* Whilst the advantages of outsourcing can be articulated in terms of scalability, service quality and cost-effectiveness, it is essential that the case for outsourcing be clearly defined, with a realistic expectation of cost savings and service delivery standards. As a precursor, it is necessary to "get your own house in order" and to understand the boundaries in terms of those services that are most likely to benefit from an outsourcing approach. Failure to do this could result in a loss of control over costs and service quality, leading to inferior service delivery and a raft of contractual issues.

3.3 The Factors Involved in the Choice of Service Delivery

This section builds upon the context and practitioner perspectives, to provide a more in-depth assessment of the factors involved in the choice of service delivery. It does not pretend to be exhaustive, but rather to highlight the key elements to assist with intelligent decision-making. A number of additional sources of material are referenced for those wishing to delve further into the subject.

Shared Services

As mentioned earlier in this chapter, cost drivers can dominate the decision to opt for shared services. Thew (2004) draws attention to an important issue:

"You have to be very clear about the messages you are sending to your staff. If it becomes clear you are thinking solely about cost, you risk tearing up the psychological contract between you and your people."

There are organisations, however, where the desire to improve the HR services has been the prime reason. Added benefits may flow from better discipline in meeting customer needs through contracting and monitoring performance, and HR may be given the chance to broaden their skills.

Perhaps the most crucial choice to be made in the way in which shared services are delivered is whether to perform tasks internally or externally. It is generally the high volume, routine, transactional activities that tend to be outsourced, because they are relatively easy to ring-fence and allocate to another organisation to perform on the client's behalf. This is examined in more detail later in this chapter.

We have already mentioned the cost motive, which can be realised in a number of ways – cutting staff numbers, reducing accommodation charges, obtaining greater combined buying power and achieving greater efficiency in what is done and how it is done. The other principal reasons for adopting shared services – quality improvement, organisational change and technological development – are also frequently seen in combination and are explained in more detail below.

Quality improvement

From the standpoint of quality improvement, shared services can:

- Make the function more professional in what it does.
- Achieve greater consistency and accuracy.
- Use better processes.
- Deliver work on time and to budget.

Through these means HR can provide a more professional, efficient and effective service. Technology can facilitate a number of these changes, as described below, but we have found that those companies introducing shared services often seek a change in attitude – a more customer-focused approach – which requires operating at a consistently higher standard and constantly seeking ways to improve. Furthermore, it means delivering services in a way that is, well attuned to the needs of line managers and employees.

Organisational change

The shared service centre concept can make it easier for HR to support customers during business change; the organisational structures might be reconfigured but a common support centre can adjust to this more easily than a disaggregated service delivery model. Given the frequency of structural change in many organisations, the structural flexibility offered by shared services can be a substantial benefit.

Another reason to deploy shared services is to reposition HR to change its role from a low-profile, fire-fighting role to a higher-profile contributor at the strategic level, well integrated with the business. More detail surrounding these changes can be found in Chapter 6.

Technological development

Developments in technology underpin many of the attributes of the shared services model. They can also support many e-HR applications – see below. However, introducing new technology is not an end in itself. It enables the organisation to complete work more efficiently through better processes and more effectively by improving quality control. However, it is an expensive venture to upgrade computing and communication devices and this has driven some organisations towards outsourcing, because they cannot fund the capital investment themselves. Outsourcing is covered in more detail below and the factors surrounding technology implementation are covered in more detail in Chapter 7.

More information about the reasons and choices surrounding the adoption of shared services can be found in Reilly and Williams (2003).

e-HR

As described earlier in section 3.1, another route for sourcing HR services is through e-HR – see Figure 3.1. This type of service provision certainly raises questions about technology, but crucially also important questions about devolvement of responsibilities to line managers and employees – matters explored in more detail in Chapters 5 and 7.

Fuelled by the claims of the consultants and technology vendors, the expectations of CEOs and senior management are high. However, in order to meet or exceed these expectations, it is vital that a number of considerations are addressed at the outset:

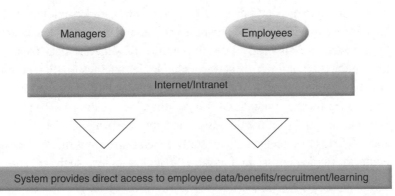

Figure 3.1 e-HR concept

- The focus on occasion is too much on the efficiencies of e-HR, that is, cost-cutting and not the longer-term gains enabled by the new infrastructure. One clear cause for concern is that discussion at senior management levels regarding the transformation impact on the HR function's capability could be too little and too late.
- The extent to which e-HR software is over-engineered and designed by IT consultants and not HR practitioners.
- The fact that e-HR is designed for the HR function and not the line managers who should be the real custodians of people and performance.
- The difficulties in securing access to the information that people really want.
- New technology does not remove poor quality data.
- Expect user resistance – unless the new e-HR-derived functionality is easy to use and seen to be relevant to the user, adoption rates are likely to be low.

In order to assess whether or not e-HR is meeting the promises, we should perhaps look in more detail at what has been achieved with the web-enablement of HR processes in practice.

e-HR processing practice

There is very little independent research on the take-up of e-HR solutions by UK-based employers. Most of the larger surveys are drawn from a predominantly North American sample and are undertaken or funded by proprietary software suppliers or consultants.

According to the European e-HR survey (2002), understanding the HR management environment of organisations, as well as existing and planned IT infrastructure, is particularly important in evaluating data regarding implementation and use of newer technologies such as e-HR. The most effective implementation of such technologies depends on several factors. Key among these are standardisation of processes, to the greatest possible extent; available IT infrastructure; data quality, and ongoing data mainten- ance. Where HR management is highly decentralised, it is much more dif- ficult to implement shared core HR technologies, such as Human Resources Management Systems (HRMS) and payroll, or web-based employee and manager self-services. In highly decentralised organisations, there is likely to be significant resistance to standardising processes. Without adequate IT infrastructure, implementing broad-based e-HR tech- nologies is simply impossible. Managers and employees must have at least workplace Intranet access, and the supporting data and telecommu- nications network must have adequate capacity to accommodate the level of usage that results from implementing e-HR services.

Watson Wyatt's survey (2002) of Business to Employee (B2E) and e-HR issues covering 173 companies in all sectors concluded that Europe lags behind the US in recognising the value of e-HR but is moving swiftly towards the change. Some 75% of participating companies plan to make changes in e-HR within the next 2 years. For the UK companies, "hard" business benefits such as reducing costs and increasing HR pro- ductivity feature highly. European companies (47%) are more likely to seek improvements in their HR service to employees than their UK counterparts (33%). Of those who have already implemented e-HR, just 8% reported that they had been very effective and 27% slightly effective in achieving the goals set. 9% believe e-HR to have not been effective at all and 23% do not yet know.

Other studies support the main themes evident from the above reports and show us that:

- e-HR will not succeed unless it is part of an employee focus culture, where people are trusted to manage their personal affairs. A corpo- rate Intranet with an employee directory will not of itself increase performance. It may save time, but it may not necessarily make people perform better (it may just give them more time in which to perform badly).

- HR needs to take ownership for establishing a relationship between the deployment of e-HR and enhanced organisational and employee performance.
- As the guardian of employee and organisational performance, the HR function will increasingly be caught up in the growing debate regarding the sustainability of the dependence upon new technologies in the workplace.

More information about the reasons and choices surrounding the adoption of e-HR can be found in the IES Report (2003).

3.4 Outsourcing

In this chapter outsourcing is defined as:

The planned transfer of a business process or function to a third party service provider in order to allow an organisation to achieve measurable business benefits.

Tactical outsourcing emerged in the 1980s as a response to the business environment of that time. Many organisations needed to reduce costs and at the same time respond to the changing nature of IT. The early benefits of outsourcing were seen as creating immediate cost savings and receiving a positive inflow of cash. Increasingly, however, the decision is based on obtaining business value rather than simply reducing costs. This reflects both the recognition of the contribution that outsourcing can make to a business, and the realisation that making outsourcing successful is not a quick and simple task. This extended contribution that outsourcing can make is often described as *strategic outsourcing*, where an organisation reorganises itself around its core competencies, and everything that is, not defined as core is a candidate for outsourcing.

In recent years more organisations have seriously considered, or indeed made a firm decision to outsource their HR services. This frequently entails entering into a contract with the chosen outsource provider for a minimum duration of 5 years, or even 7 or 10 years, and therefore should be seen as a strategic decision, as highlighted above, and not merely a tactical decision for reducing cost in the short term.

How to decide what to outsource

The benefits that can be derived from strategic outsourcing are much broader than the tactical benefits of cost reduction and cash infusion. They include:

- Leveraging best of breed suppliers who provide this service as a core part of their operation.
- Improving the focus of the organisation on its core competencies.
- Sharing risks and benefits.
- Obtaining guaranteed service levels.
- Enabling fundamental changes in business and process.
- Having access to a wider pool of experienced and skilled staff.
- Enabling career opportunities for existing staff.
- More visible and predictable costs.
- Bringing a wider range of new technologies to the attention of the organisation that will enable it to generate improvements in business value.

Outsourcing is not a magical solution

However, it is worth stressing at this point that if you have a difficult situation internally, such as broken processes or poor measurement of HR performance, do not believe or expect that an outsource provider will magically transform the situation. *It won't.* You need to do sufficient work internally so that you can understand more clearly what the HR function actually does, what it costs, and how benefits are measured and assigned.

Sorting out your own services first will also reveal opportunities for efficiencies, betterment of quality and cost cutting. This process may demonstrate that it would in fact be more appropriate not to outsource at all, or to significantly reduce the scope of any outsource contract.

In 2004, the International Association for Human Resource Information Management (IHRIM) presented an overview of the results of a new HR business process outsourcing survey conducted by Towers Perrin. The report highlighted a number of main findings, which are summarised below:

- HR business process outsourcing is delivering immediate cost savings, but has not met the transformational objectives of companies surveyed that have adopted broad-scale HR outsourcing in the past 4 years.

- A company cannot transform its HR function through outsourcing. Eliminating transactional work is a part of the broader objective, but only a part.
- Full-scale HR outsourcing demands changes in HR's fundamental role and requires people to behave differently. Companies that do not address this as such are far less successful than those that prepare internally for what everyone agrees is a seismic shift.
- More than three-quarters of the survey respondents, who collectively represent 90% of all current major HR business process outsourcing (BPO) arrangements, said that they had met short-term cost-saving goals, with 37% citing "complete success" on this key objective.
- Reductions in long-term costs are beginning to emerge as well, although 56% of the group said it was too soon to tell how their arrangement would affect the ongoing costs, and just 37% overall cited some success on this front.
- Respondents were far less positive about their results in such critical areas as transformation of the HR function, improvements in service quality, and employee and manager behaviour change.
- Significantly, companies' experiences with HR BPO differ depending on the timing of the deal. The earliest adopters did seek transformation of their function, passing both well and poorly designed processes to vendors so that they could focus solely on strategic work. The survey data show that this shift did not occur.
- Owing to the extent of behaviour change required from employees, managers and the HR function itself, companies found that they could not merely pass along staff and disorganized processes and achieve the expected benefits.
- Respondents had mixed views on one of the most controversial aspects of the outsourcing today: moving operations offshore. For the most part, the group did not have enough experience to assess either the value of offshoring or the validity of potential concerns about it. Just 45% expected to see cost reductions from offshoring, and while 29% said that they had "some to complete" success in meeting that expectation, most (57%) said it was too early to tell.
- More is more when it comes to processes outsourced. In outsourcing, the more processes moved to the vendor(s), the better the company's experience, because of the synergies that could be built across processes and economies of scale. But less is more when it comes to

75

vendors used. The fewer the vendors involved, the greater the satisfaction with the whole arrangement.

- The business must be involved. Higher satisfaction and effectiveness are also associated with increased involvement from key business leaders, especially in the most challenging area of implementation, reshaping the generalist to be more strategic and helping the organisation to rely more on self-service.
- Focus on helping generalists build new competencies. Two-thirds of the respondents agreed their HR generalists needed to develop new competencies.

Case Study

Lessons learned in the relationship between BT and Accenture

People Management (2004) reported that Accenture HR services and British Telecommunications (BT) have been working together since mid 2000 and the contract is up for renewal next year. The relationship has not been an easy one and a number of points were highlighted:

- "There is now more choice of outsourcers, so there are issues about whether Accenture is offering the best outsourcing alternative, and if so, how does BT keep them 'on their toes'."
- Difficulty in moving to another outsourcer: the commercial relationship will need to start all over again. Despite the difficulties, they now know each other as organisations.
- Imperfect communication: despite big investment in communication to keep HR managers informed, the line didn't get the same treatment and some didn't realise outsourcing had even happened.
- Time taken to establish a formal business relationship and clarify responsibilities was longer than expected.

In response to these issues various actions were taken:

- Policies were rewritten to become clearer and more user-friendly.
- Process review.
- A joint council was established to manage the contract. There is also an HR forum which aims to define the boundaries between BT work

and Accenture work and expected service levels. It also alerts Accenture to impending strategic changes that could impact the contract.

- Improved service level reporting.
- Greater clarity about service requirements, the price to be paid, role clarity and governance, and for both parties to be connected and informed about business direction or changes.

These perspectives are very helpful in highlighting some of the opportunities and challenges in pursuing the different sourcing options, particularly the outsourcing option. The next section examines in more detail ways in which you can identify the most appropriate outsource provider.

3.5 How to Find a Suitable Outsource Provider

So how do you decide whether to outsource HR services, and on what basis?

Remember that outsourcing is not the only option. All sourcing options should be evaluated against clear objectives and with an understanding of how benefit delivery will be measured. Do not assume that existing suppliers will make good outsourcing partners, and be creative in the way you define projects of "work packages" to meet business objectives.

A key decision must revolve around the perception of the degree of internal management control which is necessary to protect a vital interest or where the impact of failure is severe.

The treatment of core activities, seen as critical to the organisation or a source of competitive advantage, should be the central elements of any outsource decision. Some organisations may take the view that these should be closely guarded and kept in-house, whereas others would be only too ready to outsource these if the overall cost/benefit analysis proved favourable.

Having decided to outsource an activity, the next step is to establish your contract strategy. This helps you to decide what kind of provider you are looking for, how you make your choice and broadly, at this stage, the nature of the contract you want.

Providers offer the following broad range of capabilities:

- Niche skills: for example, recruitment and learning.
- Technical solutions: useful where technology is expensive, leading edge or complex such as supporting e-HR applications.
- Broad-based capability: this is combined with sufficient technology.

There are several models depending on whether you use one single or several best of breed suppliers, or a main contractor with subcontractors, and whether you intend to contract out part or all of the function/process. Individual suppliers will probably not be the best at everything and single supplier deals are not always the most cost effective. On the other hand, there is much more work involved in managing multiple contracts, and suppliers need to work together to provide the best service.

Settling upon the right sort of contract

There are standard terms that an effective contract should cover, but overall its emphasis should be on rewarding the supplier for quality of service rather than penalising them for failure to deliver. Many contract-related problems in outsourcing relationships stem from a failure to create a living document which is flexible and reflects the expectations of both the parties. Effective contract preparation provides a sound basis for productive outsourcing relationships. The contract should cover:

- terms of the agreement,
- minimum service levels,
- ownership and confidentiality of data,
- warranty,
- exhibits,
- transfer of assets and contracts,
- staff moves,
- termination clauses,
- incentives,
- disclaimers,
- bankruptcy,
- force majeure,

- performance measures,
- anticipating change.

It is also critical to have a clear contract specification defining the scope of the work, covering the following:

- Inter-relationship between processes.
- What work is handed over by whom to whom and at what point.
- If work is completely new, invite the potential contractor to propose the services they would choose, thereby standardising the production of an imaginative solution.

Hence it is at this stage, as part of the due diligence process, that you may want to ask the following type of questions. (This is not an exhaustive list, but provides examples.)

Commercial/pricing/cost savings

- Please provide details about any strategic relationships you have and how material those relationships are to your proposal.
- Provide a clear, transparent breakdown of your proposed price structure by function and activity, and year. What assumptions have been made regarding headcount?
- Provide examples of the level of discount we could receive.
- What is your willingness to apply a variable pricing structure straight away, as opposed to 6–12 months from transition?
- Provide a detailed breakdown of your proposed set-up costs.

Term and effective date

- Please clarify the input and dependencies surrounding the time-related elements of the proposed contract.

Service levels

- Are you willing to agree service levels upfront?
- Please provide specific service levels for review.
- Explain your rationale for your approach on service credits.
- What is your approach to operational assurance?
- What is your approach to handling ongoing and new initiatives?

- Explain your approach to and methodology of recruiting, including processes for identifying/attracting marketing candidates.

Other considerations

- In order to judge that other bids are acceptable, you need to have a detailed understanding of your current costs against your current services, otherwise it would be impossible to judge the quality of what you are being offered.
- Documentation should be in a form that makes sense to allow companies to meaningfully compare one bid with another.
- Selection of contractor will not only involve price and service offered, but also reputation, track record, one's own experience, if any, and the contractor's apparent financial stability.
- Also understand the motive of the contractor – why do they want the business, where do they expect to make money?
- Contractors may work to encourage the widest possible take-up of services made to optimise the higher value-added components. In other words, they may purport to be able to offer services at the top end of the service pyramid. Make sure you do very stringent diligence checks on these claims.

When designing the flexibility elements in the contract, make sure you account appropriately for reductions in activity levels compared with existing, as well as increases. The potential contractor may seek to impose a minimum annual commitment, a financial sum that represents the minimum value of the contract per year. This sum may seem to be fair and reasonable on the basis of current activity levels being maintained in the future, but can become a financial burden if activity levels decrease significantly.

Determining the contract length

- Generally, shorter-term contracts are more appropriate for cost-driven approaches and tend to be favoured for lower skilled or less complex tasks.
- Longer-term contracts are more appropriate for more complex tasks involving significant handover times and learning period for the contractor.

- The concept of a "strategic alliance" becomes more realistic as contract times are lengthened. Contractors prefer longer contractual terms because of increasing efficiencies over time, and also the "softeners" that can be offered in the early years.

Statement of key deliverables

These deliverables must relate to volume, training and quality of the output (see examples below). Importantly:

- These deliverables have to be buttoned down or ambiguities will later become apparent.
- If existing performance definitions do not exist, you need to establish a baseline through stakeholder perception analysis or by linking expected performance to benchmark performance of other service providers.
- Establish clear contractual key performance indicators (KPIs) to define the expected level of operational performance from the contract (see Figure 3.2).
- Consider contractual measures for dealing with success and failure; that is, withholding payments as service levels fall or providing bonus payments if performance levels improve. Whatever the regime, a regular reporting schedule is necessary, including indices of performance and progress meetings.

Service item	Service descriptor	Service measure
Resourcing services	Permanent employee – time from receipt of an approved hiring request form to offer acceptance	Average time to offer acceptance: within 20 business days
Resourcing services	Non-PAYE contractor – time from receipt of an approved hiring request form to offer acceptance	Average time to offer acceptance: within 6 business days
Learning services	L&D projects customer satisfaction	90% customer satisfaction based on post delivery survey
Reward services	Action authorised contractual salary adjustments by agreed cut off dates	90% of adjustments to be processed accurately for pay runs
Reward services	Ensure statutory compliance in all processes	100% compliance

Figure 3.2 Illustrative contractual KPIs

■ There should be an escalation clause in the contract to resolve disputes and ultimately terminate the contract if things have degraded to a profoundly unsatisfactory level.

Implementation plan

There is an ever-increasing number of organisations who have learnt that outsourcing is not a simple way of passing business problems to a third party, and some are finding it difficult to realise the benefits. The 1999 Outsourcing World Summit Survey System indicated that 40% of the 219 respondents were either dissatisfied with or ambivalent about the results of their outsourcing initiative. At the same time, many organisations are managing successful outsourcing relationships with the same suppliers. So what can we learn from these experiences? The following list highlights some of the most significant and most frequently overlooked elements of a good outsourcing arrangement. Those involved should always remember, however, that problems can and do arise throughout the process of planning and implementing the outsource.

The implementation plan should be developed once the business case has been agreed. It should take account of how quickly the process can be outsourced and of the need to prepare for the transition. Before embarking on any outsourcing project, it is important to assess the readiness of the business for the transfer of services. There may be critical projects delivering at certain times which might affect the timing of the handover.

It is vital to be clear about how the business relationship will be managed by both the supplier and the customer.

The *relationship plan* should establish how the respective parties are going to establish trust and how the initial controls will evolve to reflect the changing relationship. In most cases controls can be relaxed as trust is developed, but they are essential in the early stages of the relationship.

The customer should have a role in agreeing the supplier's account management, and key managers on both sides should be involved in the contract design and negotiation.

The transitional phase relies heavily on *trust and collaboration* between those involved, and this is where most problems arise. At this stage it is essential to establish roles, responsibilities and processes to enable a seamless transfer of service. If there is inadequate trust between the management and the supplier, things can go wrong quickly and with dire consequences.

If these issues are addressed effectively at the outset, the relationship is off to a sound start and partnership is a realistic goal. The best way to consolidate and build on such a relationship is to establish a unit in which both the customer and the supplier(s) have a stake – emotionally, professionally and financially, if not legally. This unit, which can be called the *management organisation*, is the champion of the outsourcing deal. Its objectives are determined and its performance is measured in the terms of the contract. Ideally it is answerable to a joint group comprising representatives of all the stakeholders: the business and all outsourcing suppliers.

A culture of *open information* is essential if both supplier and customer are to get what they need out of the relationship. The supplier needs to make a profit and the operating side of the business might want a share of the management organisation's gains. Practical difficulties can arise from this: for example, the supplier may have data centres containing sensitive information for more than one customer. These issues need to be identified and resolved early on in the relationship.

People management

The timing of the outsourcing implementation plan needs to take into account the demand that this will make on resources, including people from:

- the function which is in scope,
- other parts of the business which are impacted,
- HR,
- legal,
- finance,
- facilities,
- PR.

Managing by contract

A project manager may typically have had between 50 and 200 people working for him or her prior to outsourcing. This will have conferred considerable power in a traditional and hierarchical sense. In contrast, the management organisation or retained function may consist of a small team of very experienced and competent people within specific domains, of which project management may not be one. Therefore, the management of transition to new roles within the retained function and introduction of new contract management skills is a key issue that should be planned before and during implementation. It cannot be assumed that the skills required to run an in-house function will necessarily be those appropriate to managing the contract.

It is important to retain the right people to manage the outsourcing process, that is, those with the right skills, attitude and personality. The management organisation is often required to switch from a task-led environment into a service-oriented culture. It may be necessary to retrain or transfer existing employees or even to recruit new ones. The new team needs to be built and developed as quickly as possible. External advisors with experience in outsourcing can help to transfer skills using tool kits, coaching, workshops, feedback and assessment.

Summary

The advent and deployment of new technology has enabled employers to change the structure of their HR functions by creating new options for delivering HR services. Amongst these are, for example, call centres, web-enabled self-service and shared service centres. These activities may be provided in-house or in whole or in part through third party organisations, such as outsourcing.

However, technology is not the only factor in determining options in HR service delivery. The different levels of access amongst sections of the workforce and the willingness of managers and employees to use them are just as important, if not more so.

It seems likely that most HR functions would prefer to offer multiple channels at least until self and assisted service have become more culturally acceptable to the organisation. However, the key to success seems to lie in creating a strategy of self-service contact that is, driven by business imperatives, whilst being responsive to users' needs. The practitioner perspectives and the published material considered earlier emphasise the need for technology decisions to be firmly rooted in business and functional strategies and HR practices, if they are to maximise the potential benefits. HR should expect senior management to exert more pressure on HR to justify investments in HR technology through return on investment analysis (ROI) and business case developments. Chapter 4 deals with these issues in more detail.

4

Making the Business Case for Transformation

This chapter deals with a vital stage of the transformation process: the construction of the business case. To some in the organisation, the business case is *the* item that will persuade them that the changes you are proposing are credible.

Chapter Structure

Key Themes
4.1 Context
4.2 Practitioner Perspectives
4.3 What is the Purpose of the Business Case?
4.4 What are the Key Elements of the Business Case?
4.5 Target Benefits
4.6 Next Level Design and Cost Estimates

4.7 Cost–Benefit and Risk Analysis
4.8 The HR Transformation Roadmap
4.9 Achieving Real Buy-In and Ownership of the Business Case
Summary

Key Themes

- A business case serves a number of purposes. It makes the case in terms of the return on investment for the transformation. It is a tool by which HR can engage with business colleagues in shaping the future services and value that HR delivers. And it is the key control document by which the HR transformation programme guides action by throughout the life of the programme.

- The business case needs to address the "hard" ROI elements of the proposed transformation. Spending time and effort on both the costs and benefits side of this will pay dividends both in terms of the credibility that this gives to your case and the baseline that this gives you for measuring benefit delivery.
- The business case builds on the "case for change" described in the envisioning section of Chapter 2, and as such is not just about numbers but also about understanding and articulating what the nature of the change is and why it is important to the organisation. This needs to be made real for the business. Developing a roadmap of what will change, and when, provides a very tangible way of describing this change in practical terms.

4.1 Context

A compelling business case is an essential step on the way to achieving a vision of transforming the way the HR function works and to realising anticipated benefits.

This chapter examines how to make that case by defining benefits and costs – the so-called "hard" elements of the case – and engaging the various stakeholder groups so that they understand, buy in and commit to the business case – the so-called "soft" elements of the case. The key to success is to pay equal attention to both elements, and through involving stakeholders in developing and making the case, the foundations for transformation are established.

4.2 Practitioner Perspectives

Traditionally, HR practitioners have been viewed as more reticent than colleagues in other functions in developing a strong, clear case for change in their function. However, the discussion with our practitioners below shows that there is now little justification for this view. Our senior HR practitioners are concerned to make an effective case, and for this to stand up to scrutiny from colleagues within the organisation and in comparison to other investment decisions that they may be competing with for funding. The views of our senior HR practitioners in this area highlight the following themes.

■ *Gaining business buy-in is a critical step in making the business case*
Andy Field focuses on the first step in making the business case – selling the vision of the future. "When you are selling a vision, simple is best. You have to show or demonstrate how the vision is going to give you a positive business impact – so, for example, how this is going to make a positive impact on the bottom line. Changing values and behaviours hitting the bottom line gives you influence. We found that we were splitting HR in two and leaving the transactional and processing to one side. We were then left to concentrate on the business partner end, for example, strategic planning, looking at how people work together, the culture, but *always* relating to how it impacts the bottom line."

"As in any communications initiative, it works best when you are talking the business' language. So we used the same frameworks and language, but related that to the people agenda."

Maggie Hurt sees the importance of working with senior business stakeholders at an individual level in order to gain business buy-in. "I have invested a great deal of time with a small number of senior managers in getting across my vision for HR. I have been helped enormously in having senior colleagues who value HR's contribution and the difference we can make to the effectiveness of an organisation. This is true of others on the executive teams too. We have some very strong line managers in National Grid Transco."

"Our senior clients give us the air time. It is down to us to make best use of it."

■ *The business case must be rooted in addressing real business issues*
If real buy-in is to be achieved, the business demands that HR change must clearly support the business agenda. Tony Williams' case is rooted in improving business performance through managers and their teams. "Our business case is fundamentally to build upon the

shared services platform and to offer more 'assisted service' to managers and employees through e-HR. This will continue to challenge the perception that HR is a highly transactional, administrative department, and provide an opportunity to further re-shape the role of the HR business partner."

"The overall aim is to create a situation where managers and employees have the ability to access information that they need for their jobs or for personal data reasons, for example, flexible benefits, directly from their workstations or through shared services. In turn, this will encourage more self-responsibility for those tasks and allow the HR function to address more value-adding areas, such as meaningful business analysis and proactive intervention to enable line managers to achieve better performance for themselves and their teams."

Steve Ashby also builds his case on the improvement in business performance and shows how tangible measurement of this improvement is critical. "The defining difference to our business performance is the creation of world-class capability at country management level. We know through our performance over the last two years that a high performing team can significantly improve their bottom line through organic sales growth and cost management, but an average-performing team will barely break even. This is because they cannot spot opportunities and turn them into profit fast enough. Average teams lack speed, agility and the 'can do' attitude, which is our primary organisational value."

"So the recognition of this sets the key business priorities for HR and fundamentally underpins the business case. Whilst it's the same set of individual interventions that any other HR function would put in place – performance management, feedback and coaching, individual career planning, succession planning and so on – it takes on a new relevance when you are able to actually see the commercial result of building a high performing team, versus accepting whatever's there and not deliberately investing in capability. This investment consists of taking the hard calls and replacing poor performing management quickly, as well as developing those with potential. In my experience, things do not get better if you persevere with mediocrity."

"We're also using the Balanced Business Scorecard to allow effective comparison of performance across our various countries. This is particularly important for our global clients, so we get transparency of performance and can address critical issues."

At Nextel, Claudia Hall describes how the case in HR reflects the service culture that Nextel promotes externally. "The business case was driven primarily by the insatiable desire and drive to make sure that HR made it easier for internal Nextel business customers to do business with us, so that they in turn would have more time to spend on their business, which is the business of dealing with Nextel customers. Previously, under the geographically focused structure, there were considerable inefficiencies and inherent confusion in the delivery of services, and this had a detrimental impact on Nextel's customers and profitability."

"Importantly, therefore, the transformation in the HR service delivery model was not driven primarily by cost-cutting pressures or technology considerations – although understandably these were addressed as part of the whole business case. It was driven by the need to place the customer first, to have a 'single point of contact' capability, and then to push back into the HR function to see what needed to be done to achieve that."

Whilst customer service is typically a major driver of the case for change, the other major driver is efficiency improvement. For Kath Lowey, efficiency improvement that reflected the overall cost reduction drive within Marconi was critical in the first instance. "The business case supporting the changes over the past 4 years has really been driven by the need for severe cost-cutting, in response to a turbulent operating environment."

"The task now is more to do with improving the levels of HR service delivery into the business. The centrepiece of the emergent business case is a new technology platform – the move to a single instance HR information system. We now need to design a service model that will complement the system and not the other way round. So we have to show that it's about the effectiveness of line management, it's about information online, it's about Marconi online, and that's why I think we need to think more radically about how we can deliver those European-type processes across Europe rather than be too UK-centric."

■ *When you make the case is just as important as how you make the case*
Janice Cook believes that "Timing was critical. The organisation was ready to make some radical changes as part of the infrastructure review. Our business had grown dramatically, and we just wouldn't have been able to get anywhere near the scale of change now being proposed three or four years ago."

"We focused on the business and on what the business could afford from its support functions. It just did not make sense to reinvent the same activity ten times over. In making the business case, one of the key cultural issues we had to address was the lack of trust in advice provided outside a particular region or country."

Randy Harris utilised the context of his organisation in its industry, and the overall economic environment, to inform how and when he made the business case. "I knew when I got here that eventually this company was going to have to get some level of centralisation, some level of standardisation, because otherwise we were going to continue to add expense, basically at the same rate that we were adding revenue, and you would never scale the business. So I had a couple of choices: I could have pushed for that move when I first got here, but at that time the stock market was on steroids: it was growing at a rapid rate and there was no compelling reason to make a change. The reality of it was that the pain of changing was going to be greater than the perceived benefit of changing, and in my experience, people or organisations or companies rarely change until leadership comes to a conclusion that the pain of not changing is greater."

"Then a year or so later the market growth began to falter and all of a sudden those people who liked having a decentralised business with full control began looking a bit more receptive to another way of doing business. It really focused our attention on how we delivered to our external customer, and we came to the conclusion that consistency and standardisation were going to allow us to scale our business and improve our operating margin. What has happened in the last three years is that every functional leader took control nationally for the functions: the CFO took control of finance; the CIO took control of IT; I took control of HR; the Chief Marketing Officer (CMO) took control of marketing; and it was a difficult time because we shifted from that geographic-centric model to a functional model. What that did was allow each of us to really focus more inwardly on our function to get a more sophisticated model, a better service delivery model and, most importantly, to improve our services while reducing our cost of doing it."

"I don't think I would have been able to get that if HR had been trying to do it solo. It was easier to do because every other function in the company was going through a similar transformation, and it was also easier to do because there were compelling reasons to change.

We needed to: we were in a business that was heavily debt-loaded, and we needed to work down the debt, we needed to get profitable, we needed to get free cashflow, and every function was able to contribute to do that. So I think it's important that when HR tries to get through a transformation, and it's going against the grain of what the company's doing or your culture's doing, it's probably a path to failure. If you can align what you're doing with the direction that your business and business strategy is going, then not only are you enhancing the HR function but you're visibly contributing directly to the overall value creation of the company, and it's easier to get traction."

■ *Investment in HR technology must clearly link to the business benefits you are targeting*

Having considered the benefit side of the business case equation, we come to our practitioners' reflections on the cost side. A major driver of cost is clearly the investment in technology. However, there are different approaches that organisations take in how they make the case for and utilise HR information systems. For instance, Andy Field offers an incremental perspective that builds on the existing technology investment. "The LSE started with a basic HR back office system and a very elementary Intranet across the organisation. There was not a lot of development money, but enough operating expenditure to be able to do some enhancing. The initial approach was to create an HR portal on the Intranet, and then to begin pulling through HR information (procedures, policies, manuals) into a framework, and then to develop a bespoke product to develop the whole e-HR set. But our main constraint was that we did not have the money to do this on a single HR system. Therefore, we needed to look to external products and companies at the smaller end of the market and use a portal approach to bring them together into a single product. To add to that, the architecture we have inherited is fairly diverse, hosted internally and externally. But by using a portal we are able to present this as a single experience to the user, which of course is important for them."

Helen Corey links the business value of information with the investment in technology. "I think a fundamental component that no one has crisply articulated to a business is how you are actually supposed to use data. The key questions for me are: How many people do I have? Where are they located? How much do I pay them? When is the next perform-ance review and how did they do on their last one?"

"Simply adding more e-HR screens or web-enabled screens for me to look at without sensitising me to what I should be doing with it is of little use. Therefore, the provision of good useful data and then sen-sitising the management population to the data should underpin any business case."

Philip Barr sees wider benefits from the investment in HR tech-nology. "Technology will and ought to be used in HR. It can do things quicker and cheaper. Of itself, it doesn't add value. It is ques-tionable if a pure ROI analysis would justify most HRIS investments. Some of the rationale must be around 'you just have to have this functionality.'"

Finally, Miles Warner reminds us that implementation costs and cost of ownership must be considered when making the case for investment in HR technology. "Underpinning this [HR transformation] is greater e-HR functionality, although I am naturally sceptical about the cost savings claimed by some organisations. I think there is a cost saving, but in the analyses we have done that cost saving does not offset the cost of imple-mentation and investment cost. It might do in the long term, but if you're looking at two or three year returns it doesn't work."

"Where the value comes is in the quality of service. You have a more motivated set of employees and managers, because they're getting accurate reliable data, and if you use it correctly you can make much more informed management decisions."

In summary, the practitioner views emphasise that:

■ *The customers of HR services must buy in to the transformation.* Achieving buy-in is not a one-off event, but one that takes significant senior HR effort. It is not only about presenting ideas to the business on how HR can deliver greater value, but it is about involving them in shaping what this could look like and what the costs and benefits are in doing so.
■ *Buy-in is achieved through linking HR change to real business issues.* How HR can support the business in addressing its issues is at the heart of the case for change. Typically, this is a function of defining

benefits that improve service and/or efficiency combined with the timing that makes the business case compelling. There is no "one size fits all" here. The business issues are about the context of the organisation in the environment it is operating in at the point in time that you are making the case.

■ *Transformation is not just about technology.* It is easy to become overawed with the technology available to support HR transformation. This may be due to the potential costs, the plethora of tools or the sheer breadth of functionality. You need to cut through this, and implement technology that addresses the business needs you are targeting and takes account of what you already have in place. The costs of technology implementation can be high, but this does not have to be the case if you are judicious in its use.

Having seen the practitioners' views on making the business case, we now address the steps that we believe are critical in order to achieve what they have described above. We begin with considering the role of the business case in the transformation.

4.3 What is the Purpose of the Business Case?

In our opinion, the purpose of the business case is fourfold: as the next step in the change process; as the mechanism to obtain approval and funding to proceed; as a reference point for all decisions and activities during implementation; and as the next stage in the design process. Each of these is described in more detail below.

The process of business case development should be seen as the next step in the change management process. Whilst you and close colleagues have developed and fully understood the vision, you need to get others on board too. The vision needs to be "real" for them too, and to become something that they can contribute to as it develops and evolves.

This process helps identify who the advocates of the changes are, who is ambivalent, and finally those who are actively against the transformation. Identifying the members of these different camps, and taking appropriate action at an early stage, will significantly increase the likelihood of success. How to address these groups is explained in Chapter 5, where the steps in moving from resistance to commitment are examined in detail.

In addition to its role in the change process, the business case will become a document around which future programme management decisions should be based.

So the business case should be used as a reference point all the way through the programme, not just as the tool to get permission to start. For instance, when the going gets tough, it can be used to galvanise stakeholder support by reminding them of the commitments they have made.

The business case is constructed in the context of the HR value pyramid, described in some detail in Chapter 2, in terms of how HR function will move from an administrative and transactional processing focus to being a true business partner. In developing the case, that premise is taken as the starting point and each aspect of HR is then carefully considered so that the implications of achieving the desired level of benefits and of the costs involved are clearly understood.

However, despite this, many organisations have skimped on this vital area of work until relatively recently, not investing the time and resources required to put together a business case that will ensure the HR function and the wider business are clear on the costs and benefits of transformation.

Often it is prudent to develop an "initial" business case prior to a more detailed "full" business case. The purpose of the initial business case is to obtain permission and funding to do more detailed design work. As a result, every aspect does not have to be defined in extreme detail. The second, and more detailed, full business case is the document used to secure funding to do the main implementation, and to act as a reference point for all decisions and activities during the implementation, as long as any assumptions on which it is based, for example cost estimates, remain stable. Of course, not all assumptions hold true, and the business case becomes a document which is updated and refined throughout the life of the programme. This matter is also covered in Chapter 5, where programme governance issues are examined further.

The process of developing the business case takes the design articulated so far through envisioning (in Chapter 2) and defining the service delivery channels (in Chapter 3) to the next level of detail. In Chapter 1 we refer to the change cycle model (see Figures 1.3 and 1.4). It is helpful to view this process as moving from the first stage – building the case for change – to the second stage – planning the change.

Case Study

A major global manufacturer had a vision for a "global e-HR transformation", but during the development of the business case the initial definition of "global" was constantly challenged, with different stakeholders querying the definition as there were potential legal, cultural and practical implications for each definition. For example, the global design required one set of employees to have access to information on colleagues of a more senior grade. In one country this was inappropriate under the current ways of working.

It took a considerable amount of work with stakeholders in that country at an early stage to get agreement on this aspect of the global design. However, this was achieved and reflected in the full business case, thus providing a reference point for future queries with respect to this decision.

4.4 What are the Key Elements of the Business Case?

The previous discussion highlights the purpose of the business case as being: the next step in the change process; the mechanism to obtain approval and funding to proceed; as reference point for all decisions and activities during implementation; and as the next stage in the design process. Clearly the key elements of the case need to address each of these areas.

Involvement of benefit owners and change sponsors in developing the business case is the important next step in the change process (see Section 4.9). Approval and funding usually requires a cost–benefit calculation (see Section 4.7) including a definition of the risks and assumptions used in developing the cost–benefit analysis.

For the business case to act as a reference point it must articulate the plan for delivery and the principles by which benefits will be delivered (see Section 4.8). Finally, the next level of detail for the design must underpin this by defining how benefits will be achieved (see Section 4.5) and what investment is required in order to deliver the benefits (see Section 4.6).

The following case study illustrates a typical business case structure and how the elements outlined above fit into that.

Case Study

The HR leadership team of a major UK government department wanted to seek ways of reducing resources engaged in routine administrative tasks, and to concentrate resources on supporting departmental managers in delivering government targets.

Therefore, the objective of the business case development phase was to provide:

- The identification and detailed financial analysis of the benefits in relation to HR process areas.
- The integration of the related people programme initiatives into the implementation plan setting out the linkages with the business case.
- HR organisation structure proposals and benefits integration with the business case.

The department was able to produce a three-tier business case that included:

- Executive summary – setting out the key factors for executive decision-making regarding this programme.
- Main body – defining the specific costs, benefits and risks associated with the project in the context of the proposed delivery approach.
- Appendices – providing the detail behind the body of the report, including detailed cost analysis, benefit calculations and assumptions.

Following approval of the business case, the programme team used it as the key control document throughout the implementation.

We now explore each element of the business case in more detail.

4.5 Target Benefits

The process of defining target benefits is an iterative one, working from the whole to the part. This approach provides a good example of how a systems mindset can be employed in practice. The process is one of setting macro-level targets initially and then breaking those targets down into specific benefits that can be attributed to changes that will be made through HR transformation.

An excellent starting point for defining targets is the business drivers model described in Figure 2.2. This model links HR's contribution to business issues across the three drivers of organisational effectiveness, namely, revenue growth, cost efficiency and brand identity. Having worked with this model during envisioning, HR's priorities for change will have emerged across these three drivers. The next step here is to attach targets to those priorities that will articulate the level of ambition for HR transformation. The organisational levers model introduced in Figure 1.2 provides further assistance here. The model is used to articulate the "as is – current HR" and the "to be – future world of HR" and therefore provides a good description of the magnitude of the change. By considering the magnitude of the change for each of the priorities, ambition levels and hence targets can be set.

So what do the targets look like? If we take an example from the cost efficiency driver, typical targets could be a reduction in the HR budget of 30% or a change in the ratio of HR staff to employee base from 1:70 to 1:150. The key in setting targets is to make them challenging enough so that it is not possible to achieve them without significant change (otherwise why would you embark upon HR transformation?) whilst ensuring that the targets are realistic enough to be achieved, as this will be a measure of the success of the transformation.

To assist in setting targets it is often helpful to compare yourself to best practice found elsewhere. Benchmarking where you sit in comparison to other companies will give you an indication of what realistic targets for your transformation programme should be. However, the risk with using benchmarks is that you may have to dig very deep into another organisation to find whether you are comparing like with like. So we advocate using benchmarks as a guide only, and spending enough time collecting your own baseline data so that you know where you are now and can then set targets in relation to that baseline.

Once the targets are set, the next stage is to break them down to determine the detail benefits that will collectively contribute to meeting the overall target. A good way to do this is to consider the services that HR offers and the service elements and HR processes that constitute each service. Figure 4.1 provides a services model of HR that we have found effective for doing this. For further information on this model please refer to Chapter 6 and Appendix 3.

Before considering what those benefits are in detail it is worth spending some time defining what we mean by a benefit, particularly the difference between tangible and intangible benefits.

Tangible benefits form part of the cost–benefit analysis (see Section 4.7) at the heart of the business case. It is something that can be measured and attributed to the transformation programme, and crucially to *particular budget holders*. Therefore, as well as identifying the benefit, it is important to determine the recipient or recipients of that benefit and ensure that they buy in to it, as they need to be accountable for the delivery of that benefit. For example, if we consider e-recruitment, who will be the beneficiary of reduced agency fees: the HR function or a business unit? The answer depends on how costs are allocated in the organisation but, whichever it is, a tangible benefit will accrue to the budget holder(s) for those costs. The table below shows examples of tangible benefits for a selection of HR services' constituent processes and potential beneficiaries.

HR service	Constituent process	Tangible benefit	Beneficiary
Resource management	Recruitment and selection	Reduced agency fees	Business unit heads
People development and performance management	Training and development	Reduction in external training costs	Vice President, L&D
Retention and reward	Reward strategy and reward levels	Manual reward data processing eliminated	Compensation and Benefits Manager

Intangible benefits can often be estimated but not attributed to particular budget holders. They should not therefore be included in the cost–benefit analysis, as accountability for the delivery of that benefit is diffused

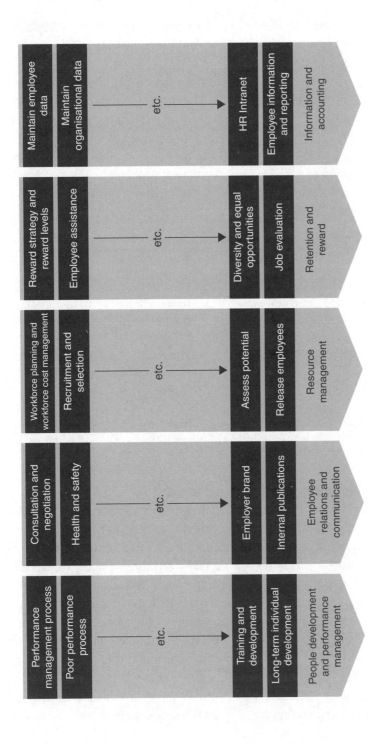

Figure 4.1 HR scope of services

across the organisation, making it extremely difficult to attribute the achievement of a benefit to a particular change that the HR transformation programme has made.

Again, if we consider a move to e-recruitment, there should be a reduction in the time from a vacancy arising to when a new recruit arrives, starts their induction process, and subsequently contributes to the business. In this case, it is harder to pin down to whom this benefit accrues. The table below shows examples of intangible benefits for the same selection of HR services' constituent processes. However, whilst beneficiaries are identified, it is at the business function rather than budget holder level.

HR service	Constituent process	Intangible benefit	Beneficiary
Resource management	Recruitment and selection	Reduced time from vacancy to hire	All business units and functions
People development and performance management	Training and development	Improved match of skills to roles	All business units and functions
Retention and reward	Reward strategy and reward levels	Improved retention	All business units and functions

Whilst intangible benefits are not included in the cost–benefit calculation, beware of thinking that they are not as important as tangible ones. Intangible benefits that contribute to the revenue growth and brand identity drivers of the organisation are often strategically significant. Therefore, it can also be useful to further distinguish intangible benefits in terms of their strategic importance. In the case of transforming the HR function, these are often the benefits associated with how the HR function will add value to the products and services that the company delivers to its customers. Often the benefits sought in this area are delivered through the business partner role, and it is here that measurement of these benefits usually takes place. However, this area of benefit is one that does not lend itself directly to quantitative measurement, and comparative and qualitative data are often used here.

Case Study

Consider a major Internet Services Provider whose strategic vision was to operate an e-enabled environment internally so that it would be second nature for staff when they sold and delivered these services externally. When rolled out to managers and employees, e-HR would touch the whole organisation and would therefore be an excellent catalyst for e-enabling the organisation internally. The company recognised this, and saw it as a key intangible strategic benefit. Whilst significant tangible benefits had been identified and quantified, the e-HR implementation clearly demonstrated to the wider business that e-enablement was a realistic proposition and, more importantly, was capable of being delivered to all within the organisation. Thus, e-HR was able to add value not only in terms of predicted cost savings but also in terms of enhancing service delivery to the end customer.

Having considered the changes that each process will undergo and determined what the benefits are, whether each benefit is tangible or intangible and who the beneficiaries are, the next step is to determine when you expect each benefit to be delivered and what its magnitude is. The milestone plan described in Figure 2.7 provides a starting point for estimating when benefits will be achieved, taking into account the fact that usually benefits are not realised immediately upon implementation, but there needs to be a period of transition.

Estimating the magnitude of benefits depends on the nature of the benefit. For example, reductions in cost may be calculated by estimating how much less effort the new way of working will involve, and multiplying that by the number of transactions made and the unit cost of performing each transaction. However, it is critical to have baseline measures of process performance from which estimates can be made.

In determining and estimating benefits a number of assumptions will be made which need to be recorded. If these assumptions change through the course of the programme then that particular benefit may need to be revised. Taking the e-recruitment example, typical assumptions include:

- How much do you plan to use the web to recruit rather than agencies?
- Will agencies perform any pre-screening?
- Will you continue to use specialist agencies?

Once the benefits identification and estimation process is complete across all process areas, then the individual benefits should be aggregated together to determine if the targets set at the macro-level can be supported by the benefits at the detail level. Typically, this process of aggregation and benefits identification and estimation is iterative.

Finally, one of the main levers for influencing achievement of the targets is flexing the scope of HR transformation. Clearly increasing the scope should increase benefits and decreasing the scope should reduce benefits. However, this will of course have an effect on costs.

4.6 Next Level Design and Cost Estimates

The identification of detailed benefits necessitates a more detailed understanding of the design of the HR transformation solution. In Section 4.3 we defined part of the purpose of the business case as the next stage in the design process. It is through the identification of benefits and their associated costs that this is achieved. The benefits identified will require certain elements of the HR transformation solution to be in place in order to deliver them. Therefore, a good starting point for the estimation of HR transformation costs is to first articulate the design at the next level of detail based upon the detailed understanding of benefits that has now been developed. In order to ensure that this is sufficiently comprehensive, the design across each HR service area (see Figure 4.1) and the process, people and technology elements that make up the HR transformation solution in that area should be defined.

In a similar way to the identification of detailed benefits, the constituent processes within each HR service area provide the best starting point for this next level of design. It is through a clear understanding of how each process will be executed in future that the organisational and technology implications can be determined. Taking what has been documented in a narrative and bullet-point format during envisioning and service delivery definition and defining the specific organisational and technology implications gets to the level of detailed required. Then mapping this out into process flowcharts helps the linkages between elements of the process to be defined. When this has been done for each HR service area the "end-to-end" solution can then be aggregated from this detail to ensure the consistency and effectiveness of that solution. This then provides the design framework within which the detailed design and implementation can be addressed as described in Chapters 6 and 7. Using this framework, the detail designers can be confident that benefits will be achieved providing they remain within the boundaries defined by the framework.

From a cost perspective, defining the technology and people implications of the processes means that overall HR transformation costs may be estimated by considering these two elements only. However, in order to ensure that an estimate of HR transformation costs is made over the same time period that the benefits are anticipated (required for the cost–benefit analysis), both one-off costs – that is, those attributable to the delivery of the HR transformation programme – and those costs that are ongoing – that is, those required in order to maintain the HR transformation solution – need to be estimated. The following table provides guidance on this classification and example technology and people-related costs.

Cost	Description
One-off/transformation programme-related costs	
Capability development	Development-related costs, redeployment and redundancy costs
Labour	Internal and external labour costs on the programme team, also including wider business costs covering design workshops, testing and training
Content	Development of initial e-content
Hardware	Server and associated implementation costs
Network	Costs of capacity to deliver e-HR to the desktop, telecommunications-related costs for service centres
Method of access	Providing sufficiently high specification machines and software to access e-HR functionality
Licences	Initial software licence costs
Ongoing/maintenance costs	
Content	Maintenance of content
Support	Both IS/helpdesk support and business support
Operational	For example: software upgrades and licence maintenance costs, costs of running a service centre, outsource charges, HR staff costs

Often some of the most significant one-off costs are those surrounding the people element of the solution or the capability development costs that support the main tenet of HR transformation – that is, the move from the administrative and transactional to business partnering (see the HR value pyramid – Figure 2.3). The components of the capability development costs typically include:

1. A decrease in the resources dedicated to HR transaction support. Whether the HR service delivery solution is based on e-HR, shared services, outsourcing or a combination of these, the cost efficiency driver implies that transactional support can be provided at lower cost and therefore a reduced level of resources. Provision needs to be made for the costs of redeployment or redundancy.

2. An increase in resources dedicated to senior management support in the form of internal consultancy and business partnering. Some of these resources may already exist within the organisation, some may require a capability development programme, and others may need to be recruited externally. The cost implications are that whilst a smaller number of business partners may be required than the current HR generalist population, the total employment costs for this group may be as great as or greater than the current HR generalist population.

3. The combination of a reduction in the administrative and transactional resources and an increase in the consultancy and business partnering resources. This implies a reduction in the requirement for traditional HR management. Clearly some HR managers will move to business partnering roles, but this will not be the case for all, and provision needs to be made for the costs of redeployment or redundancy.

4. An increase in line managers' capability. Investment in increasing line managers' HR capability, required to ensure the benefits of e-HR, and HR business partnering, is realised.

Estimating the technology costs clearly requires a good understanding of what technology is being deployed and how it will be used. This provides a good opportunity to engage with colleagues from the IT function at an early stage. Do you enhance what you have by upgrading or e-enabling? Or is a new system the only feasible option? Working with your IT colleagues here will assist in getting the right solution and builds buy-in with the IT community.

Technology providers will usually be pleased to demonstrate their products and this can be an excellent way to capture the imagination of colleagues. However, make sure that the technology provider covers their implementation strategy and other non-technical areas, as the technical elements of the solution are only one part of the costs.

The largest one-off cost is usually *labour* and will involve HR, IT and business staff as well as, usually, external consultants on the core programme team. To cope with this, the costs of providing cover or backfill for the HR and business people seconded to the programme team may be needed. Also, it is important not to overlook "hidden" costs such as HR and line people participating in workshops, testing and training.

The cost of *developing content* is also often overlooked. e-HR technology is no use unless the content supports the new ways of working, for example, e-learning materials or performance management tools. There will be both one-off and ongoing maintenance costs associated with content.

The costs of *software licences* are a significant cost of access, along with others described below. However, it is important to consider the net effect of these, which is netting them off against the costs of the systems you are removing. This is usually done by including the removal of the other systems in the benefits calculation.

There will almost always be *hardware costs*. However, look out for opportunities to share costs and economies of scale with other programmes that are in progress. Another cost that can be overlooked is the provision of a suitable *method of access* in order to interact with an e-HR system. Clearly it is critical that employees have access to it. Costs will potentially need to cover laptops, desktops, personal digital assistants (PDAs) and other mobile devices, kiosks, and possibly even home PCs, depending on the access solution defined.

HR and IT employees will be required for the *ongoing support and maintenance* of the solution. There will also be contractual costs if you embark on any outsourced arrangements here as well as the costs of system upgrades and other maintenance going forward.

Often, as you involve your colleagues in IT in the process of technology design and costs estimation, they may suggest additional benefits that had not previously been considered. These should, of course, be added back into the benefits table, estimated and have beneficiaries identified. This reinforces the point that identification of benefits and costs is an iterative process as you develop the business case.

4.7 Cost–Benefit and Risk Analysis

By this stage, you should have a financial estimate of benefits and costs, and when these will be incurred. These are now brought together in a cost–benefit analysis. This is not a financial analysis textbook and therefore the details of how technically to perform cost–benefit analysis are not covered in this book, rather it is the principles that we wish to establish here.

In many organisations the method of performing cost–benefit analysis is often prescribed. Typically the approach will be based on net present value (NPV), internal rate of return (IRR), payback or a combination of these. If you have a choice in this, it is generally considered better to use either NPV or IRR analysis as this considers the time value of the investment. For detail on these techniques please refer to the recommended text in the Further Reading section, *Accounting for Non-Accounting Students*.

Just as you have engaged with your IT colleagues in defining the technology design and costs, it is important to engage with Finance function colleagues in cost–benefit analysis in order to develop a robust and defensible case. The allocation of capital expenditure is usually managed through the Finance function, and therefore getting assistance from colleagues there will enhance your likelihood of success.

The cost–benefit analysis is not the only factor that will be taken into account in approving the business case. The risks in achieving the predicted benefits need to be considered. Risk and issue management is explored fully in Chapter 5 but it is important that an initial appraisal of the major risks and potential mitigation is made during the development of the business case so that the results of the cost–benefit analysis can be weighed up against the risks involved.

Case Study

An ex-nationalised – now FTSE 100 – company wanted to identify and rank benefits and to plan in detail how they would be realised. To rank them, they used a weighting process, where quantitative information (payback period, cost of implementation, ongoing cost of operations) was weighted against qualitative information (improved operational effectiveness of business units, delivery of value-added HR services, fit with IT strategy, business risk). They were then able to prioritise the benefits and the investment in the project.

4.8 The HR Transformation Roadmap

Towards the end of envisioning we recommend that a "90-day plan" is developed (see Figure 2.7) that defines the key milestones required to bridge the gap from current to future HR. Through the course of developing the business case, much more is now understood about the HR transformation solution and when its various elements will be delivered. Therefore, the plan for transformation can now be articulated in greater detail – we term this the "HR transformation roadmap".

Physically, the roadmap is in the same format as the 90-day plan. However, the content within each segment changes as those initial high-level milestones are now broken down to the next level of detail. The process, people and technology theme introduced earlier in this chapter and expanded upon further in Chapter 5 is used to segment the roadmap horizontally so that in every 90-day period there are specific milestones for the process, people and technology elements of the programme. Further views of the roadmap can also be developed. For example, a view that defines when the different elements of the new HR service delivery model will be delivered from a senior management, line manager, employee and HR practitioner perspective for each 90-day period provides a tangible plan by which expectations can be set across each of those groups. Through creating these different views the roadmap becomes an important communications tool in engaging people in the programme.

In the first part of the roadmap, it is often preferable to split this into individual months for the first 3 months of the roadmap in order to provide month-by-month clarity over that period. Similarly, for the later parts half-yearly periods may be more appropriate. After the business case has been approved and the roadmap becomes a working plan, keeping the first part at an individual month level of detail for a rolling 3 month period is very effective for managing expectations across the business and the programme team.

In the first parts of the roadmap the delivery will typically be around "quick wins" or "early implementations". Quick wins typically begin to put the new process and people elements in place supported by existing technology that has been tuned and modified ahead of the longer term, enduring technology implementation (if this is what is planned). This provides the opportunity to deliver benefits early, build the credibility of the programme and encourage behaviour change throughout the life of the programme rather than in a "big bang" at the end. Also, if the "initial" and "full" business case approach is being taken, it is possible to deliver some quick wins whilst the full business case is being developed in parallel. When the full business case is then taken for approval, the programme will have already delivered some benefits, building confidence in the programme for the next level of investment.

Developing and viewing the roadmap in this way enables senior stakeholders to see what HR transformation will deliver to them, their managers and their employees over each period of the roadmap. This builds momentum for the change across all these groups by ensuring that they each have some benefit delivery in each segment of the roadmap.

As the roadmap is defined the interdependencies between HR transformation and other programmes and initiatives within the organisation emerge. It is important to record and track these interdependencies as they can potentially affect both the cost *and* benefit sides of the business case. For example, there could be costs incurred when another programme places an unexpected requirement on the HR transformation programme, or there may be a need to interface with other solutions being developed elsewhere in the business. On the benefits side, other interdependencies could delay the delivery of benefit or even invalidate a benefit if it is already being delivered through another programme.

Listed below are some common interdependencies we find with HR transformation programmes.

Interdependency area	Description
Technology	Linkages to programmes that upgrade network capacity and PCs
Interfaces	Systems interfaces with other core systems, for example Finance, Procurement (especially workflow/organisation structure)
E-enablement programmes	Integration into the Intranet and content, and how support is provided
Change programmes	Change projects in other functional areas
HR programmes	Other initiatives within HR
Other HR transformation work streams	Typically work streams are interdependent

In the Section 4.6, we noted that changes to PC desktops and other upgrades are typically going on all the time. These technology changes could affect the roadmap and plan, as desktop specifications, for example, might not be the same at the point when go-live is planned as they were when the business case was first being developed. This is another reason for getting IT people involved from the beginning and keeping them involved.

Interfaces are particularly important for the e-HR elements of the programme. There are interfaces with Intranet applications, phone lists, e-mail directories and security systems, to name but a few. All of these interdependencies need to be taken into account.

Other transformation programmes may be underway at the same time that are outside of HR but will affect the HR transformation programme – for example, in the Finance or Procurement functions. Look out for duplication. If at all possible, seek out opportunities to make changes at the same time for groups impacted by those changes.

Finally, many people overlook the importance of timing when choosing to propose and then embark on transformation. The right timing is dependent on business, organisational and political factors which all need to be taken into account. Getting the timing wrong will cause the programme to falter and potentially fail if the business case is not strong. The degree of buy-in to the business case is a good barometer to determine if the climate is right for HR transformation and we examine this in the next section.

4.9 Achieving Real Buy-In and Ownership of the Business Case

One of the main tenets of this book is that successful HR transformation is achieved through the effective management of change. In order to do this, the principles and practice of change management must be an integral part of each element of the transformation, in particular through the adoption of a process consulting mindset (see Chapter 1). The development of the business case is no exception and in this final section we explore the elements of change management that are particularly pertinent in business case development.

In business case development, it is important to identify who the main benefit owners are as they must buy in to the benefits predicted in the business case and will therefore be highly influential in driving the change to achieve those benefits. The mechanism for achieving that buy-in is their involvement in developing the business case so that it is something developed collaboratively rather than imposed.

The impact of HR transformation on both HR and the line in many cases goes to the very core of people's working lives, and therefore taking the opportunity to involve individuals from these groups in the business case development process will begin to lay the foundations for their embracing the changes that HR transformation will bring and reducing resistance.

Through this process of involvement it is useful to identify change sponsors and change leaders. They are the people who are going to play key roles in implementing HR transformation within the organisation, and will occupy a range of roles throughout the business rather than being members of the programme team itself. It is vital to get them involved in the development of the business case so that, by the implementation phase, they are fully engaged and able to demonstrate their understanding of the impacts of change to their functions and to the wider business.

Change sponsors provide "public" support – both in their actions and in what they say. Sponsors must be capable of representing the transformation to colleagues in a convincing way. They are usually in senior roles, and as such often provide staff and resources to support the change within the business. They must demonstrate "publicly" that they buy in to the consequences of the change proposed in the business case,

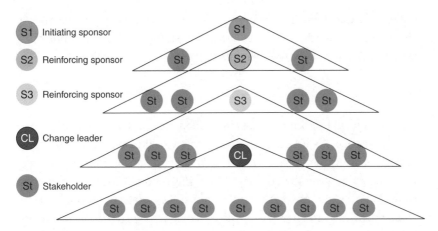

Figure 4.2 Sponsorship and change leadership, based on Daryl Conner, Managing at the Speed of Change, Wiley, 1998

and often members of the programme team will support and coach the change sponsors in the execution of their role.

As you cascade further through the organisation, you will identify change leaders who are usually part of the change sponsors' organisations and who are in a position to help drive the change within their areas. Change leaders will be in a variety of roles, for example, business partners or line managers, but they will all be respected by their colleagues and be working at the local level. If they can be identified and involved in the business case, they will be able to work with you in moving from planning towards implementation from their positions at the heart of the business. The role of change leaders in the implementation is covered in detail in Chapter 7 and the relationship between sponsors, change leaders and the organisation is illustrated in Figure 4.2.

Here are some practical approaches to involving HR and line managers in developing the business case that we have found to work effectively.

Speak the business' language

It sounds simple, but unless you communicate in a way that your business colleagues will understand, the message you are trying to give will be lost. This is a familiar issue, but in our experience not enough emphasis is put on this area. Consider involving a group from your target audience to check and rewrite the message. Why not ask them to take responsibility for it? In doing so they will become engaged in the programme.

Lead by example

This is an ideal opportunity for HR to demonstrate its change leadership role in practice. As we have discussed, many of the benefits of HR transformation lie in how effectively line managers and employees address what was previously the domain of HR. Engagement with line managers when building the business case demonstrates that HR is both serious about the change and that it is concerned that managers believe in and buy in to the benefits that HR transformation will bring to the organisation.

This approach is also an excellent way of ensuring that HR does not develop the business case in isolation from the rest of the business, and that the business stays involved after the initial engagement in the envisioning process. This reduces the risk that the business perceives that the programme has gone into a black hole and is then suddenly hit by implementation. Also, it tests the HR transformation solution from the business perspective, providing the mechanism for the business to raise potential design issues early in the process.

Use demonstrations of new service delivery channels

Demonstrations given very early on can be extremely powerful in getting people excited about what the transformation could look like. They help people really to understand what the e-HR delivery channel in particular will look like and what their role in that will be. Demonstrations can be easily organised – in fact, many software vendors will stage them for you.

Similarly, opportunities exist to demonstrate shared services and outsourced delivery channels. Site visits provide a good opportunity here, as do conference room pilots (physical demonstrations of how a process will work with simulated hand-offs and processing).

Ensure the commitment of those who have responsibility for benefit delivery

Ensuring that benefit owners include in their budgets the effect of the anticipated benefit accruing to HR transformation is a highly effective way of demonstrating their commitment to HR transformation and of concentrating their minds on the implications of the changes. This approach is particularly effective where cost savings are concerned. Working with benefit owners here to commit to business case cost savings by taking these costs out of future budgets predicated on the savings that HR transformation will bring sends a very powerful message.

Deliver some changes early in the programme

The roadmap can be used to encourage positive behaviour change across the organisation. By stratifying the roadmap by level within the organisation and by functionality in process areas, you will be able to deliver tangible HR transformation change in chunks very early on in the programme. It is not only possible to deliver concrete benefits before the whole programme is completed but, even more importantly, by doing so, behaviours can start to change, so that when the larger changes happen, people are ready for them.

Summary

This chapter shows that robust business case development provides a firm foundation for HR transformation, both in terms of the "hard" and the "soft" elements. For instance, thorough preparation of the business case significantly increases the likelihood of meeting or exceeding the benefits case, whilst the inclusive and consultative approach taken in developing the case continues the focus on HR transformation as a process of change, developing real commitment to the changes proposed.

Through the development of the business case, the design of the HR transformation solution is taken to the next level of detail driven by what is required to achieve the target benefits. The cost implications are then determined and the process of assessing the comparative costs and benefits completed.

In a similar way, the initial transformation plan first developed during envisioning is taken to the next level of detail to form the HR transformation roadmap. The roadmap enables senior stakeholders, to see what HR transformation will deliver to them, their managers and their employees over each period, becoming a key tool for communications with stakeholders across the organisation.

5

Stakeholder Engagement and Programme Management

The preceding chapters have all made reference to the crucial importance of securing the commitment of managers and employees to the human resource transformation process and to do so within an overall project or programme management framework. The formalisation of this should be a feature of the HR transformation business case, covered in Chapter 4.

We advocate that stakeholder engagement should not be conducted in isolation but as part of an overall governance approach. You may have everyone bought into the new vision of HR and built the finest and most watertight business case, but if you have doubts about the programme management capability, you should put off the start of the programme until you have the right person or team in place.

To achieve successful programme outcomes, particularly in respect of highly complex programmes extending over many months or even years, it is vital that appropriate disciplines are in place to ensure that costs, benefits and implementation time scales are carefully monitored and managed.

Chapter Structure

Key Themes
5.1 Context
5.2 Practitioner Perspectives
5.3 Stakeholder Engagement
    Tools

5.4 Programme Governance
    Tools
5.5 Managing Risks and Issues
Summary

Key Themes

- A review of some perspectives on human change and how these can help to map out the stakeholder topography.
- How the stakeholder mapping process can inform the change sponsors and agents about the most effective ways to manage resistance and reduce negative impact on the programme.
- The programme governance framework is explored from the perspective of practical steps that can be deployed to secure the best possible programme outcomes. All programmes give rise to conflicts with the attendant risks and issues. Knowing how to manage through these is crucial to success.

5.1 Context

You will know that the ability to manage change effectively is regarded as a crucial skill. Vast amounts of resources are expended by organisations to adjust employees to a new way of achieving desired goals. The natural propensity for individuals and groups to "defend the status quo" presents a set of challenges that HR management must overcome in order to bring about desired change. In addition, your management must also seriously take into account and consider the myriad of problems that may result if they are not responsive to issues in the workplace.

The change cycle model and process consulting mindset described in Chapter 1 also touched on these points and contribute to the view that in the context of HR transformation, change management includes:

- Getting all those involved and affected to accept the changes and the results of the change process.
- The effective management of resistance.

We argue that viewing resistance and commitment together leads to a better understanding of the nature and dynamics of these factors in change management and the tools and techniques required to deliver successful outcomes.

We also stress the point that stakeholder engagement is not conducted in isolation but as part of an overall project or programme governance model. This reinforces the advice given in Chapter 1 about adopting a systems mindset, so that you are keenly aware that a number of interrelated elements need to be managed well to bring about successful HR transformation.

The practitioner perspectives that follow provide an array of insights, which add variety and richness to these considerations.

5.2 Practitioner Perspectives

The Importance of Understanding Stakeholder Topography

Randy Harris clearly identifies different stakeholder groups in the HR transformation at Nextel. "As we made the transformation, there were people who got it: they understood directionally what we were doing and why, and enthusiastically had the ability to make the transition of functioning in a more consultative role, delivering services that other people were providing, tapping into this myriad of resources that we've created."

"The next group said, 'I understand it, but I don't necessarily know how to do what you're asking me to do. I'm not sure, as you take some of these things off my table that I used to do and you're asking me to broker services that the functional parts of HR are going to provide. You're asking me to get out of the transactional world that I used to live in, in terms of helping my people process new hires and terminations and stuff like that, because we're going to do that in a shared services environment.' That group is one that I'm willing to make a strong investment in, because they have the desire – they just need help in the ability to make the journey."

"The third group is probably the toughest group. They give you the appearance of wanting to support the direction you're going, but they really don't like it and they go 'stealth'. You think everything's OK, but below the waterline there's a whole different story going on. That's the audience that you have to convert upstream to one of the two groups that I mentioned, or to the fourth group that I'm about to describe, which is: don't have the ability and don't want to, or even if they have the ability, they don't want to."

"What I can't allow, and what I don't think the organisation can allow, is to be undermined by people who really don't want to support the direction that we've determined. So that group you have to drive to the surface and help them make a decision, and in a constructive way invite them on board and show the reasons, rationale and benefits of going down that path, but at the same time, if they don't want to, then agree that we're both better off finding a new direction."

Fear of Change

Vance Kearney makes a very telling observation on this subject when describing the reaction of Oracle employees to the notion of online pay-slips. "Technology literacy is very high in Oracle, and indeed our users tend to ask penetrating questions about data standards, privacy and security. An example of this could be found in our decision to move to automated payslips, viewable online, to replace the hard copy payslip. Initially, there was a good deal of opposition to the move, because people were emotionally attached to their physical, hard copy payslip and did not want to see its demise."

"People would ask the following sorts of questions:

■ But surely the hard copy payslip proves that I've been paid?
■ Don't I need a hard copy payslip for supporting mortgage/loan applications, etc.?"

"In the first case it was explained that the hard copy payslip simply proves that the payslip has been printed. Actual payment is performed by BACS separately. In the second case we explained that you can print your own payslip and lenders ask for confirmation anyway (also to be automated)."

"This small example highlights a more general point, which is: fear of change is always worse than the reality, and employees can always cope with more change than you think they can."

The Deployment of Surveys

Steve Ashby explains how surveys can help the management team of ESS worldwide services relate better to its employees and customers. "We use an employee satisfaction questionnaire (ESQ) that we send out to all our employees annually. We have discovered some consistent responses from across our directly managed business and we have received inter-esting and different responses from those businesses, which we run as joint ventures. As part of our Corporate Social Responsibility (CSR) commitments, we ensure that all countries create measurable action plans to address the issues raised by employees."

"The ESQ results are also used in the formulation of HR strategy right throughout the Group. I have never seen such an effective response to the issues raised by employees. This stuff is discussed at senior board level and the solutions cascaded right through the entire organisation. This creates a huge alignment between management and our associates, and explains why such a high proportion of our staff feels so loyal towards the organisation."

"We are expected by the governments in all the countries in which we operate to have a Social Uplift Programme. This centres on the replacement over time of expatriates with local management who we have brought on and developed. Increasingly, governments are asking us to report on our progress against the targets that they expect us to put in place. Our global clients have also made commitments to their governmental partners about their own Social Uplift Programmes. Therefore, we have an added impetus to achieve these aspirations because what interests our clients fascinates us endlessly."

"From an HR perspective, I ensure that local national managers are properly selected, have detailed induction and career development plans and that they take on real jobs. I will not accept the appointment of token managers simply to make our statistics look good."

At SchlumbergerSema, Miles Warner explains how perception surveys have been used to inform future developments. "We have recently performed a comprehensive manager perception survey in some of our UK businesses, and the results showed that some e-HR applications were very highly regarded, such as our career centre and performance management tools, but it also showed us that we need to pay more attention to overall training and support, to enable our managers to get the most out of the tools. These findings will inform our next stage investments in e-HR."

Tony Williams refers to the discovery of some highly important insights into the perceived performance of business partners at RBS. "In a recent survey of several hundred managers, designed to gauge perception of HR service delivery, it was very interesting to note that overall the line managers were more satisfied with shared services and e-HR than the HR business partners themselves. This drew attention to the relative lack of enthusiasm for conveying a positive message into the business by our business-facing team, a problem that was symptomatic of the concerns and resistance they felt towards the changing face of HR."

Supporting People through the Change Process

Kath Lowey places great emphasis on supporting managers and employees through the change process. She comments on the introduction of e-HR and "single point of contact" HR. "From a manager perspective, we have access for managers on two levels. The first is a Manager 1 access, which is all compensation data, so those managers are given direct access (via e-HR) to change compensation and benefits; the second is team leader type access, and they have a Manager Workbench. That has all our key people processes, and we have pitched our third release of this as 'How Do I?' It is basically: How do I recruit somebody? How do I put through an annual pay review? How do I change a benefit? It's very simple, but there are global processes delivered at a local level and interpreted very simply. Managers can call a single point of contact if they've got a query, but they have all their data on their staff, they can see it using an org charting tool, they can go in and now even decide on the pay review we're currently doing. The line manager can go online and actually check names and do a salary and benefit comparison online almost immediately."

"However, because of the reduction of staff and the pulling into the central team, how do we get to the line manager what it is they need to know? We've also done other things, because it's not good enough just suddenly giving them all this information when we're releasing our global processes. Because we do certain things at the same time each year round the world, we've designed training which we call manager tool kit training, and we've designed and delivered five modules. This is critical to the transformation process, because we've got to train our managers how to be managers again. So my plan this year is to bring the line managers up to speed in terms of how they do their job, and they understand that's their responsibility. We need now to move on to process improvement, quality, so it's all designed to aid the rollout of the tools to our line managers and our employees."

Securing Unwavering Support

Tony Williams stresses the importance of securing unwavering support from senior management. "It's vitally important with any major programme to have unwavering support from senior sponsors, and at RBS my boss, Neil Roden, has been banging the HR Shared Services and e-HR drum for about 5 years. He's definitely a big, big driver of it. This in turn has convinced his peer group and his boss that this is something that the organisation will benefit from. A factor in that has been the use of the term 'internal process re-engineering', which has familiar linkages with the concept of manufacturing in RBS, rather than e-HR, which sounds more jargonistic."

"Equally, my professional background in re-engineering processes and business management serves to underpin personal credibility in carrying these changes through. If somebody has operated in business and changed processes and changed structures and changed the way you deliver service and you apply this back to HR, then you've got an edge. I think many HR people lack these attributes."

"However, there can also be other major perception hurdles to overcome. One of these can be that line managers perceive HR as dumping lots of work back on the business and on the individual as assisted service is rolled out, and I am at great pains to say, 'No, it's actually the same as you should have been doing it, it's just quicker and it just happens to be on a system.' This kind of attitude can also be symptomatic of wider reputational issues."

Keeping an Ear to the Ground

At SchlumbergerSema, Miles Warner describes an open policy of engagement with managers and employees. "We have a very open policy. Whenever HR managers travel, they always have what we call 'round tables' in all the different locations they visit, and a round table is essentially a discussion where anyone who is around comes in and just has an informal chat, presentation of results. Any question goes, but let's say you want to talk about career development and then somebody wishes to raise the fact that their salary was wrong last month, you get into a discussion that goes down a totally different track from the one you actually wanted to talk about. This underlines the importance of getting the basic transactions right."

Helen Corey also expresses the importance of reliable feedback. "A key challenge is being able to filter out 'noise' from stakeholders, so that genuine concerns can be identified and acted upon. Ultimately, one is seeking to achieve strong, unwavering support from key stakeholders, and it is helpful to have a reliable 'ear to the ground' so that as project sponsor you can anticipate issues before they arise, or react very quickly if they do."

Understanding the Psychological Relationship between People, Processes and Technology

Richard Brady underlines the importance of understanding how people relate to new technology and processes.

"Let's take recruitment as an example. HR may wish to improve some synergies and economies of scale such as through preferred supplier relationships with staffing agencies, etc. The perception from the management population can be, 'yes, this is a good thing because as it's offering consistency, you've got a good relationship and our source of talented people is enhanced.'"

"The prevailing view of managers, I fear, is, 'this doesn't give us the flexibility we need as managers to find the best people. We used to have this relationship ourselves, and surely it's the role of a manager to source talent, and how can our colleagues in resourcing add any value?'"

"So there's then a desire to work around what may be a perfectly well-established, well-considered process. The HR community may have communicated and engaged with its stakeholders and customers in putting this together, but the need for a rapid solution (depending on the industry) and the complexity I've described may lead to some disagreement about whether this changing supplier relationship can actually deliver results. A prevailing mentality seems to be (as a line manager), 'I can do it myself, HR is over-complicating it and I wish they wouldn't try to bring too many things onto my radar screen, which I really don't understand and the technology isn't intuitive enough. What I've been given to work with on my desk top, it's like too complicated, so I'll switch it off, I won't go to use it and I'll subvert it.'"

Helen Corey also brings a perspective to this issue. "One of my key issues is how to source the right people for the projects within my remit. I have to work backwards from my business vision and goals and ask, 'What are the types of people that I actually need, or what are the profiles of the individuals? And do they fit into that budget?' No one starts with, 'OK, we have this really great group of people and they have these wonderful skill sets and are basically really creative once given an opportunity … put them in a room to see what they can come up with.' We just don't have the data on the HR system to enable informed decisions. People typically go to someone they know in the organisation, and then perhaps seek validation through HR by looking at performance reviews or whatever."

Communicating the Business Vision

Claudia Hall explains how Nextel communicated their new "One HR" philosophy to the business. "We had a very varied audience that we had to communicate to. We developed a communications plan, we developed a strategy, we put everything in place, and Randy Harris, the senior vice president (SVP) HR, and his direct reports went on a road show, visiting major cities and touching every single employee in HR. We presented to them what the organisation would look like, what the purpose was, what the rationale was, and we provided them with a high level calendar of the phasing for implementation. At this point, the idea was to let people know what was going on. Yet it was a change management operation of major proportion, because you had significant role changes in the HR organisation, in some cases leading to the perception of loss of control, ambiguity and so on."

"For the rest of the organisation external to the HR function, we took a similar approach to our HR road shows, and we obviously would not have begun this if Randy Harris had not first sold it to the chief executive officer (CEO) and chief operating officer (COO) of the company and then to the executive team. And when he sold this idea to them, it was consistent with the business strategy that had been developed by our COO, so we were rolling out an organisation structured similarly and under the same philosophy as our business strategy. So from an executive standpoint they agreed that it was the right thing to do and the right way to go, and then the next level down in the organisation, through pretty much from the executive to senior management, were briefed on what we were doing. The cascade to the general employee population was a bit shakier. The HR 'single point of contact' role holders, having been fully briefed through the HR road show, attended staff meetings and spread the word throughout the organisation, teaching our business units exactly what the look and feel of HR was like and all about."

Educating People in the Art of the Possible

Andy Field underlines the importance of articulating the art of the possible during the HR transformation process at the London Stock Exchange. "Previously the organisation had no e-HR, but now managers are getting views of their teams that they did not have previously. They are also seeing it freeing up HR professionals to work on higher value-add activities. Many managers do not realise what they do not have and also what HR can offer. It is as much about educating them in the art of the possible. They also trust HR as professional because we talk in a professional manner – again, speaking the right language is important."

"But once you show them that there are possibilities, you both realise that there is more work to be done."

"We have invested in this. We created new full-time business partners in order to work on very strategic, real issues. This has involved long-term planning. Critically, they are defining the future requirements for e-HR. For example, how do we want to view the organisation in the future? The e-HR will need to deliver on this. Also, in the future, we will need to link processes together. Investing in business partners drives e-HR, and it must be responsive in return. We must listen to what they want to use things for rather than letting ourselves be driven from a product perspective. In essence, don't try to be systems and processes led, but be transformation led, let the systems support the transformation, not the other way round."

Listen to Concerns – Identify Resistance

Janice Cook explains the value of listening to concerns and acting upon them. "At the time of the HR review, NCH was a highly devolved organisation. A fundamental tenet of the future HR organisation was a move to 'whole organisation' working. Whilst this approach operationally mirrored changes in the core service delivery area – Children's Services – we encountered significant stakeholder resistance to the proposal. It was as if the lid of a pressure cooker was lifted and the underlying opposition to a more coordinated way of working became concentrated in opposition to the proposals for HR transformation."

"NCH has a strong consultative and participative culture, and this approach is hugely important to us. Faced with a strong emotional resistance to proposed changes in HR, senior management resisted the temptation to steamroller change through the organisation. Instead, top management spent a lot of time listening to the concerns being expressed about whole organisational working. This decision to engage in a meaningful dialogue with people in the organisation through face-to-face conversations was a critical factor in helping people to work through the implications of change for themselves. The bottom line was that despite being given many opportunities to come up with alternative proposals, in focusing on the business rationale for change, no significant alternatives were forthcoming."

"Consultation was initially planned for three months. In reality, it has taken around fifteen months to secure full organisational buy-in. This is a good example of how change needs to be considered within the context of the broader organisational system: we couldn't just do HR differently without taking into account the broader organisation and its culture and ways of working. That had to change too."

"It may appear to be something of a cliché, but getting the senior executive team behind the proposals early on was critical in making change happen. There were two main consequences. Firstly, the HR review became bigger than HR. It was a business decision and the senior team talked about it in terms of a business decision. Secondly, it was about the organisational development of HR, and the leadership team led."

"We could have improved our communication with management in the devolved organisation. What we didn't do well enough at the early stages was to set out our expectations of the two most senior operational directors and the part they needed to play in communicating and engaging with their teams. We assumed too much and didn't see the world sufficiently from their perspectives. Although we rectified the situation later, a lot of resistance had built up which, with hindsight, we hadn't expected and needed to have addressed earlier."

"I was generally surprised at how poorly NCH embraced change. We work in an environment in which there is, and has been, enormous flux, and we assumed that the way we dealt with change professionally would be transferred to the internal change agenda. This did not happen in practice. When push came to shove, the organisation's values were put under pressure and, as happend in times of stress, some entreme behaviours were demonstrated. This is a huge learning for us, and one the leadership of NCH are taking to heart."

Maggie Hurt also remarks about the resistance at first line manager level at National Grid Transco. "Further down the organisation, we need to work harder in getting across our vision for HR. I can't say that we have found the answer yet, but a combination of the culture being promoted by our business leaders, investing in manager development and our own efforts to shift the centre of gravity in HR is starting to pay dividends. The main issue is tackling resistance at the first line manager/supervisor level, and this is where we are focusing our biggest investment currently."

Andy Field describes resistance as being grounded in suspicion of another HR initiative, often leading to the question from managers, "This is not core, have I got time for this?" Andy stresses that it is about proving that it *is* core – good statistics, good business knowledge that will, at the end of the day, affect the bottom line.

However, Philip Barr sounds a cautionary note about attempts to immerse the business in the HR vision. He takes the perspective that you don't need full business buy-in into the HR vision, mainly because you will never get it. His view is that the way you want to change HR will be anathema to many managers who are comfortable with a more traditional HR support.

Good Governance is a Prerequisite of Success

Randy Harris explains the importance of HR being a good role model during the transformation process. "You want to provide the right front to your customers internally and be a role model for helping other functions in the company to change. I think HR needs to do both: we need to be effective in making our own transformation, but if we can't be a role model for how other parts of the company should be transforming themselves, I'm not sure who can. I think we've been diligent, but at the same time I would say not cut-throat, in terms of our treatment of people who seem unenthusiastic about the transformation. There have been times when I have knowingly tolerated those people, in the hope of being able to move them over to the positive side."

Kath Lowey reflects on the business case development for the next phase of e-HR design at Marconi. "To assist in the plan going forward, we have recruited an expert to look at the ERP design within the broader context of transformation. This will be an element of the business case that will be presented to the main board for approval. HR will be seen to sponsor the programme, but there will be significant input from around the business."

Tony Williams stresses the important role of governance surrounding the HR transformation programme at Royal Bank of Scotland. "With any programme of this type, good governance is a prerequisite of success. In my capacity as Head of HR Shared Services, I have an overarching governance role, to ensure that appropriate processes and disciplines are enacted around cross-functional programmes."

Miles Warner draws attention to the involvement of the business in the programme development. "The only point I would make here specifically is that the programme must be built with the business managers and their businesses closely involved – HR cannot do it independently."

Claudia Hall underlines this point. "Randy Harris, the HR SVP, acted as the primary catalyst to kick-start the project. The overall mandate to proceed was granted by the executive board, on the basis that the HR transformation project was in full alignment with the overall business strategy."

"A wide range of senior stakeholders were also involved in refining the overall business objectives, mapping out processes and delivery schedules."

"Throughout the project, the HR function has worked hard to maintain the unwavering support of the business and has placed a high priority and importance around professional governance."

Vance Kearney illustrates Oracle's adherence to a disciplined project governance approach: "A good example of our approach can be found in the recent project to automate the appraisal process online. The steps to take are:

- Set out the idea of what we want to do.
- Involve the business process owners and users.
- Distil the process to global core plus allowable local variations.
- Involve the system team – can the new process be configured easily, or does it need to be revised for system reasons?
- Form a global project team to manage trial and user acceptance (involving HR and line).
- Pilot in two to three countries.
- If acceptable, make new functionality accessible to the wider business."

"Importantly, Oracle 'rolls-in' users – we don't 'roll out' systems. Users will be able to access online training material and have access to a 'super user' (from HR) for more difficult issues."

Finally, Janice Cook raises the very important consideration of taking accountability for decisions. "The corporate HR director and one of the directors in Children's Services were the principal sponsors of the HR review, and were actively involved in the delivery of work. They were supported by occasional members of a project team. The HR review was accountable to the infrastructure review programme team and the senior management group."

These practitioner perspectives raise a number of critical considerations in respect of stakeholder engagement and programme governance:

- *The importance of understanding stakeholder topography.* The ability to identify and engage different stakeholders, as individuals or groups, is seen as absolutely fundamental to any transformation effort. Unless you can secure the unwavering commitment of the primary sponsors of the transformation programme and address concerns or resistance from those most impacted by it, serious issues will arise.
- *Communicate the business vision.* To help "win over" opinion on your side, it is essential that the transformation programme is perceived to be relevant, in alignment with the business vision and that people understand their role within that vision. Otherwise, tensions can surface, often fuelled by suspicion based upon ambiguity or rumours.
- *Programme governance is the overarching framework for success.* For HR to be perceived as professional in its transformation efforts and establish itself as a role model for the business, adherence to good programme governance is a pre-requisite. This is the means by which the different facets of the transformation programme are managed with the overall aim of achieving successful outcomes in terms of cost, benefits and time scales.

These considerations are now explored in more detail.

5.3 Stakeholder Engagement Tools

We think it is useful at this point to expand on the concept introduced earlier in this chapter that resistance and commitment to change should be seen as a dynamic continuum. This is illustrated in Figure 5.1.

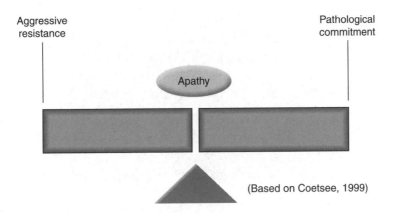

(Based on Coetsee, 1999)

Figure 5.1 Securing commitment

Aggressive resistance is regarded as a destructive opposition, reflected in destructive behaviour such as purposely committing errors and spoilage, subversion and sabotage.

The neutral or apathy zone represents a situation where people are informed about changes, but their perceptions and attitudes regarding the changes are neutral and their behaviour is characterised by "passive resignation", representing a transition between resistance and acceptance of change.

Pathological commitment represents the final phase of acceptance to change. In this context, it is characterised by passion for the change process, associated perhaps with obsessive and compulsive behaviours.

Between these poles are various "shades" of resistance and commitment.

We believe this model provides a diagnostic framework to identify the extent of acceptance or rejection of change in your organisation. Mapping individuals, groups or business units onto the continuum may be difficult and should not be attempted lightly. But it is a powerful tool if used wisely. For example, following the use of one of the survey/measurement tools described below, you could map individuals or groups onto the scale. This provides a basis for meaningful discussion about what needs to happen in order to move those stakeholders into the more positive, commitment end of the continuum, if it can be shown that unacceptable levels of resistance are evident.

You should, of course, be prepared to justify the reason for any assumptions you have made when plotting stakeholders onto the continuum.

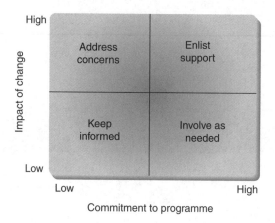

Figure 5.2 Stakeholder mapping

The Stakeholder Topography

One of the key themes raised by the senior practitioners was the importance of constructing a view of the stakeholder population so that these individuals/groups/business units can be characterised in terms of their importance to the change process and how they are impacted by it. This is assisted by using the stakeholder mapping framework shown in Figure 5.2. A sample is shown below:

Stakeholder group	Example impacts
Employees	Maintaining their own data rather than relying on HR administration to do it for them
Line managers	Increased people management responsibilities supported by e-HR rather than HR consultants
HR consultants	Move to added value business partner roles rather than administration comfort zone
HR administration	Expert support rather than re-keying administration
HR specialists	Demand driven by business partners rather than line
Payroll	Data from e-HR system rather than separate re-keying
External recruitment suppliers	Reduced number due to e-recruitment functionality

Those individuals or groups that are seen to display high impact and high importance are the most significant in terms of securing acceptance of the change process. Those positioned elsewhere in the matrix present different levels of significance. In these cases it may be acceptable simply to achieve modest support or even neutrality.

To expand on these points, let us look in more detail at some of the stakeholder groups illustrated in the earlier sample:

- It is evident that line managers are both highly important to the transformation process and highly impacted by it. As such they warrant careful and considered attention. A failure to engage properly with this group and secure a good degree of acceptance to the transformation process will create significant issues, such as poor utilisation of e-HR tools and a failure to adopt more people-centred practices within their role profile. These will at best stifle the transformation process or at worst sabotage it completely.
- The HR administration team are important and may be highly impacted if the intention is to reduce headcount based on the assumption that more HR administration is performed by managers and employees using e-HR self-service tools. This could raise morale/retention issues at a critical time when the new services are being introduced, requiring higher levels of support to users. In this situation, it may not be possible to persuade this group to warmly embrace the transformation process, but it will be necessary to move sentiment into the mildly resistive/neutral zone of the continuum in order to maintain decent service levels.
- The reductions in the number of external recruitment suppliers may antagonise those suppliers eliminated from the new list, but conversely may also provide an injection of encouragement to the group chosen to continue (and possibly enhance) their contribution. These different impacts need to be managed. Those suppliers who are expected to maintain their contracts post HR transformation must be clear and accepting about what is expected of them. The rejected suppliers need to understand the rationale for their exclusion, but may never be accepting of them. This will not impact the HR transformation process in the short term, but may be an issue in the longer term if you seek to re-engage their services.

These examples show the value of stakeholder mapping as a way of categorising the different groups, and informing you about the level of effort and priority that needs to be invested in ongoing activities to bring about desirable outcomes necessary to support the HR transformation programme objectives.

How to Enlist Support and Overcome Resistance

You should be prepared to invest in meaningful stakeholder engagement at the start of the change cycle and continue, relentlessly, throughout. It will be worth it.

The biggest single contributor to success is securing the unwavering commitment of the senior change sponsors. Without this, the HR transformation programme becomes vulnerable to attack and disruption. We strongly recommend getting this in place early as a priority.

You may have to be creative to win an audience with the most senior stakeholders. If you can, arrange one-to-one meetings and use these opportunities to present a compelling factual case in support of the programme. If this is not possible, then gain access to the next reporting level and seek to influence this group of people so that they in turn can upwardly influence their superiors.

Whilst one-to-one meetings can be extremely impactful, think creatively about other channels:

- Team meetings.
- Invitation to a steering group (covered in Section 5.4).
- Making sure the PA includes a brief on the HR transformation programme in essential reading material.
- Requiring a response through an auditable process, such as electronic tagging, so that the respondent is aware that simply refusing to reply will create an automatic elevation to the steering group or higher.

Of equal importance to understanding how individuals or groups show their attitudinal stance for the change initiative, it is necessary to monitor and measure behaviour. You will almost certainly identify what we call "secret subversives" – people who appear to be on your side, but then undermine the programme. They should be identified and dealt with as quickly as possible.

Developing a list of actionable items that demonstrate behaviour is essential. It should include:

- Demonstrating that they are accurately communicating the change initiative to their teams.

- Showing endorsement of the newly created HR processes.
- Signing off key documentation that allows financial investment.

It is important to stress again that investment of time and effort in the segmentation and characterisation of the stakeholder community, combined with techniques to understand their position on the resistance to commitment continuum, will repay itself in terms of dividend many times over. *This is not a task that should be undervalued, misplaced or subordinated to a low level in the priority order.*

Often in change programmes these "soft" or human issues – which is essentially what stakeholder engagement is all about – become subordinated to the technical issues and considerations surrounding system choice and implementation. Beware of allowing the technical issues to take over for too long. Without the people on board, no system will deliver the benefits you promised in the business case.

Once you have mapped out the stakeholders, the next task is to understand where they lie on the resistance to commitment continuum, and this in turn will determine where effort should be prioritised.

How Do We Test the Temperature of the Business?

There are various techniques that can be used to test the temperature of the business and in particular the stakeholder groups that have been identified using the tools described earlier. A number of different types of survey tool can be used to capture information about attitudes and behaviours. Figure 5.3 illustrates some of the different types that can be used.

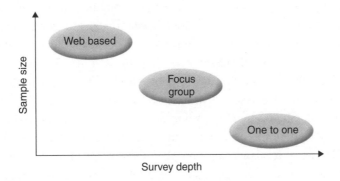

Figure 5.3 Testing the temperature

The techniques that combine both qualitative and quantitative outputs can be very useful indeed. So, for example, a survey could be constructed that requires the respondent to indicate their perspective on the change process by answering questions based on the Likert scale (strongly disagree $\Rightarrow$ strongly agree). In addition, free text boxes can be used to allow the respondent to provide a more in-depth response around particular issues or concerns. Analysing these responses will provide a good indication of the issue types and the strength of feeling or importance surrounding these.

This kind of survey works well in a web-based format. The results provide a preliminary indication of any issues and/or concerns and allow a judgment to be made in respect of the position of individuals/ groups on the resistance to commitment continuum. It may then be appropriate, particularly with the significant stakeholders, to probe these issues in more detail. This is usually best done in the form of focus groups or one-to-one interviews.

A sample web-based survey can be found at www.getcommitment.com and is designed as a generic tool to ascertain the level of resistance or commitment to a change programme. An example of a shorter survey, specifically tailored to ascertain perception towards the implementation of e-HR, is included in Appendix 2.

It is also very important that appropriate ethical behaviour and standards are observed at all stages of the process. For example, if you say survey results will be treated in confidence, make sure they are.

The Global Dimension

The different segments of the stakeholder population within a global or multinational programme could have radically different views of the same change process. This means that the stakeholder engagement activity needs to address those different entities or jurisdictions, and you should not slip into the comfort zone of thinking that a very professional and comprehensive assessment of the situation in, say, the UK can then naturally map onto Japan, USA or other countries in continental Europe.

It may well be the case that data protection issues receive a heightened degree of focus in Germany than they might in the UK. A global HR process that would allow, for example, someone in Italy to view the personal details of an employee in Japan might cause enormous consternation. The degree of ambiguity around different aspects of the programme may raise concerns in one area, but be accepted as the norm in others.

You should investigate these factors thoroughly. It is stressed again that the *stakeholder engagement process needs to be applied with equal rigour to a multi-jurisdiction programme.* In this way, you get an informed opinion on issues in each of those jurisdictions. Subsequent efforts to address those issues can then be more closely tailored.

Case Study

A global manufacturer implemented e-HR, including employee self-service and manager self-service, to around 8000 employees in the UK and a similar overall number in other parts of the world. In combination with the delivery of new technology solutions, the HR organisation also transformed into the business partner/specialist model described in Chapter 2.

Research was conducted before implementation to ascertain the views of both HR and line managers towards e-HR to discover any issues of major concern so that the senior programme sponsors could address these. Additional research was also conducted during and after implementation. Various survey methods were used as described above.

The results of the surveys pointed to the need for a focused effort in respect of the new capabilities that managers would need to be able to use the new tools to optimum benefit. As a consequence, a blended approach of online, telephone and face-to-face training was undertaken. Additionally, it became necessary to stress the critical importance of data maintenance and accuracy, and to reinforce the accountabilities of managers in this respect.

Expressing Stakeholder Engagement in Terms of Value

The benefits that you will articulate in the business case (covered in Chapter 4) are planned on the assumption that stakeholders will embrace the new ways of working. You should be aware that failure here could, of course, destabilise and reduce the anticipated benefit stream upon which the investment has been made.

This fundamental link between stakeholder commitment and benefit delivery underpins the importance of expressing stakeholder commitment in terms of its value contribution to the HR transformation process. For example, it is essential to secure the commitment of the key stakeholders who sign off the business case. Without the signatures of those principal sponsors in the first place and indeed their ongoing unwavering commitment, there would be an interruption to financial investment with an attendant knock-on to benefit release.

The maintenance and accuracy of the organisation structure, configured in the human resource management system, may be dependent on managers maintaining their particular part of it on an ongoing basis. This organisation structure will no doubt be used to feed many other processes and systems. Therefore, its accuracy and integrity is paramount. If managers fail to do their own maintenance, this will then create a higher maintenance burden for other functions in the business, adding layers of cost.

These are just some of the expressions of value that can be directly linked to stakeholder engagement – hopefully its value to you in your organisation can be readily appreciated.

5.4 Programme Governance Tools

Building upon the attention given in this chapter to stakeholder engagement, it is worth being reminded that all of this activity should be housed within an overarching governance framework that provides a vehicle for effective management of HR transformation. We start with the business case for transformation, the constituent parts of which were described in some detail in Chapter 4, but now we view that activity from the perspective of the wider governance framework.

Business Case Framework

It is usual for business cases to go through a sequential phase of development. This is elaborated on in Figure 5.4.

Reinforcing the points made in Chapter 4, the initial proposal may be a short document that highlights the overall costs, benefits and risks associated with the programme. If the proposal looks reasonably promising,

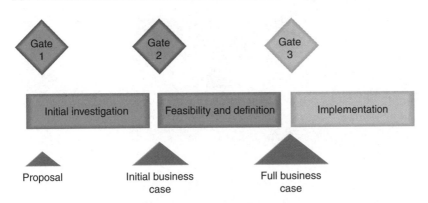

Figure 5.4 Programme business case framework

it can then be developed into an initial business case, at the conclusion of which one should have a 60–70% confidence level in respect of the main costs, benefits and other outcomes. After that, a full-blown business case, with associated confidence levels in excess of 90%, can be worked up, and it is this that forms the ultimate touchstone for investment decisions and benefit expectations.

But who is applying the overall guidance and inspection needed to ensure that the HR transformation is not only well conceived but has a good prospect for delivering value to the business? How is the implementation monitored and measured? How are problems dealt with? To look at these matters, we need to delve further into the composition of the governance structure.

Steering Board

We strongly make the point that programme governance should not simply be confined to the identified programme team, dealing with the day-to-day implementation. There should be other layers of governance, as illustrated in Figure 5.5.

The programme director should be answerable in the first instance to a steering board which provides a higher level inspection of costs, benefits and delivery milestones and becomes an issues and risks resolution forum if matters present themselves that are beyond the resolution of the programme director.

Chaired by the senior programme sponsor, the steering board should comprise a broad range of talent: senior HR people, internal audit, line

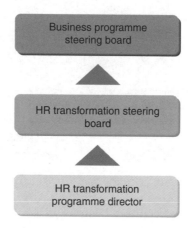

Figure 5.5 Steering boards

managers and finance. At a higher level still, it would be beneficial to have an overarching business programme steering board that looks to see how the HR transformation programme dovetails with other change programmes that may be going on in the business at that time. It also provides a further opportunity to inspect cost benefits and delivery milestones.

The emphasis around periodic inspection of cost benefits and delivery milestones cannot be overstated. Whilst some may view this as an unnecessary administrative burden that simply detracts from "getting on with the job", it is undeniably the case that without these disciplines in place the risks to the programme outcomes can become massively magnified.

Frequent inspection of costs, benefits and delivery milestones can provide comfort and assurance that the programme is basically on track. Furthermore, it can pick out those things that, if unchecked, are likely to destabilise the programme at a later point in time.

Early identification and remediation of these kinds of issues provides enormous dividends. Left unchecked, however, such issues could cause significant ramifications, if not a crisis, for the programme in its later stages.

Programme Team

Extending the theme further, look at the composition of the team in Figure 5.6.

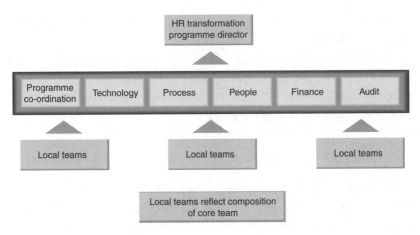

Figure 5.6 Programme team

Clearly, the programme director has overall responsibility for managing the different elements of the programme on a day-to-day basis and keeping it in good overall shape. This person will have a major influence on the way the programme is characterised. For example, if the person is known to have a particular leaning towards technical issues, it is possible that they will be allowed to be the dominant consideration and skew the activities of the programme team accordingly.

We are not saying that someone with a predominantly technical background is not fit to run HR transformation. Rather, we are making the point that the person chosen for this role must be capable of understanding the need to keep a number of work streams properly aligned and not fall into the trap of allowing personal preferences or comfort zones to drive the programme in a particular direction, to the detriment of others. The best way of achieving this is to keep the overall customer experience "front of mind" and use this as the basis for driving the programme forward.

Crucially, as we have discussed earlier in this chapter, the person must have exemplary stakeholder management skills; it is likely that these will be tested to the limit!

Reporting to the programme director, you would have, in an ideal situation, someone whose sole focus is on the day-to-day co-ordination of the plethora of activities that are associated with a major HR transformation programme. This individual would be very much at ease with one of the recognised programme management tools such as MS Project, and be in a position to advise the director of any apparent slippages or problems that might arise that would ultimately affect the declared programme milestones.

Chapter 2 raised awareness of the need to split HR transformation into three main areas of *technology, process* and *people*. Here we look in more detail at the sorts of activities and people profiles that you would typically align to those areas.

Technology Work Stream

The person responsible for technology would be expected to be a principal point of engagement with the systems integration provider, whether this is the internal information technology function or an external party or both. This person is ultimately responsible for translating the HR processes into a technological solution, involving configuration of the main system. In addition, there would be considerations surrounding the suitability of the Intranet or people's ability to access that system through their desktops, laptops or phones.

Process Work Stream

The person responsible for the process work stream is the person who will effectively manage the process re-engineering work to ensure that in the "new world" HR processes become as lean and efficient as possible. There are a number of ways of approaching this. One way, for example, would be to approach the work with literally a clean sheet of paper, calling upon various people in the organisation to contribute their view of a particular process and constructing the new process from scratch.

Whilst this has undeniable benefits in terms of creating a perception of inclusion, by engaging a wide stakeholder audience and appearing to be genuinely in line with the concept of meeting customer expectations or being customer driven, there are also a number of potential major pitfalls with this approach. One such pitfall is that, having created or crafted a new process based on this highly inclusive clean sheet approach, it then becomes eminently obvious in consultation with the technology department that to configure such a process in the system would require considerable time and expense. This realisation then might prompt the need to go back out to the stakeholders who contributed to the original process to say that it is no longer applicable – with the subsequent dissonance this would create.

Another way of doing it would be to adopt as a baseline the standard "out of the box processes" that associate with the new system, and only to permit variants to those standard processes where it can be demonstrated that a significant business benefit would result. These variants may take the form of observance or compliance with legal requirements, or where a judgment could be taken that for cultural reasons it is necessary to do things in a particular way and that enormous offence could be caused by overhauling or retiring that particular process.

One of the drawbacks of presenting baseline core processes in the way described is that it could appear to senior stakeholders to be a *fait accompli* and might therefore create a backlash from stakeholders, with associated disruption to the programme.

On balance, therefore, it is probably the best tactic in most situations to engage the appropriate stakeholders on process grounds by presenting the overall picture. In other words, to explain that whilst their views are being sought to help refine and better the existing processes, there are nevertheless frameworks within which those betterments or changes need to take place to take account of the issues surrounding configuration within the main system. These issues carry a cost implication now and in the future.

People Work Stream

The people aspects of the programme deal with the human capability enhancements or changes that are needed arising from the business change process, and also address organisational design issues. As stated earlier, however, this critical area of an HR transformation is often overlooked or subordinated in favour of technical considerations.

Taking this a stage further, it may be tempting to confine the discussions and the initiatives around people enhancement to within the HR function itself. Quite properly, the HR function undergoes major change in an exercise of this kind, seeking to move from being predominantly administrative in its persona towards being a more strategic value-add contributor to the business – as discussed at length in Chapter 2. The skill sets, therefore, of the newly formed HR function are markedly different from the historic situation, and a good deal of time and effort and planning needs to go into securing these capability enhancements.

However, that is, not the entire story. The line managers are an absolutely critical component in the overall success of the programme, because they will be in the front line for dealing with the business changes as they happen, taking more responsibility for day-to-day HR matters, using the new e-HR derived tools, such as employee self-service and manager self-service, and acting as ambassadors for the change process throughout the business. It is critical, therefore, that line managers or representatives of the line become involved in the programme at an early stage so that their views are taken proper account of.

Crucially, the technology, process and people enhancement work streams must be kept in close alignment; the importance of this will be demonstrated a little later in this section. As a consequence, it is highly desirable to have these three core aspects of the programme incorporated under *one* "governance umbrella".

Case Study

The HR department of a major pharmaceutical company wanted to improve its efficiency and effectiveness in support of the global business. They planned to introduce greater efficiency through employee self-service and assisted service, but to become more effective and to deliver greater value the function needed to ensure that best HR practice was being shared across the organisation.

The business wanted the programme to be mobilised quickly, and identified an internal programme manager to lead the initiative. A transformation team of ten people was set up, drawn from the HR function worldwide. After defining priorities for transformation, they split these into work streams, and each team worked together to understand the benefits that could be derived from each work stream. Implementation plans were then developed, and these were combined into overall implementation roadmaps for each work stream team.

Processes were set up to support the programme sponsor, the executive VP for HR and the stakeholders, including the HR VPs and the business level VPs who were eager to start seeing benefits.

The company's emphasis on rapid mobilisation, sponsor and stakeholder management was achieved because they were able to develop multiple perspectives and to structure the plans accordingly.

Potential Conflicts

It is worth mentioning again at this point that potential conflicts can arise between the technology, process and people work streams. This is linked to a tendency amongst many programmes of this type to devolve towards a technology-based solution whereby the programme becomes a technology-driven implementation and the "system" becomes the main focus of attention. Instead, of course, the programme should be characterised as a business change programme. As mentioned earlier, it is important for the programme director, at an early stage in proceedings, to stamp his or her authority on this situation to ensure that the programme is led very much from a customer perspective.

Certain solutions to fulfil customer requirements could prove to be very expensive to translate into practice, requiring system customisation, for example, that carries a heavy price tag, not only at the outset but also into the future. So one of the roles of the technology head is to ensure that the customer requirements are assessed in terms of cost and benefit and that the most appropriate technological solution is ultimately performed. However, this is different from the technology department deciding at the outset what the solution is going to be and then essentially requiring the customer to be a "forced fit" into the technological environment.

Many so-called "skirmishes" occur on this point. These can become a focus for inherent tension and conflict within a programme, and the programme director needs to understand this, to be prepared for it and to make sure that the technology function does not dictate the overall programme outcomes.

Other Considerations

Equally importantly, the finance team, the audit team, the procurement team and other support services as deemed necessary should form part of the overall HR transformation programme team. These support services provide the disciplines around cost, monitoring and control, benefit measurement and the measurement of benefit realisation, the very ingredients upon which the business case depends for its validity and upon which the business took the decision to make the investment.

If the programme encompasses more than one country, or a series of sites in one country, it would be helpful to have locally based teams responsible for the delivery of the programme in those individual sites or in those individual jurisdictions. The local teams would need to have a skilled composition that reflects the overall mix of the core team that has been described earlier. There should be no dispute about the local teams acting as the principal conduit into those site-specific businesses or in individual jurisdictions; the main debate surrounds whether or not the local team should "pull through" the final solution from the core team or whether the core team "pushes out" the solution through the local teams and into those businesses.

The best advice here for the core team is to make sure that it sets up the appropriate common standards that will apply across all aspects of the programme. In other words, the overall governance framework, the style and tone of the programme emanates from the centre, but the local teams working within that framework fashion the solution to meet the local requirements – with those requirements being assessed, tested and analysed by the core team. In this way, the local implementation would appear to be more in touch with the requirements of the local business whilst at the same time being backed up and supported by other resources.

The problem of risk destabilising the programme outcomes is examined in the next section.

5.5 Managing Risks and Issues

Risk Management

Risk is any uncertainty, potential threat or occurrence that may prevent you from achieving your objectives. It may affect timescale, costs, quality or benefits. All programmes are exposed to risk in some form, but the extent of this will vary considerably.

The purpose of risk management is to ensure that:

- Risks on programmes are identified and evaluated in a consistent way.
- Recognised risks to programme success are addressed.

You cannot use risk management to eliminate risk altogether, but it will enable you to avoid it in some instances or minimise the disruption in the event of it happening in others. When a programme sponsor approves a programme, he or she does so in full knowledge of the stated risks, and accepting the consequences should things go wrong.

The steps are:

- *Identify*: Log all the risks that may potentially jeopardise the success of the programme.
- *Estimate*: Review each risk in turn:
  - assess the likelihood of the risk occurring,
  - assess the severity of the impact on the programme if it occurs.
- *Evaluate*: Use a risk matrix to determine the "risk category" (high, medium or low) to help you assess how acceptable the risk is.

Depending on the risk category, take action as follows:

High risk: Take definitive action to prevent or reduce risk.
Reconsider the viability of the programme before proceeding further.

Medium risk: Take action to prevent or reduce risk where appropriate.
Prepare a contingency plan if risk cannot be reduced.
Manage risk and implement contingency plan where necessary.

Low risk: Take action to reduce risks if cost effective.
Monitor risk – it may become more significant later.

Taking positive steps to reduce the possible effects of risk is not indicative of pessimism, but is a positive indication of good programme management. Many possible options exist for reducing risk, including:

- *Prevention*, where countermeasures are put in place either to stop the threat or problem from occurring or to prevent it having any impact.
- *Reduction*, where the actions either reduce the likelihood of the risk developing or limit the impact on the programme to acceptable levels.
- *Transference*, which is a specialist form of risk reduction where the impact of the risk is passed to a third party via, for instance, insurance.
- *Contingency*, where actions are planned or organised to come into force as and when the risk occurs.
- *Acceptance*, where the organisation decides to go ahead and accept the possibility that the risk might occur and is willing to take the consequences.

Consider also:

- Bringing risky activities forward in the schedule to reduce the impact on the programme outcome if they are delayed.
- Modifying the programme requirement to reduce aspects with inherently high-risk, for example, new, leading edge technologies.
- Allowing appropriate time and cost contingencies.
- Using prototypes and pilots to test the viability of new approaches.

Issues Management

An issue is something that has happened, and either threatens or enhances the success of the programme. Examples of issues are:

- the late delivery of a critical deliverable;
- a reported lack of confidence by users;
- a lack of resources to carry out the work;
- the late sign-off of a critical document or deliverable;
- a reported deviation of a deliverable from its specification;
- a request for additional functionality;
- a recognised omission from the programme scope.

When an issue is identified you should:

- record it in an issues log;
- agree and take action to resolve the issue;
- regularly update the progress commentary on the log;
- once the issue has been resolved, record the method and date of resolution in the log;
- report new, significant issues in a regular programme progress report.

You should expect a large number of issues to be raised at the start of the programme or at the start of a new stage within the programme. These will mainly be queries from people seeking clarification that aspects of the programme they are concerned with have been covered. This is a rich source of feedback on stakeholder concerns as well as a check on completeness of the programme plan and scope.

Make sure you record issues, even if you have no time to address them or cannot yet find a person to manage the resolution. Just making them visible is sometimes enough to start resolving them. Also, many issues cannot be resolved on their own simply because they do not reach the core problem; they are merely symptoms. Once other "symptoms" appear as issues, it is possible to start making connections that can help to identify the core problem. Once this is solved, a number of issues can be struck off in one go.

"Scope creep" is a phenomenon where a programme over-runs its agreed timescale and budget due to many extra (often minor) "features" being added in an uncontrolled manner. For this reason, it is often easier to bundle a number of small changes together and assess them as a whole, choosing to implement only those that will further the objectives of the programme. At the other end of the scale, it is wise to consider delaying the addition of a major change until after the programme is completed and introduce it as a second phase programme. Remember, the primary aim of a programme is to fulfil a stated business need. As long as this need is satisfied, fine tuning, enhancing or embellishing the outputs is a potential waste of resource.

At some point, a time may come on a programme when an issue arises that cannot be resolved whilst keeping the programme viable. Either a time window will be missed or costs will be so high that even a marginal cost analysis leads to the conclusion that it is not worth continuing. In these cases, a decision to terminate a programme might be treated as a success, as there is little point in continuing with a programme that is, not viable in business terms. However, such a situation would demand serious questions being raised about the risk and issue management regime in place at the time.

Figure 5.7 shows how a well-managed programme retains a decent shape all the way through, meaning that key activities in the programme are being well-managed and aligned and harnessed. Benefit delivery is good and on track and the governance structure is able to contain the complexity to within manageable proportions. On the other hand, if the complexity becomes unmanaged, what then happens is that a significant shortfall of benefit takes place: either benefit streams themselves are delayed, or costs rise significantly as efforts are made to contain the event or sequence of events that have created the unmanaged complexity situation.

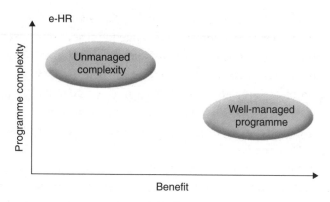

Figure 5.7 Risk and issues management

This point illustrates something mentioned earlier about the need to retain a highly diligent focus on costs and benefits, and also to make sure that key milestones are achieved and to be in a position to have the processes in place to take swift remedial action if it is recognised or identified that things are moving out of kilter.

An unmanaged complexity situation can be very draining and very wearing on members of the programme team and indeed the higher steering boards. Therefore it is highly beneficial and desirable to prevent those situations happening in the first place than to have to deal with them, although it is almost inevitable there will be occasions during a complex programme extending over many years when unmanaged complexity will strike. The ability to be able to deal with that situation is absolutely fundamental to the over-arching programme governance framework.

Returning to the theme of keeping major items in alignment, Figure 5.8 shows how the three core pillars of the HR transformation programme – technology, process and people – are kept in alignment around a particular milestone.

The point of this is really to show how a number of inter-related activities need to be carefully managed in the build-up to a critical go-live situation, and how the state of each of those major activities would need to be regularly tested and assessed as the days tick by, in order to minimise or eliminate risk. Chapter 2 made reference to organising these bundles of activities into 90-day periods, to give more visibility and focus around deliverables.

Finally, it would be highly recommended for practitioners to constantly review and assess a number of questions listed below. Having

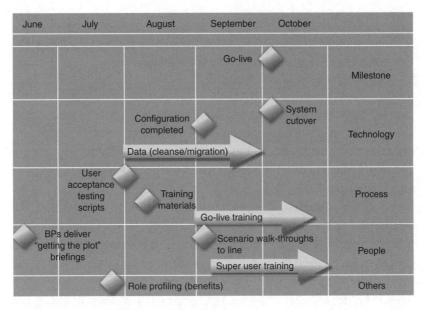

Figure 5.8 Making it happen – illustration

reliable answers to these questions provides an insightful perspective on the programme overall.

Business management

- Is the programme still a good business proposition; are the risks acceptable?
- Is the business ready to take on the operation of the solution?
- Are the benefits/results monitoring systems in place?
- Are current estimates of the costs and benefits in the business forecasts?
- Are all internal and marketing communications designed and ready?

Programme control

- Has a programme health check been done and found to be acceptable?
- Are you sure beyond reasonable doubt that the solution will work?
- Have all stakeholders reviewed and approved those deliverables requiring their input?
- Have all purchases that affect service delivery been properly completed?
- Are all support agreements in place?

Ongoing evaluation

■ Are resources in place to monitor adequately the costs and benefits against the business case?

Summary

Our own experience and indeed that of the senior contributing practitioners underlines the critical importance of good stakeholder engagement as a major element of HR transformation from day one. You neglect this area at your peril.

A number of tools and approaches can be applied to determine the disposition of stakeholders towards the change process, and from this it is possible to plan stakeholder campaigns to address their issues and concerns. Invest most time and effort in securing the commitment of the stakeholders you have defined as highly important.

Stakeholder engagement does not happen in isolation, however, but as part of the wider HR transformation programme and we have emphasised the need to put in place appropriate governance, to ensure from the start that you monitor costs, benefits and key delivery milestones. Never be afraid to admit to problems before they reach a serious and disruptive level and make sure that that the conditions of success of the programme remain clearly articulated and understood.

6

Implementation: Structure, Culture and Capability

We turn now to the implementation aspects of HR transformation – the third phase of the change cycle presented in Chapter 1. This chapter looks at issues from an organisational and capability perspective; Chapter 7 covers the implementation aspects of the process and technology side. For the purposes of the book it made sense to split these, but in real life they are, of course, linked closely together and should be part of an overall programme, as set out in Chapter 5.

We look first at the practical issues of:

- Who does what in transformed HR?
- How will the culture of transformed HR need to change?
- What new capabilities will HR professionals need to acquire?
- How do we develop these capabilities?

Chapter Structure

Key Themes

- The impact of HR transformation on each delivery channel needs to be assessed in order to inform future organisation and capabilities.
- The culture of HR needs to become more customer-focused, with a stronger emphasis on internal consultancy and marketing.
- HR professionals will need to develop stronger capabilities in strategy and organisational development, client relationship/consulting and project management.
- Organisations need to be prepared to invest in developing the capability of HR professionals and line managers.
- HR must demonstrate strong leadership if transformation is to stick.

6.1 Context

A question line managers frequently ask HR professionals in a newly e-enabled environment, or where transactional/operational/advisory HR activities have been passed to a shared services centre, is: "So what does HR actually do now?"

One of the main points we have made throughout this book is that HR transformation is about the transformation of the whole HR function. The question posed by line managers is fair and reasonable – what value are they going to get from HR professionals employed by the organisation? And it is no good HR professionals shrugging their shoulders and saying, "Oh, we are going to be more strategic now." This will not wash. It is important to be helpful, to work effectively with managers to address their critical issues, to show value in tangible ways. Indeed, there is a paradox in the HR value model: in many ways we act most strategically when we are most focused on addressing current critical organisational issues. The strategic bit is being able to address current critical issues within the context of the bigger organisational picture and to help internal clients implement whatever change is needed.

In Chapter 2 we used the HR value pyramid to illustrate how e-HR enables the organisation to deliver excellence in administrative and transactional areas; it is about process efficiency, improved data and information management, more cost effective solutions and better decision support. To manage e-HR will require people who understand the process, information and technology. This is about doing the HR basics really well – and our clients want us to do this, make no mistake. HR administrative excellence generally figures in the top five things that senior executives want HR to do well.

Then there are the things that HR needs to do at the top of the value pyramid. The next chapter deals with implementing changes in technology and process. This chapter deals with the organisational levers – structure, culture and people. Our aim is to present tried and tested approaches that will help you to accelerate the implementation of the HR value model. But first we will present what some senior HR practitioners have to say about implementation.

6.2 Practitioner Perspectives

Practitioner themes already captured in this book – such as "no one size fits all", "the need for HR to align itself with the business", "change needs to be delivered quickly", and so on – are not restated and should also be borne in mind as an important backdrop to the comments made below. Our main themes for this section are:

- *Line managers must become good people managers and HR must help them achieve this – through coaching, training and better policy guidance*

Philip Barr puts this clearly. "It is essential that line managers fulfil their responsibilities for people management. It is the line's responsibility to manage and HR's to advise them to do that. Generally, line managers are better than 20 years ago – they are better educated and have greater responsibility earlier – which means that there is less need for HR to push and prod them. However, we are still some distance away from the time when line managers are delivering their people management responsibilities in full. Partly this is a question of skills. More often it is about desire and the collusion between line manager and HR professional in maintaining the status quo."

Janice Cook is candid about the challenge facing HR. "To be honest, we still have a way to go in enabling our line managers to take on their full responsibilities around people management, and there is still a reliance on HR support. We have realised that part of the issue is knowledge and skill, and we plan to address this. Arguably, more important is changing the way we do HR – becoming less rule-driven. We believe that part of the reason why managers find it hard to take on board the people management bit is because HR clouds their ability to manage through introducing far too many rules and procedures. Rules and procedures create dependency on HR expertise to interpret and advise on these rules and procedures. Instead of empowering managers, we create a culture where managers are insecure about how best to act. Our message is that HR does not exist in its own right. It is there to help the organisation succeed."

Randy Harris articulates a hope that employees will not "think of me as the Chief HR Officer for the company. I want them to think of their managers as their Chief HR Officer. This means developing and supporting our managers and giving them the skill set that they need to meet the people needs of the employees who work for them. Then the high-tech approach to employees works, because they are getting high levels of contact with their manager."

Claudia Hall highlights the need to invest heavily in engaging with the line about their future role, especially with first line and middle management. Maggie Hurt underlines this, and points to the investment being made in first line manager/supervisor level development in order to communicate expectations about their role and equip them with the skills to perform.

- *We must attract high quality people into HR and HR professionals must develop new business-focused capabilities*

Randy Harris believes that "the HR generalist role will not disappear. I think that there will be probably fewer of those roles, but more senior. These people are going to be more forward-looking in terms of: where their internal customer's organisation is going, how they need to allocate resources, what's the strategy, what's the need going to be in terms of human capital, how do you anticipate that, and if you are going to restructure how do you do it in a proper way? We will still need functional specialists like recruitment and compensation. But the general side I see as becoming more involved, integrated and aligned with the business, and that is, going to require HR people to have some business experience."

Maggie Hurt argues that the need for a strong operational focus is particularly true of HR business partners. "They need to be attuned to the needs of the business. Specialists can be remote, and this is not a good thing. Those specialists who work well behave like internal consultants. They work hand-in-hand with the business and HR business partners. One of the things we need to stop doing as HR professionals is to think that we only exist for our specialism. Fundamentally, the HR professional needs to be an operator, not a theoretician. Knowledge of the business is a key capability." She adds, "We have been working hard to help our HR professionals acquire the language of our business and develop the skills to influence effectively. To add value we need to help our clients develop and execute strategy – so there is a huge organisational effectiveness/change agenda for us. We also need to build strong client relationships, and we need to deliver our work in a way that makes value transparent. So we are drawing on the lessons of external consultants and also developing our client relationship and project capabilities."

Philip Barr is clear about the challenge facing the HR function. "We need to get higher quality people into business generally and into HR in particular. Where are the stars in our organisations? Why are there so few stars in HR? We face a number of challenges as a function. We need to overcome a belief in many senior executives that HR really isn't essential to the organisation. I also believe that not enough HR folk in the private sector really believe in the need to drive profitability and performance."

Vance Kearney makes a strong case to build organisational development capabilities in HR. "I don't know any HR development department that really does organisational development. They do individual development, team development, but I don't think they truly do organisational development. CEOs develop organisations and HR helps."

Richard Brady calls for "ongoing development around the skills of internal process consultation. I see very little evidence of that. There are efforts to communicate to the customers internally saying, 'this is what we've done and this is the new vision for the future – Human Resource is here to help'. The capability to understand the business issues and how people management impacts on these is likely to be based on process consultation."

Miles Warner stresses that "HR must earn its place at the most senior decision-making level. HR has to talk the language of the business. But it also needs to articulate its view from a human standpoint, because we are bringing something to the table that the financial people and other managers won't necessarily have considered."

Steve Ashby argues that our focus should be to "build a team of HR professionals who are business builders, rather than people who know all the ins and outs of classic HR, because where they will add value is in being business coaches and partners to the in-country management teams to show them how to do their business better. So I expect all my HR team to have commercial targets, and they have got to demonstrate that what they are doing has a clear 'line of sight' to the bottom line."

■ *Line managers need to be involved in implementation*
Janice Cook highlights the different ways line managers have been involved in implementing the new HR delivery model. "The HR customer has been strongly involved in the HR transformation journey from the start, and we can point to numerous ways in which the line have been involved. For example: active, hands-on senior level involvement in the project team; a customer reference panel that has engaged with the proposals throughout; three more customer groups that looked at particular aspects of the proposals, for example, shared services; involvement of three directors on the implementation group, and early consultation with all managers. We have worked hard to ensure that our new HR delivery model is client-centred."

■ *Partnership must be built between HR and the line and between HR and external suppliers*
Maggie Hurt makes the point that in a world where a sizeable amount of HR will be delivered by external suppliers, "the principle of partnership must apply also to our relationship with external suppliers. We will continue to use external support into the future, but want partnership with people, not entities."

■ *Selection into new roles needs to take account of new capabilities*
Janice Cook stresses that "the appointment process needs to be seen to be fair. We took into consideration past performance, self-assessment and a capability-based interview. The HR director was not on the interview panel. The key capabilities that were assessed were the ability to

work strategically; execute strategy and support effective organisational change; build strong client relationships and implement the new HR model."

Richard Brady presents a tough challenge for the HR function to rise to. "I think that there is a lot more that can be done to help to train and develop people to make that journey, and also to face up to the fact that some people are not necessarily cut out for and don't have the knowledge, skills and capabilities to become business partners."

■ *Implementing HR transformation is not fundamentally different from implementing any other organisational change*

Maggie Hurt points to the use of an HR capability framework and structured interviews based on this framework as a basis for selection into new roles. "In implementing HR transformation we will meet with resistance, and HR professionals can be as conservative and change-averse as any other managerial group. As with all organisational changes, there is a strong pull-back to the status quo."

Claudia Hall illustrates this point extremely well. "In making changes to the way we recruit, the initial transition was very hard. It was hard because we had to deliver recruiting services to the organisation at the same time as we were transforming the organisation. We also had many HR folks who did not want to give up the control of recruiting: they didn't want to source the candidates, but they did want to interview and do the transactional piece around recruitment. A particularly interesting lesson was that we rolled out a new recruiting process. We had a process flow-map developed in cross-functional workshops. So we had one recruiting process across the organisation. However, after a few months I found that there were internal customer issues, the reason being that each recruiting team started to customise our standard processes."

■ *HR business partners can get bogged down in the administrative/ transactional tasks*

Maggie Hurt notes that there is a transition period for administrative/ transactional work to pass from HR business partners to either a shared services centre or self-service. "We are trying to shift ownership for transactional/administrative work to a shared services centre. For various reasons – work processes, communication, capability, etc. – there have been shortfalls in service levels, resulting in errors. Managers are, rightly, not prepared to tolerate errors, so HR business partners take on the responsibility for sorting out issues. This means that the administrative and transactional workload of business partners increases and we are having to work hard to build sufficient trust to shift responsibility and ownership back to the shared services centre."

Claudia Hall notes that "for some of the HR business partners it took a considerable amount of time before they embraced the new role. Some just didn't understand it, and if you don't understand it you are not going to communicate it effectively."

So what additional reflections can we draw from the viewpoints expressed above?

We would like to highlight three areas.

Firstly, implementing a new HR delivery model has all the markings of any other large and complex business change. There will be enthusiasts and resisters, and those involved will each have to work through their own personal readjustment to change. HR functions are sometimes not so good at looking after their own. We need to accept that HR people are like any other employees, and need to be supported through the change process. This raises issues around change leadership, which we discuss further in Section 6.7.

Secondly, the focus on the business and the relationship HR needs to have with its internal clients. Delivery of people management is, as we have noted earlier and will discuss in greater detail in Section 6.3, a shared responsibility, executed via a number of delivery channels. Effective HR will therefore be the product of partnership, and the HR function must ensure that it does not leave its line colleagues exposed.

Thirdly, change does not happen in tidy, neat steps, and some things can take a while to change. The easiest area to effect change is structure, and this is often the starting point. People are appointed into new roles and are expected to perform according to the new specifications. But the systems and process changes may not yet be fully implemented, so there are stresses and people become frustrated that they are being pulled back into old ways of working – or they are quietly pleased that the reality of change has not actually hit home. Additionally, the development of new capabilities and acceptance of a new way of working takes time. There is no easy solution here, and the reality is that HR professionals are likely to have to cope with high levels of ambiguity during these periods of transition. For those involved in steering transformation, they need to be mindful that they are likely to hit such a "messy" period during implementation, and that whilst this is normal, they will need to focus on taking enabling actions that will help HR to deliver its new operational model quickly.

6.3 Who Does What?

Delivery Channels

Different service delivery approaches were covered in Chapter 3 and it is evident that HR management in organisations is not just the domain of the HR function. As we have already noted, there are many players in the delivery of HR in organisations:

- Employees (through self-service),
- Line managers (through self-service and their people management responsibilities),
- Outsourcers (back office, recruitment, training, etc.),
- External consultants,
- Different internal players in the HR function (shared service centre, specialists and generalists).

Collectively we refer to these participants as "HR delivery channels". During implementation it is important to take decisions concerning where responsibilities for service delivery will change.

We can be certain that HR transformation will shift accountabilities for HR management. What each organisation will need to work out is how far these accountabilities shift and to whom. This is the purpose of this phase of work in the transformation process.

We do not start this thinking about future accountabilities with a blank sheet of paper. Some of the transfer in accountability will be directly related to e-HR and will be known. So, from a technology perspective, there will be core HR processes/activities that must be embedded in the HR Information System (HRIS) backbone. These (such as responsibility for personal data) will be e-enabled and move to employee self-service. There will, in all probability, be e-tools on top of the HRIS backbone that will embed other HR processes. There will be the opportunity for greater self-service concerning policy/procedural advice, and so on.

In addition to these shifts in service provision that are linked explicitly to e-HR, we also need to take into account other organisational drivers that will shape the way HR is delivered. In one organisation, for example, the debate about the delivery of HR management was linked to a broader discussion about enhancing the people management responsibilities of line managers and a desire to increase the level of external provision of HR services. So some changes in the delivery of HR management were made on the basis that either "this activity should be undertaken by the line" or "this service can be better provided externally".

In Chapter 2, we stressed the importance of HR tuning in to the critical issues faced by the organisation. What we want to do in this section is to explore how to work through the "who does what" question and, in particular, to ensure that the HR function ends up being focused on those areas that will contribute most value in the organisation.

Understanding that HR is delivered through a number of channels is the first step. The second step is to scope, at a relatively high level, the services embraced by HR management – not just what the HR function does – for your organisation.

Scope of HR Services

The *scope of HR services* document is the second key input into this process. The example shown in Figure 4.1 in Chapter 4 sets out HR services under five headings:

- People development and performance management,
- Employee relations and communication,
- Resource management,
- Retention and reward,
- HR information.

Some examples have been provided with the content (and level of detail) that should be shown under each heading. In developing your scope of HR services document, the important things to consider are the following:

- Focus on the full scope of HR management, not just what the HR function does, and remember that HR management includes training and development.
- Do not aim for an exhaustive list of every activity undertaken in the realm of HR – keep labels at a high level.
- Aim for no more than ten labels, and ideally around five to ten, for each heading.

A "straw man" scope of services document is presented in Appendix 3.

Accountabilities Workshop

As a precursor to organisational design, we have found it helpful to combine the work on HR delivery channels and scope of HR services to ascertain where responsibilities change for HR service delivery. Our suggested forum to complete this work is through a workshop.

The key input to an accountabilities workshop is a template that consolidates both the above. Appendix 4 shows an excerpt from an accountabilities workshop. We have shown the impact of HR transformation on the role of manager and employee, as this illustrates well how some responsibilities may strengthen and others weaken as a result of proposed changes.

In preparing for the workshop, focus on completing two straw man templates, one template showing the "as is" and another presenting the known accountabilities in the "to be" delivery model. Through desk research and interviews, it should be possible to develop a very robust picture of the "as is" and a good starting point for the "to be". What this preparation work is likely to highlight are inconsistencies in accountabilities across the organisation. These templates can be tested in advance with participants and any outstanding issues can be presented for discussion/resolution at the workshop.

The reason for completing both the "as is" and a "to be" template is to be able to manage implementation more effectively. Knowing how HR transformation will impact different organisational roles will enable communication to be tailored and subsequent interventions to be structured to secure stakeholder buy-in.

We have found that an accountabilities workshop works well when participants are drawn from the HR function and the line and comprise typically around 15–20 people. Participants do not necessarily need to be the most senior people, but should have a grasp between them of the full range of HR services. In the workshop, the aim is to validate the "as is" template and to finalise a "to be" template. The balance of time should be spent on considering the "to be" template.

At the workshop, a process we have found that works well is to:

- Create a large version of the template straw man (sheets of brown paper work well).
- Organise participants into five small groups.
- Introduce the task, setting out the aims of e-HR-led HR transformation, givens, etc.
- Allocate a heading per group.
- Ask each small group to complete their template, identifying where they believe accountability will lie.
- Rotate groups to comment on the work of their colleagues (a sticky dot can be placed alongside a statement requiring clarification or which needs to be challenged; anything missing can be written on a post-it™ note).
- Work through each of the templates and reach agreement where issues have been flagged (with dots and post-it™ notes).

The outputs from this workshop will then need to be socialised with key stakeholders.

We have found that the workshop outputs are helpful in framing a number of interventions that need to be undertaken as part of the HR transformation process. For example:

- high-level activity analysis (supporting analysis of future resource needs);
- HR process mapping;
- accountability mapping and role definitions;
- capability identification and training requirements;
- stakeholder communications;
- structure design.

Structural Issues

We have already noted that where structural lines are drawn between HR delivery channels the structural issues will vary from organisation to organisation. The main questions that will need to be addressed are the following:

■ What activities need to be centralised to take advantage of economies of scale and consolidation of expertise?

■ Where do we need to decentralise to ensure that we remain close to the business and take account of the unique needs of different parts of the organisation?

■ Where do we draw the line between those activities that are performed internally and those that are better performed externally?

■ Where do we draw lines of responsibility for people management between internal organisational boundaries – both between the HR function and line managers/employees and within the HR function itself?

■ How do we leverage technology to deliver HR services?

In answering these questions, there are many contingent factors, such as the ambition or ability of the organisation to implement e-HR solutions; current capability of line managers in people management; attitudes to in- and outsourced provision; maturity of the HR function; suitable outsourcing options and so on. This means that your decisions around HR delivery will ultimately be the product of trade-offs and contingencies that reflect the situation your organisation faces.

We have already explored issues around alternative sourcing, and earlier in this section we set out the need to achieve clarity around the broader delivery of HR management, as it is an important building block in being able to define the scope of the transformed HR function. We now turn our attention to the HR function itself and emerging structural solutions – remembering that structure is but one piece of the broader organisational system (see Section 1.4).

In our work with a wide range of organisations, we are finding that two main HR professional roles emerge. The first is a highly skilled generalist role – the *HR business partner*, who is the primary client interface and who provides leadership and support on the full range of HR issues, including training, learning and development. The second

HR business partners
- Provide leadership on a broad range of HR issues
- Develop and implement business-focused people strategies
- Build human capital
- Support clients in developing higher levels of performance
- Provide coaching on people and organisational matters
- Ensure HR is adding value

HR specialists
- Demonstrate deep subject matter expertise/thought leadership
- Develop "toolkits"
- Own relevant HR processes
- Commission external resources
- Represent the business externally

Figure 6.1 HR business partner and specialist – key accountabilities

role is an *HR specialist* role – typically in areas such as learning and development, compensation, HR information, etc. Figure 6.1 sets out high-level accountabilities for each of these roles.

We now reach the "so what" question. So what if there are two main HR roles? Hasn't this always been so?

At a superficial level, this is certainly true. But we are seeing some significant changes in the way the HR function is working, what HR professionals are doing and how they are contributing. The "what" and "how" questions are key to the HR value model and will be explored in Section 6.5. Below, we explore two of the main issues faced by HR functions in implementing the HR value model from a structural perspective. The important point to note is that it is not the labelling or even where organisational lines are drawn that is, important. What is important about the structural dimension is the alignment of HR delivery with the strategic goals of the organisation and the focus on the internal business client.

Where should HR professionals sit organisationally?

In truth, this varies from organisation to organisation. Some favour HR professionals reporting directly into the same senior executive (typically HR director or equivalent), whilst other organisations prefer to run a virtual HR function with a range of reporting accountabilities: for example,

HR business partners reporting into their client; shared service centre reporting into a central support services function; and where they are not outsourced HR specialists reporting into a senior HR executive. The shades of HR organisational design are many.

A number of themes emerge. They include the following:

- Key is the primacy of the business partner role in managing the client interface. This is a significant change and shifts power within many HR functions away from the specialist to the business partner. As such, it is both a substantive and a symbolic change representing a cultural shift to a more client-centred approach. For many HR functions, this change has involved a difficult transition for specialists and can be a significant point of resistance during the early stages of HR transformation. We have found that this is particularly true of training and development areas, which may have previously had account management posts and may have been organisationally distinct from HR.
- A structural shift towards a common administrative/transactional function, whether through an in-house or an outsourced shared service centre. The implications of this structural change are that there will be one common HR information system and that local employee databases, personal files, administration and other local systems and fragmented administrative resources will cease to exist. Again, the building of trust in a shared service approach is critical, particularly as the benefits of scale often err towards a geographically centralised service centre.
- The specialist role is being increasingly provided externally through outsourcers, consultancy and specialist providers.
- Areas previously staffed by HR specialists (e.g. HR policy) are increasingly being led by HR business partners. For example, in one organisation the development of new HR policy will be led by an HR business partner and run as a project involving a variety of stakeholders on the project team. In another organisation HR business partners may have responsibility for leading an HR process or policy area, for example resourcing, performance management, diversity.
- Whether HR professionals report through a business unit or the HR function, there is a need to develop an HR community – for development, networking, knowledge sharing and learning.

Managing the boundaries between HR business partners and
HR specialists

This is an area of difficulty often faced by HR functions. The underlying issue is primarily about which role is the tail and which the head. Does it matter? Ultimately the function needs to develop an HR agenda which will support and help the business succeed. So what matters is that the function works through issues around the client interface and how work is commissioned and then delivered. In our experience, if HR specialists are business-focused, boundary issues are less of a concern, as their work will be inexorably linked in with business priorities. Problems arise when HR specialists are semi-detached from the business, pursuing their own agendas and priorities rather than those of the business. For example, in one organisation some learning and development specialists had invested significant time in developing a whole range of training workshops which were not a priority. There are many other examples outside L&D, such as the development of inappropriate policy, investing in unnecessary external research, participating in external bodies of dubious value to the organisation, and so on.

One of the ways HR functions are resolving this organisational boundary issue is through adopting aspects of the consultancy model. Below we offer two examples of how this works.

In this first example, the business partner has the key client interface and works with the client to address their critical people and organisational development issues. Sometimes the business partner is able to work with the client without additional support. However, where additional support is needed the business partner agrees with their client terms of reference for a "consulting project". The business partner then contracts for additional resource, either other business partners or specialists (or even line managers). Specialists may be in-house or external consultants. The business partner then ensures that the consulting project delivers to client expectations.

In this second example specialists, through their subject matter expertise and focus on external developments and trends, identify opportunities for change, which are taken to the business. Once the business signs off the work, the specialist then owns the "consulting project", which will be developed in collaboration with business partners and line managers. In this instance, the HR specialist brings new ideas into an organisation that will challenge thinking and add value in much the same way that a good consultant will. The organisation has the right to reject the idea or to decide to pursue it. In this sense, specialists should be thought of as leaders and will proactively seek to introduce world-class practices to help the business to perform better.

Few HR functions have moved to a pure consulting model (a model which would encompass timesheets, internal charging, resource pooling, account management, etc.) and indeed aspects of the consulting model, like internal charging, have dubious value. Yet there are three aspects of the consulting model that are helping business partners and specialists to work together more effectively:

- The acceptance that HR professionals need to be addressing those issues that are most critical to their clients. This is an important way in which value is expressed and is based on the principle that there will be a *commissioning* of work by the client.
- This work will be packaged as a *project*, with clear terms of reference – including deliverables, timescales, resources, costs, etc.
- HR participate fully in these business critical projects because they have *valuable skills* that will help their client to make progress.

6.4 HR Culture

We will not labour the point about the need for HR to change its own culture, as the points are well made elsewhere in this book. When discussing culture with HR teams, a typical picture of the challenge facing HR is summarised as: "We need to be less reactive and more proactive." What this encapsulates are three significant cultural challenges for the function:

Challenge 1 – to become more client-focused: We will discuss the new capabilities HR professionals need to develop in Section 6.5. Client management is clearly one of the core capability areas. Internal HR must learn the lessons from its competitors – external providers – and develop a consulting mindset that thrives on anticipating and solving client problems. This will also mean learning to question and challenge what clients are asking for. Although difficult at times, partnership must be built on a relationship where challenge and support are expressed in equal measure.

Challenge 2 – to articulate a clear value proposition: Linked to the need to be more client-focused, HR professionals must be able to articulate how HR adds value. This means getting better at measuring outcomes and estimating inputs. It means being able to have a sensible discussion about the use of resources and priorities. It also means being able to articulate what will be delivered, by whom, at what cost and when. In this way, the organisation will be able to make better choices and will see the amount of perceived low-value work diminishing.

Challenge 3 – to market and sell HR better: This challenge is, of course, linked to the previous two. Lawler and Mohrman (2003), in their recent survey of trends and directions in HR, point out that perceptions concerning the contribution made by HR are not changing as fast as the actual change on the ground. This is clearly a cause for concern. Part of the problem is that HR professionals have not traditionally thought about how they market and sell themselves. For example, during our client relationship workshops we spend time thinking about HR's value proposition and about the way HR sells itself to the organisation. Generally speaking, this is often the first time HR professionals have thought about themselves from a selling perspective. They are not very good at thinking about their experiences and packaging them in a way that enables clients to see what they are capable of contributing.

All the above are, again, lessons that can be learned from external providers to help us shape a culture that is confident and proactive.

The point we make on all HR transformations is that whatever cultural attributes the function wishes to develop, they need to be hard-wired into the other organisational levers – the way you organise, use technology, manage your work processes, lead, develop people and so on.

6.5 New HR Capabilities

Our work on defining and then developing HR capabilities for the new world of HR has been the product of a number of conversations that went along the lines of:

"We buy into HR transformation. We agree that we need to make our contribution as strategic partners. We accept that as HR professionals we need to understand the organisation and its priorities better, and demonstrate value through our work. But what we are not clear about is what will be different about our day job? How will we know that we are performing differently? What help will we be getting in order to make the changes we need to make?"

Reflecting on these conversations, we agreed that there was little value in just saying to HR professionals, "Go forth: contribute strategically and add value." Part of implementation must include clarifying the performance expectations around the new professional HR roles and, as a consequence, being prepared to invest in the development of HR professionals and managers.

From our practitioner discussions so far in this book, we can draw some clear conclusions concerning the terrain that HR professionals need to occupy. They need to:

■ understand the business, and be respected as business people;
■ be able to contribute to the development and execution of strategy – which means that organisational development/change management expertise must come to the fore;
■ act as internal consultants, able to build strong client relationship skills;
■ articulate and demonstrate value through each intervention made with clients;
■ influence rather than depend on positional power.

Knowing about HR rules, policies and procedures is no longer good enough.

We come in a full circle, back to the three mindsets introduced in Chapter 1 of this book. As we argued in that chapter, the tool kit that HR professionals need to draw from in order to execute effective HR transformation is the same tool kit it needs to take into the business each day to work effectively as strategic partners with clients. Whether the HR professional is in a generalist or specialist role, the tool kit is the same. The only thing that changes is the breadth or depth of subject matter expertise that is, needed.

What we intend to do in this section is to focus on the capabilities HR professionals need to develop. We will present a best practice capability framework and show how this sits within an overall capability development process, and we will draw on the experience particularly of National Grid Transco to illustrate implementation. We have chosen to highlight the work of National Grid Transco because the work undertaken by the HR team over a period of time and through a significant merger demonstrates well the building blocks that need to be put in place to achieve a step change in HR capability.

Case Study

The initial work on the HR capability framework was undertaken with National Grid plc before it merged with Lattice plc. Work was undertaken envisioning the new HR delivery model, and the business was well advanced at the point of merger. One of the decisions taken at an early point in the transformation journey was to invest in developing the capability of the HR team. This decision sat alongside other decisions to implement a business partner model; establish a shared services centre; consolidate key HR processes and start the process of e-enablement.

The National Grid HR team had performed a traditional HR role well. However, as the business embarked on an ambitious change agenda, a HR capability framework was developed in order to set out the performance expectations for the HR team at all levels.

When National Grid merged with Lattice and became a FTSE top 20 business overnight, a decision was taken by the new National Grid Transco HR team to continue implementing the new HR delivery model, including the adoption of the HR capability framework and development programme.

Architecture of the Framework

Capability areas

The HR capability framework has eight HR capability areas. Five of these capability areas are linked to the traditional skill areas of HR and are shown in Figure 6.2. These capability areas express *what* HR does. The terminology reflects the needs of National Grid Transco; other organisations have used different terminology broadly within the same architecture.

These traditional skill areas also relate to the scope of services template presented earlier in this chapter.

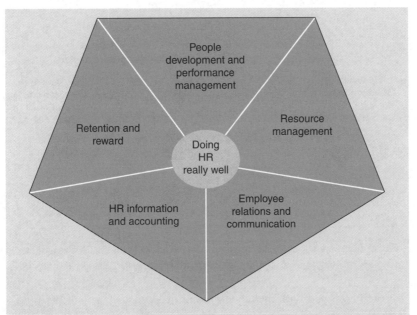

Figure 6.2 Core HR capability areas linked to the traditional skill areas of HR (Taken from the National Grid Transco HR Capability Framework.)

In addition to the business of HR, there are also three newer capability areas specifically linked to the changed role of the HR professional. These are shown in Figure 6.3.

These three new capability areas express *how* HR works with its clients and are described as follows:

Strategy and change implementation: Understanding the business and the critical business issues; being able to deploy appropriate tools, frameworks and models to help clients respond to these issues; developing the skills and capabilities that place HR at the heart of organisational development and change management. This capability area is strongly aligned with the development of a systems mindset discussed in Chapter 1.

Client relationship management: Creating impact and developing the influencing skills that will enable HR to work in partnership with internal clients; developing coaching and facilitation skills; using a process-consulting/client-centred approach. This capability area is

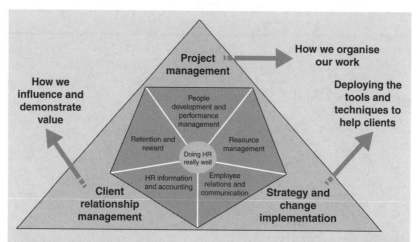

Figure 6.3 Core HR capability areas specifically linked to the changed role of the HR professional (Taken from the National Grid Transco HR Capability Framework.)

strongly aligned with the development of a process consulting mind-set discussed in Chapter 1.

Project management: Organising work more productively through using the principles of project management. This approach is based on the consultancy model where work is typically parcelled as a project, with specific terms of reference. Whilst we accept that not all the work of HR will be able to be packaged in terms of a project, the development of a project mindset increases the amount of work that will be structured with a clear value proposition and approach to assure delivery. This capability area is strongly aligned with the development of a project mindset discussed in Chapter 1.

Capabilities

Linked to each of the capability areas is a small number of capabilities, shown in the table below:

Capability area	Capabilities
Strategy and change management	■ Contributes to/develops business and HR strategies and plans ■ Facilitates effective change ■ Shapes the organisation's culture

Capability area	Capabilities
Client relationship management	■ Builds strong client relationships ■ Challenges and influences client thinking ■ Demonstrates value to internal clients
Project management	■ Applies project management tools and techniques ■ Manages projects
People development and performance management	■ Supports managers in building the performance of individuals ■ Works with managers to ensure that succession pools underpin key posts ■ Facilitates the development of effective teams
Resource management	■ Sources vacancies ■ Manages employee release ■ Develops workforce plans
Employee relations and communication	■ Builds a strong employer brand ■ Ensures the employment framework is compliant with prevailing law and aligned to business needs ■ Promotes effective consultation and communication processes
Retention and reward	■ Works with managers to ensure appropriate retention strategies are put in place ■ Ensures an affordable and competitive reward package
HR information and accounting	■ Provides effective decision support information ■ Delivers to high service levels ■ Promotes the e-enablement of HR service delivery

These capabilities provide a next level of detail and are the focus of capability development.

Performance levels

Set alongside each of the capability areas/capabilities is a set of four performance levels – fourth being the highest level. The performance level descriptors have been written so that they can be evidenced whether

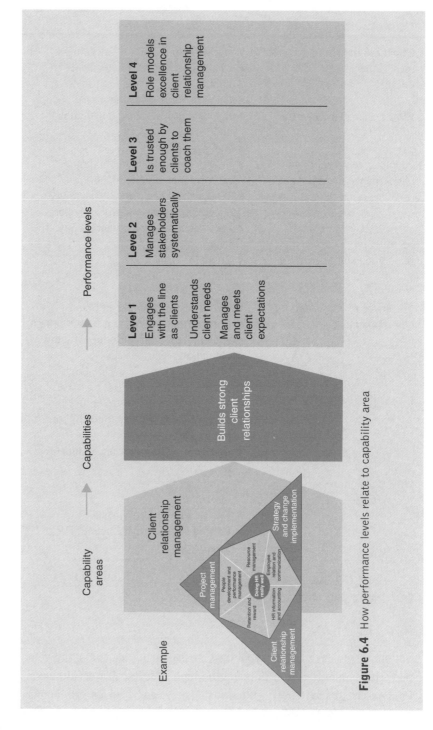

Figure 6.4 How performance levels relate to capability area

self- or manager-assessed. An example of the performance levels is shown in Figure 6.4, which relates to the client relationship management capability area and the capability "builds strong client relationships".

Although not specifically highlighted as a capability area, the theme of *business focus* pervades all aspects of the framework: it is what HR capability is focused upon. As such, the need for business focus is integrated into all the performance levels.

Using the HR capability framework

The capability framework is used in three main ways:

Firstly, to enable the HR leadership group to assess the bench-strength of the HR team through establishing a functional profile against each of the performance levels.

Secondly, to support performance review/performance development discussions. The framework has been written so that HR professionals can evidence each of the performance descriptors. For example, using the performance level 2 in Figure 6.4, someone can show how different tools have been used to manage stakeholders systematically.

Thirdly, to shape a development programme to enable the bulk of HR professionals to be operating at the middle two performance levels – levels 2 and 3.

6.6 Developing HR Capabilities

Where possible, we strongly recommend that HR professionals achieve professional qualifications and accreditation through their relevant professional institute or governing body. This is important in building the credibility of HR, in ensuring professional standards and in developing a community of influential HR professionals.

However, the acquisition of a formal professional qualification does not always address sufficiently the full range of capabilities that HR professionals need to acquire to operate as effective business partners. In our work with a wide range of businesses, the development of capability has been run in-house with a strong focus on applying knowledge to the circumstances of that business.

We will continue to use National Grid Transco as our case study to illustrate how HR capability has been developed.

Case Study

A straw man discussion document was written and used to stimulate debate and shape the capability development process. This was an important step in building business commitment to the programme approach, content and investment.

The two main building blocks that underpin the capability development process have been:

- capability workshops,
- learning groups supported by individual coaching.

This programme has been delivered during a time when finance has been tight. The programme has been developed with cost effectiveness very much in mind. As a result, a programme has been delivered that is, high value, challenging, intensive and streamlined. We describe these two building blocks below.

Capability workshops

All HR professionals attended three capability workshops linked to the areas of strategy and change, client relationship management and project management. These workshops were pitched at levels 2 and 3 of the HR capability framework described earlier.

These workshops have had a number of beneficial outcomes in addition to the explicit aim of developing HR capability:

- They brought different levels of seniority and different areas of expertise within HR together for a shared learning experience.
- They created a powerful environment for dialogue and experience/ knowledge sharing.
- They helped build a common language around the core capability areas – within HR and, as HR use the tools and frameworks with clients, within the business itself.
- They have been an organisational development intervention as they aided the HR function to understand the change process it was going through.

The strategy and change and client relationship workshops were run over 2 days, whereas the project management workshop was a 1-day event. All were very practically oriented. Where a tool, model or framework was presented, there was the opportunity to explore its practical application.

The workshops covered the following broad areas:

Strategy and change:
Understanding the business environment/critical issues
Linking HR priorities to critical business issues
Key change management models and their use
The change cycle
Structure-driven change
Shaping the organisation culture
Dealing with individual transitions and change.

Client relationship:
Understanding the different roles we play (process/expert)
Making more effective client interventions
Developing a value proposition
Contracting with clients
Influencing skills
Basic facilitation skills
Coaching the client.

Project management:
Project management principles
Applying the project approach
Developing terms of reference
Effective time management
Project management tools.

Learning groups/coaching

As the focus of the workshops was on knowledge and skills acquisition, there was recognition that HR professionals needed time to apply what had been learned on the job with clients and to reflect on that learning. It was agreed, therefore, to use the action learning group approach to follow through and consolidate the initial workshop inputs. How have learning groups worked?

From a practical point of view they comprise around eight HR professionals (range of seniority and area of expertise), who have met around five times over a 6-month period and have worked on a theme: for example, marketing the HR function; knowledge management in HR; the employee of the future. The decision to run theme-based learning groups as opposed to more open, learner-driven groups was due to two main reasons. Firstly, the group participants themselves preferred a more structured approach and secondly, the organisation could see a tangible return on the investment that was being made.

Learning groups have four main areas of focus:

1. To pursue personal development goals within the context of the learning group task.
2. To reflect on how the group is working and to learn about how we learn.
3. To achieve a deliverable related to the learning group theme.
4. To apply and consolidate the use of the tools and techniques acquired during the capability workshops.

The learning group has been supported by an external facilitator, who has helped the group to keep on track, to achieve the above goals and to make the most of the learning opportunity.

Personal coaching has been wrapped around each of the learning group meetings. This decision recognised that some personal development was not suited to a learning group environment. Additionally, it was put in place to address an issue which arose from previous experiences of running learning groups, namely, that after the first couple of meetings operational priorities tended to encroach on the learning group and attendance/momentum diminished. In addition, the coaching provided the opportunity to reflect on what happened at the previous learning group meeting and to consider how to use the next learning group to best address development objectives.

Key learning points that have emerged from this process can be summarised as follows:

- People were able to experiment in a risk-free setting.
- Recognition (after about two meetings) by the group that it was *their* group and that they needed to own the agenda, the process

and the outputs. The group saw this as a key point in realising that their capability development was their responsibility.

■ Considerable insights into the culture of HR were made: for example, the good (e.g. supportive, encouraging, willing to share knowledge and experience) and the not-so-good (e.g. over-committing and under-delivering against promises; poor time management).

■ Genuine improvements in capability were experienced, with learning group members making more effective interventions with clients.

■ Momentum was sustained throughout and, indeed, by the end of the process the groups were successfully self-managing.

■ The experience boosted the ability and confidence within HR to take the learning group approach into the business.

The National Grid Transco experience has been extremely successful in moving HR capability. The approach taken has been successful partly because of the recognition that people need to be accountable themselves for their own learning (thus a high contribution level throughout, giving the whole process good momentum) and partly because we took an approach that left no one out of the process.

6.7 HR Change Leadership

The main focus of this chapter is on the tools and approaches that we have used to implement the HR value model. What we have not touched on in any depth is the role that the HR leadership group needs to play throughout the process of implementation. That it is a key role goes without saying, but we set out below a few of the things that we have found effective HR leadership groups have done well during implementation:

■ provided strong and visible personal commitment to a transformed HR;
■ worked collaboratively to create a vision;
■ engaged actively with the implementation process (they have not just delegated and walked away) and put at risk their own personal credibility around delivery;

- seen HR transformation as a process, impacting the whole HR terrain, and been prepared to work through the process with the HR transformation programme team;
- led from the front, taking an active role in influencing and communicating with key business stakeholders and the HR function;
- given time to regular workshops and other interventions throughout the process;
- remained patient – things do not always go to plan – and been prepared to address unexpected challenges;
- used external facilitation and consultancy well – consultants have supported the internal team and have not replaced them;
- acknowledged that members of each team need to work through the implications of change and transition for themselves;
- recognised that they are, themselves, part of the transformation process.

We would like to amplify the last two of the points above. The first point is around the way individuals are supported through transition. We make quite a big deal of this in our capability workshops, and draw heavily on the excellent work of William Bridges (1993) in this area. In providing good change leadership there is a need to help people with endings: to help them to come to terms with the fact that the way things were has gone for good. Some of the things that have been done to help with this include practical actions like changing job titles, working environments and reporting lines. But they also include things like "end of era" celebrations or the symbolic binning of old material. In helping people with beginnings, things like the capability framework, conferences and symbols (a visual representing the HR capabilities was used very effectively by National Grid Transco) help people to understand the *purpose* of transformation; engage with the *plan* to implement it; see a *picture* of the new world of HR and the *part* they will play in it. Good change leaders make this happen.

The last bullet point above is really important. A huge amount of credibility is gained when the leadership group themselves acknowledge their need to change and then do something about it. Particularly good examples of this have been when the leadership group has participated in the capability development workshop and is seen to be working through the issues of behavioural change as much as the rest of the HR team.

We have also seen some very poor things happening during implementation – and often outside the direct control of HR. We hope that you will not identify with these, but some examples are set out below:

- The capability development programme was split so that senior people participated in learning groups and the remainder of the function in capability workshops.
- A travel ban was imposed just after learning groups had been set up on a cross-national basis – which prevented non-UK participants from attending.
- A participant was made redundant during a workshop.
- An outsourcing solution for transactional and advisory activities was adopted against the will of the leadership group.

The reality is that HR leadership matters. If the HR leadership group does not step out with enthusiasm and keep the drumbeat of change pounding, then your best plans will flounder. It can often be a cliché to talk about the need for senior commitment to a change programme. With respect to HR transformation, we can say with a high degree of confidence that this is true, and we hope that in this section we have set out some of the things for the leadership team to focus on.

Summary

The real value of HR transformation happens when HR professionals work in partnership with the business. Implementation of the HR value model does not just happen. There needs to be a process, and that process needs to be integrated into the overall HR transformation programme. In this chapter we have presented the main process steps and tools to help you implement quickly and effectively. The main focus is on what business partners do and how they will know they are performing effectively. At the heart of the HR value model is therefore the development of HR capability. We have shown in this chapter how this may be reflected through an HR capability framework and capability development programme. Finally, we have presented the important role the senior HR leadership group have in providing change leadership throughout implementation.

7

Implementation: Process, Technology and Benefits Realisation

We turn now to the process and technology side of implementing HR transformation. Whilst implementation is of course about delivering the changes you have planned, there is no purpose in delivery unless it achieves sustainable business benefit. Therefore this chapter also covers how to manage the realisation of sustainable business benefits.

Chapter structure

Key Themes

■ The implementation of HR process and technology needs to be true to your original vision for HR transformation. The alignment of implementation with your vision and plans needs to be explicitly addressed so that you do not inadvertently diverge and risk the success of your programme.

- The detailed design and implementation of the processes and technology are important elements of HR transformation. However, it is the adoption of those processes and the supporting technology by HR, employees and line managers that defines whether the change has taken root in the organisation. Therefore continued involvement of all those impacted by HR transformation in the implementation is critical.
- Delivery of sustainable business benefit is at the heart of successful HR transformation. However, expectations need to be managed in terms of the level and timing of benefit delivery. This is done through a benefits realisation plan that explicitly defines when and where benefits will be delivered and who is accountable for their delivery.

7.1 Context

This chapter considers the implementation of HR process and technology; both individually and how they interact, particularly with respect to the impact on the HR function, employees and line managers. Implementation is about realising the vision that you have set out for HR and moves from detailed design, through building and testing, to "cutover" to the new solution.

Of course, implementation is only part of the story. The realisation of the benefits envisaged when constructing the business case is vital. Therefore we explore how to track key benefit areas and ways to measure and evaluate implementation effectiveness. We consider ways to lock-in and sustain the benefits of HR transformation, delivery of sustainable business benefit being the ultimate measure of success.

7.2 Practitioner Perspectives

- *Implementation of new HR processes and technology changes the roles HR, employees and line managers play*

Kath Lowey considers the change from an HR and line perspective. "It's about shifting the HR back office operation to the front, and it's about being online – we're a technology company, after all. But you still see this desire underneath for people to have a person alongside them to help them make decisions. The key is how do you get that with a small team, and not align to each organisation a team of HR people, because they'll end up doing things differently, it'll cost more money and you've lost them."

"We have delivered a different way of doing service, but the *critical* thing going forward is training in terms of how they use the new services. Unless you can achieve that, significant benefit will be lost. I'm quite amazed, with what we've been through, that I still have managers, and senior managers in some areas, who just don't understand. On one hand, they will talk in figures about the general and administration cost being too high for the organisation, but they also want personal service from HR, which costs more, and that's been a real issue."

"When we put everybody in the one (HR) team, they felt, 'Well, we're going into a service centre and you're cutting us off from our business contacts.' Absolutely not. What you get now is that you can be working in a service environment, you can be working in product engineering or you can be working in the corporate centre, so you're going to get a much broader view, and I've really tried to encourage my team to be out with the business, to find out what we're doing, but it's not about doing the managers' jobs for them. However, my view is that as more and more transactional HR is delivered through self-service, our model will move more towards specialisms."

Vance Kearney believes HR has a standard-setting role. "It's not about administrating salaries, it's about policing people standards, so quality of selection is a very important area, as is the development of people. I think the HR function should be *very, very* strong in standards of selection, whether that's in hiring standards or in promoting standards. Too often we compromise standards. We should take the hard choice, and if we can't find somebody who meets our standards we shouldn't hire anyone until we can find somebody who does."

Claudia Hall focuses on the change from a line manager perspective. "The line managers need to become familiar with our 'One HR' philosophy and understand the benefits that can be derived from streamlined core processes and single point of contact access into HR services. They also need to become more efficient users of technology, whether it is Interactive Voice Recognition (IVR) services or web-enabled self-service."

"However, there are a number of cautionary signs that indicate managers are exhibiting dissatisfaction with the apparent progression towards ways of doing things that erode the level of human contact.

We must have the 'H' retained in Human Resources, or you may as well dissolve the organisation and e-enable everything and put in consultants to help the organisation."

Randy Harris takes this further. "I think my mindset is that in a perfect world we will be high touch to our management community. We'll become a bit more high tech to the employee base because we're geographically dispersed; we'll have 1000 retail stores at the end of this year with three, four, five employees in each of those stores. We have over 400 locations: there's just no way I can deploy enough HR people and trainers to be high touch to every single employee. The concept of high tech to the employees is to push more technology out there so that employees can be more self-sufficient. The concept of high touch to managers is that if we can develop our managers, support our managers and give them the skill set that they need to meet the people needs of the employees who work for them, then the high tech approach to the employee works because they're getting high touch from their manager which is really where they want to get it; they don't want to get it from me or my team. Most employees want their manager to be a positive and constructive point of contact for them."

- *You cannot consider e-HR alone. Data and information is a key result of the interaction of HR processes and technology*

Vance Kearney addresses this. "To provide a complete solution requires quite a sophisticated set of technology … and partial e-HR doesn't change much at all. I can give you an example. I have countries that have HR and payroll, and they do salary increases through manager self-service, which sounds great, and indeed it is: the salary increase gets processed and it goes to payroll automatically and the HR database records the history and all relevant data. But then I have other countries where payroll is not an integrated system, so the manager goes through the web-based self-service and changes the salary, and at the end of it someone in HR sends an e-mail to payroll to change the salary. Before web self-service the manager rang HR and they sent the same e-mail to payroll, so a web page has only replaced a phone call, which isn't real automation. Without full systems interaction the process remains fundamentally manual."

"I don't think that the HR department has ever really been that interested in processing transactions; the transactions have often been a means of access to other issues. So the fact that a manager wants to change somebody's salary or change somebody's status is an indication of dissatisfaction with a grading or a pay structure, it's an indication of a potential change in the market or an organisational issue, so quite often the transactions were really only little things that we did that led us on to the real work of HR. They were never really the real work of HR; they were kind of a necessary evil that we had to perform. So I think it's a good thing that we're not having to do that, and the debate about whether it's automated or whether it's outsourced or whether it's a bought-in service is not very interesting."

"So the technology's great, it's taken away the transactions... but it does then lead us to the key question, 'so what is HR going to do to add value?'"

Helen Corey fully supports this view. "I return to my points about HR making better use of data and supporting managers in making business decisions and employees in feeling more in touch with the business. Instead of saying, 'We should be doing an e-HR initiative so that management has a better view or transparency,' does HR ever look at it from the other point of view and say, 'We actually want employees to have better transparency to what their bosses are doing?'"

"The company's greatest assets – people – walk out of the door every day and evaluate their relationship with the company. In my view, HR can make a beneficial contribution to the business by encouraging greater loyalty and commitment from its workforce, effectively through enhancement of the company brand. That's what HR should be striving to do: finding ways to help managers and employees perform better and experience loyalty to the company brand, which in turn will positively impact the bottom line."

"From a technical systems perspective, the constant challenge is trying to align HR processes and data with the real needs of the business. Managers need to be able to access data that supports their business role and gives them insights to deliver better performance. HR needs to demonstrate closer alignment to the business and earn credibility through providing services, whether data or consulting advice, that show a clear link to the business. Too often, so-called 'best of breed' HR systems fail to provide the required business functionality; the so-called 'vanilla' or prebuilt components have been designed without sufficient appreciation of the real work of the manager or the needs of the employee."

"In terms of professional support to the line, whether it's via HR business partners or specialists, they must be aware of and understand the business imperatives. Fluffy HR will not do."

Miles Warner is equally forthright. "We go to great lengths to encourage employees to supply data via e-HR, this also raises important issues in terms of how that interaction translates into benefits. For example, there's a huge amount of data coming into the system, and once you have a huge amount of data people want to use it in all sorts of different ways. I think the biggest challenge we've got now is convincing the employee population that all this data that's coming in through career requests and performance management is being properly managed by HR. The employees know that the organisation has it because they put it in the system themselves; they then say, 'Right, you've got it all – now what are you doing with it?' So you've got to make sure that you've got processes to feed back to them what they need. If you don't move quickly, the organisation will start to demand information, leading to a massive increase in workload."

"To give you an example, the career centre emerged well in the recent perception survey. This online facility allows people to see generic careers that they can take in the company, on a global basis, anywhere you want, and they're all putting into the system what they would like to do. Naturally, if you offer someone a new role, you have to be very careful you don't offer them a role that's not included in their personal choices, otherwise the whole thing collapses, so you've got to be able to continue to encourage the use of the system by making sure that the population is seeing some return for what they're putting into the system."

"This principle holds true for other areas, too. Where the value comes is in the quality of service and how you use the data. Let's take an example of a manager you are seeking to appoint to be in charge of the business somewhere. If you've got three or four different candidates who come up and you've got a lot of independently sourced data, that encourages objectivity and a much more informed decision about who is best for that role, rather than relying on someone's 'best mate' type system. So you can manage that whole process of succession planning and talent management. This has huge value to the organisation, simply because the self-service process has sourced so much more data, and then it's used intelligently."

"Another example is in a downturn situation. If you've got a good set of data in the system that's been input by managers and employees, you can identify your bottom 10%, or whatever percentage you agree on, much more clearly. Also, in the realms of discipline, you can discipline someone more effectively in line with the local regulations without any of the potential costs of tribunal, passage rumours and all that other stuff that can be motivated and cost an organisation money."

■ *The redefined processes and supporting technology must contribute to wider business benefit through their alignment with the vision*
Claudia Hall is very clear on this. "The benefits stem directly from the creation of our 'One HR' philosophy – reducing confusion for our internal customers and enabling the delivery of services that improve business performance. This has been achieved to date largely through changes in organisation structure, processes and HR roles, but we shall be looking to achieve additional benefits from improved technology, such as the deployment of web-based self-service tools for managers and employees, based upon our PeopleSoft system."

"The benefits of HR transformation have underpinned the highly successful growth of Nextel in the last few years, helping to propel it into the Fortune 250."

Janice Cook strongly supports this view. "The continuous development of HR must have inbuilt evaluation and review. What was key in NCH was the ongoing need to manage expectations and communication in the organisation, particularly in checking that the vision for HR was still aligned to the overall business vision."

"The need for tracking against the vision is illustrated by the lessons learned from an earlier attempt to develop the HR function. A radical vision for holistic HR was agreed, but was implemented at a time of organisational devolution. Without the proper checks and monitoring, the function became very localised and the vision for HR was lost. Part of our challenge recently has been to recover ground lost in that first attempt to change."

"At the outset we agreed a set of criteria against which we would evaluate the new HR model. Although the HR review was as much about cost control as cost cutting, we will achieve a modest 20% reduction in HR costs. Monitoring and tracking implementation is very important to us, and we learned from previous attempts to change HR the downsides of not doing this work."

Tony Williams reflects, "I was brought in as a catalyst to change the way that HR was delivered in this organisation and we've been very fortunate, partially because the business context has gone in our direction anyway to allow us to do what we want to do and partially because I think the organisational context has also given us plenty of opportunity to prove where HR can add more value. If you buy an organisation and you're charged as a business, as a group, to save £1.4 bn over a two-and-a-half-year period that was a galvanising objective for us all, to actually make it happen. The primary response and contribution from HR was to look at delivering efficiencies through shared services and to support the people issues involved in such a major transaction generally."

"I don't think we've gone far enough through our formal e-HR programme for me to have all the answers. I'm predicting what the answers are going to be and predicting where the issues are. I could have come into my organisation 3 years ago and said, 'I'm going to drive out 30% of your costs' and I'd be sitting here now saying, 'I've still not saved more than 5% of your costs – in fact, I've probably met cost.' I simply don't believe the e-HR hype from a cost-saving perspective."

Steve Ashby comments, "Our business is like a tornado; it moves and grows rapidly and a little erratically because generally when we win a contract we don't have much time to mobilise it. We were building complete catering facilities and staff accommodation in the desert last year with 14 days between contract award and first meals served. So we don't always know what's coming up next; and thus we don't have a precise flight path."

"The benefit realisation process is linked to the technology-enabled development of KPI definition and measurement, standard operating processes, business reporting and so on. These act like a flexible sleeve around the tornado, assisting it to keep growing rapidly. Our business is rightly concerned about being constricted by processes and systems and bureaucracy. If we build an external skeleton around the business that consists of bureaucratic systems and processes and 'one size fits all,' we'll suffocate it. What we need is flexible enabling structures that support the business and never slow it down."

"That flexible structure will enable us to manage the outputs of the HR function around the globe, to have the right KPIs in place, and have a deep understanding of our business, performance and financial trends.

Done properly, we can then get the benefits that we need: real-time information about performance by country against a whole set of KPIs that link to the balanced scorecard – without asking people to change the way they do things every day. Process and technology is only relevant and useful if it helps people do things better, faster and easier."

"Our clients will see the trends at the same time as we see them, which will make sure that everybody stays focused on a small number of highly meaningful KPIs, as opposed to a very long shopping list which may or may not consist of the right things."

"Smart processes and technologies engender confidence and trust, leading to greater business value and improved client delivery."

■ *Effective measurement of benefit delivery cements the achievement of HR transformation*

Randy Harris comments, "Importantly for me, our CEO makes it easier for me to do what I do because of the concept of PSV (people, service and value); as a CEO, he is very balanced and understanding of the needs of customers, shareholders and employees. I was the first person he hired when he became CEO and he consciously wanted someone sitting in this chair who had run a business somewhere along the way in their career. Because let's face it, at the end of the day, there's not a CEO in North America that looks forward to seeing the head of HR on their calendar for the day so that they can come in and have an HR conversation. They just don't want to. If I can go and have a conversation with him about how we're going to drive earnings per share (EPS) or how we're going to help contribute to our operating margin going from 39% to 44%, he's real interested in having that conversation."

"So if I can package what I'm going to do from an HR point of view in a way that gets his attention at the outset of what we're doing, it's no different from talking to the Head of Engineering Operations and Head of Sales and Marketing, HR are not a drag on the bottom line by spending dollars, but we're contributing to the value creation. You can see that in the return on investment. Everything we do within HR, we qualify with the return on investment; we set it up front and we apply the same accountability to ourselves that I would if I was putting a sales comp plan together for our sales force. That makes you a whole lot more credible."

Steve Ashby says, "Line managers will know that their performance against KPIs will be visible and compared with similar measures in other parts of the world, leading to a competitive spirit of sorts. Similarly, their own career and remuneration will depend on how they do against these KPIs. The executive team can portray the business strategy through the KPIs that we agree with the line managers and the way that we measure performance. It's frustrating for line managers who tell us that they've done really well in a particular area, only to find out that it's not strategically relevant! It's also terrifically wasteful of resources, energy and manager motivation."

"So the new approach to performance setting and measurement is a very elegant way of skilfully influencing what people focus on, and I can't think of a more powerful way that I've seen in the last twenty or twenty-five years of being in HR. Regular and focused performance feedback, visible progress against targets on the 'league table', line of sight between manager KPIs and strategic objectives – sounds so easy, but it's amazing how few organisations crack it."

"Line managers can rightly expect HR to provide a set of core and common processes which support them in pursuit of their KPIs. Processes such as performance management; setting high-quality KPIs, which focus people in the business on the correct things; good feedback and coaching methods which improve individual capability; regular review through performance appraisals of results; development plans which are put in place for those people to become better at their jobs; and the succession planning process where you look at the overall health of the organisation, where your gaps are, and where your gaps are likely to be as the business grows and develops and moves in new directions."

"Whilst this may not be revolutionary in approach, it takes on a new relevance when you are actually able to see the financial or commercial result of building your high-performing team versus accepting whatever's there and not actually investing in capability."

Richard Brady adds, "It's easy to generalise, but I think that there are some tremendous and exciting examples of where HR is delivering value. The relationship between HR delivery processes, be that value through other internal consulting efforts and customer perception at the employee and manager level, is being measured more effectively. Also the linkage between that HR capability and so-called 'human capital' and external customers' loyalty is being measured more effectively. The concepts of employee engagement offer a huge opportunity for human resources to focus on how their efforts link to not just satisfaction of their internal customers but also external customer loyalty and then profit and other financial and non-financial metrics."

"I think it's a sea change really for HR to move from a gatekeeping, decision-making, parent relationship to one where they are serving internal customers who can be very difficult as all customers can. In society our expectations as customers have increased exponentially over recent years with the advent of the Internet, speed of access to services and progress in delivery of goods and services in the market-place. We expect immediate answers and we expect our suppliers to treat us in a way that we want to be treated or we'll go elsewhere."

"I see efforts to measure satisfaction but often we measure things which seem to be important like recruitment cost to hire, duration to hire and training delivered. These are very often 'lagging', process-focused and historical measures rather than 'leading' measures (such as levels of skills and capabilities). In learning and development, for example, there is a need to go well beyond the 'happy sheets' immediately post event, to look at the relationship between acquiring new knowledge, skills and attitudes and improvements in customer service, satisfaction and other measures of organisation performance. A major skill set lacking in HR professionals is that area of predictive statistics and measurement."

"HR needs to become more measurement focused. Efforts are quite haphazard in that area at the moment except within organisations that benchmark either internally or externally. This is still something that I rarely see. It would be good to see more of this because how else do we know if we're delivering on our customers' expectations?"

Tony Williams reinforces the importance of the balanced scorecard. "I have a balanced business scorecard now that I put on the internal HR Intranet, covering things such as payroll errors, payroll queries, all kinds of volume metrics. There is some qualitative stuff but it's more efficiency qualitative than effectiveness. Just to give you a quick example – the efficiency and speed by which I produced a new hire contract is measured, the end-to-end timescale of recruiting and embedding a new start is not measured. The ideal that we're aiming for is an effectiveness measure that allows us to analyse the performance of new hires, such as out of the last hundred people that we recruited, 98 are performing at above average performance and adding extra value to the bottom line. That's the ultimate effectiveness measure."

"As we roll out the systems that allow us to measure things much more robustly, workflow management and so on, it will give us a really good opportunity to demonstrate tangible benefit from our operations."

In summary, the practitioner views emphasise that:

- *HR process and technology implementation impacts both HR and the line.* Clearly HR's move from the transactional to the strategic and the supporting processes and technology that surrounds this significantly impacts the HR function. However, it is equally important that the impact on the line is considered and addressed, because if buy-in and commitment is not secured here then the new processes and technology will not be adopted. The implication here is that HR cannot then move to the strategic role because the transactional role is not being effectively addressed.

- *The development and implementation of HR processes and technology are inextricably linked.* There is a symbiotic relationship between HR processes and technology. Often the link between them is the data and information that drives the business process. Neither process nor technology can be addressed independently and an iterative approach that drives opportunity from both sides is the best way to address this.

- *Continued focus on the delivery of benefit is vital.* Whilst target benefits have been set out previously, if the process and technology implementation does not reflect these then the work put into the vision and business case will have been wasted. It is through effective implementation that the vision and benefits are realised.

Having considered the practitioners' views on the implementation of process and technology, we now address the steps that we believe are crucial in order to achieve this. We begin by considering the three broad stages in implementing the process and technology solution, namely: detailed design; build and test; and cutover. In doing so, and in keeping with the main thrust of this book, we consider both the tasks involved and the business change aspects at each stage.

7.3 Detailed Process and Technology Design

Through envisioning, defining the service delivery approach and building the business case, the HR transformation solution will have become ever clearer. Careful consideration will have been given to the people, process and technology elements such that the overall solution defined is one that will deliver the vision and benefits targeted. The first stage of implementation therefore is to finalise the design at the detail level. This means addressing the people and capability elements (see Chapter 6), the process elements and the technology elements both individually and together.

Detailed design follows the principles of the systems mindset (see Chapter 1) by considering the multiple linkages between elements of the solution, working from the whole solution to the details of the constituent parts. In Section 4.6 we described how to develop a design framework that defines the "end-to-end" design. By utilising this and the target benefits, those charged with developing the detailed process and technology design can begin.

During business case definition (see Chapter 4), the technology solution that best fits your specific needs will have been identified. The task in detailed design is to specify the configuration of this technology solution right down to the level of the system screens on which the transactions are performed. The main decisions that need to be made at this stage are:

1. Which elements of the process will be performed by the system and which elements need to be performed outside of the system?
2. Which data fields must be completed in order for the process to work and which are optional?
3. Can the technology solution be configured to support the new processes without needing to modify the underlying code or programming of the system? Often this is termed the "vanilla" system. Modification over and above the "vanilla" system means that additional implementation and maintenance costs will be incurred. If the business benefits can be delivered with the "vanilla" system then clearly this is the ideal route. If this is not the case then the costs (including maintenance costs) of making the modifications need to be weighed against the reduction in benefits if the modifications are not made.

195

4. In the case of global or multinational implementations, are there local country or regional differences that need to be addressed? Ideally these should only be local statutory differences as these should already be "pre-configured" in the technology solution. Any additional differences will need to be developed and maintained separately. In a similar way to the "vanilla" system debate above, modifying the system for local requirements adds to both the initial implementation and the ongoing maintenance costs.

The decisions around detailed design are usually made in workshops with HR and the line, or by the HR and line representatives on the programme team. Involvement of HR and the line is crucial in this process as it provides both a check that what is being designed is pragmatic and workable and that those who will need to operate the new processes and systems are engaged to promote commitment (see Chapter 5).

As the detailed design proceeds, where resolution on particular design issues cannot be achieved through the workshops or the programme team it may be necessary to take some of these decisions to the steering board for direction. This "design authority" role is one that the steering board should play by exception but it can be critical particularly in providing guidance and direction on the degree of customisation or local variation.

From a process design perspective, the main task at this stage is to map the processes onto a diagram that shows what the system will do and what the responsibility of HR, managers, employees or external agencies will be. Figure 7.1 provides an example of how this may be mapped.

In developing this diagram it is important not to fall into the trap of merely refining existing processes and responsibilities and essentially promoting the status quo. HR transformation is about the shift from the transactional to the strategic and therefore HR involvement in data entry and checking at the transactional level should be minimal, if at all. Sometimes organisations take this further still by removing HR involvement from every stage of the transaction processing for some processes and instead it is line managers and employees supported by the e-HR system that take responsibility for the entire process. This understanding of how responsibility for processes changes is vital for moving to the next stage in the change process, that of determining the impact of the new processes

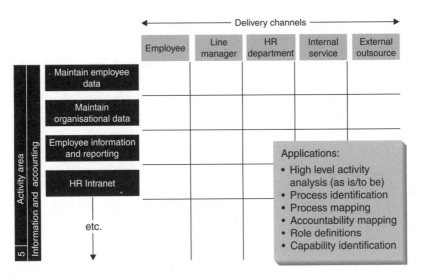

Figure 7.1 Identifying who does what

and systems on the organisation and the readiness of the organisation to adopt them.

The starting point for assessing impact and readiness is the stakeholder identification and initial impact and resistance-commitment assessment already completed (see Chapter 5). The task at this stage is to take that initial analysis down to the next level of detail both in terms of the stakeholder groups themselves, the understanding of the impact on those groups and the levels of resistance-commitment. For example, during initial stakeholder analysis all employees may have been treated as an homogenous group. This would now be too broad for the differing impacts that they may experience. Therefore, the employee stakeholder group may, in this case, be subdivided into office-based employees and shop floor based employees in order to take account of the differing impacts of e-HR technology in their respective areas. The key here is to balance the degree to which stakeholder groups are subdivided. As a rule of thumb, the level of department on a particular site is usually the lowest level of subdivision necessary.

Then for each of the detailed stakeholder groups, the impacts are recorded for each relevant process in terms of change from the "as is" way of working to the "to be" way. Clearly, not every process impacts every stakeholder group and the degree of impact differs in each case. From this, a picture of relative impact emerges. Those groups with the greatest impact are often those where most attention must be paid in the change planning that follows.

At this stage it is also useful to assess the readiness to change for each detailed stakeholder group. This readiness assessment concentrates on the attitude that the detailed stakeholder groups have towards the new processes and systems. There are a number of factors here:

1. History of change within the organisation: Has change been managed effectively previously?
2. What is the capacity for change in the organisation? Have major change initiatives been recently completed or are under way?
3. What is the level of awareness of the detailed stakeholder group as to the nature of the change for them?
4. And finally, "what's in it for me?" On balance, will the detailed stakeholder group view this as a positive or negative change, bearing in mind the nature of the impact on them?

Through this readiness assessment, likely levels of resistance can be determined at the next level of detail. As in the case of the impact analysis, those stakeholder groups who are likely to be the most resistant are the ones where most attention needs to be paid in change planning.

Often the employees within organisations are less resistant to HR transformation than the managers. For employees, the benefits tend to outweigh the negatives as they take control of their transactions. For managers their perception tends to be the other way round with the perceived disadvantages outweighing the advantages. Their instinct is that they are being asked to do more and that their workload is increasing. On the surface this is the case, with e-HR transactions required to be input or approved. The reality is that these transactions needed completing previously using phones, faxes, e-mails and paper-based forms, often through a significantly more inefficient, lengthy and circuitous route. However, business change is not only about facts but about perception, behaviour and culture. In some organisations a rational argument that these transactions were performed by managers previously via different means will prevail and in others it will not, sometimes the culture of the organisation is such that managers will work online themselves and in others the culture is for managers' assistants and administrators to do this. A contingent approach is of course necessary focusing on how business benefit can be achieved and ultimately how the organisation's managers can become more effective people managers.

Clearly, it is not only line managers who may feel uncomfortable. The move to managers and employees executing transactions that were previously performed by HR will also take some people within the HR function outside of their comfort zone.

Case Study

When designing its HR transformation solution, a global IT services organisation considered the different processes and ways of working within the operating units in each country. These processes were very different and it wished to move to a global approach. Through the innovative use of e-HR technology and service centres and the processes and information surrounding them, global consistency was achieved through managers and employees using the global Intranet for standard transactions and the regional service centres for the more complex ones.

This was a major change in approach in many of the operating units and considerable time and effort was spent supporting the managers and employees through this change from the early stages of design and consultation through to embedding and sustaining the change post-implementation. Whilst the change from a process perspective was significant, from a cultural standpoint it was commonly accepted and expected that managers use the Intranet to perform transactions.

The change management plan is the means by which the issues identified through impact and readiness assessment are addressed. It is normally developed in a tabular format recording:

- Detailed stakeholder group.
- The impact or readiness issues that have been raised for that group.
- A measure of importance or priority for each issue.
- The action that needs to be taken for that issue, by whom and when.
- How feedback on the success of the action is to be gathered.

The types of action vary depending on where the stakeholder group falls along the resistance to commitment continuum and how far the group needs to move (see Figure 5.1). Actions may be around communications, such as raising awareness, explaining the benefits of the new process or reinforcing "what's in it for me" for the stakeholder group, or they may be around tangible design elements such as modification of performance management objectives. Typically the actions are executed through the sponsor and change leader network described in Section 4.9. Sponsors work at the senior levels in the organisation, demonstrating their commitment to HR transformation and the benefits that it will bring to the organisation and cascading this to their teams.

From the detailed design stage onwards the role of the change leader is particularly important. They deploy their strengths very much at the local level, working on business readiness, the impact of change, making sure activities around communications are working, and representing their areas in the design workshops. Crucially, they will also be trusted to give feedback to the programme team, effectively providing the link between what is needed for their stakeholder groups and what the programme team delivers. This is an excellent opportunity for HR to "walk the talk" in terms of its prospective business partners enacting their role as leaders of change within the organisation. If those business partners are responsible for change leadership with their group of line managers, this has the dual benefit of HR really demonstrating that its role is changing and begins to cement those relationships between business partners and senior line managers.

As feedback is gathered on the level of success that the actions have achieved then further actions will become necessary. Similarly, as more is known about the detailed design, further impacts may be identified. Clearly, this is an iterative process with the objective of moving the various stakeholder groups to the point where they are ready to move from awareness and understanding of the change into readiness for implementation. The following case study provides an holistic view of the business change approaches discussed.

The theme of iteration during process and technology detailed design applies not only within the process and technology areas themselves but also to the interaction between them. This takes the form of determining what should be performed within and outside the system and what rules should be followed in each case. Therefore, in addition to the process diagrams described in Figure 7.1, it is also useful to record the rules by which each process operates. This is invaluable during the next

Case Study

A large manufacturer of consumer pharmaceutical products wanted to introduce e-HR, and quickly realised that it needed to understand where various elements of the organisation stood on the issues. It put together a plan to gather information, which included the following elements:

1. *Stakeholder analysis*

   A "first-cut" view of the identity of the main stakeholder groups, where they were located, what they stood to gain/lose as a result of the programme, and hence their most likely disposition.

2. *Impact of change assessment*

   A summary of the way in which each of the main changes resulting from the programme would impact each of the stakeholder groups. This enabled some assessment to be made of the depth and breadth of change impacting that stakeholder group, allowing the appropriate involvement to be planned.

3. *Change readiness assessment*

   This examined the organisation's readiness for the overall changes resulting from the programme. It looked at many factors potentially influencing the outcome of the programme, and it was used to shape the overall business change approach.

4. *Change planning*

   Change-related risks were identified, and some early assessment and risk mitigation planning and actions begun.

5. *Change leader network*

   The network of "local" change leaders was designed, and candidate individuals identified. Through this the actions to mitigate the risks identified were executed.

6. *Sponsorship and commitment strategy*

   Built from the stakeholder analysis to identify *influencers*, *lines of influence* and *basis of influence*. This started to shape the initial stakeholder management plan and the support of sponsors in the actions they were taking to advocate the implementation and adoption of e-HR.

7. *Initial communications planning and delivery*

   Developed in order to ensure clear communications to the organisation concerning the existence of the programme and the design work under way. Whilst its focus was on the future communications, it also summarised the communications that had already taken place and the feedback obtained in order to guide future activity.

One of the key lessons that the team learnt was that whilst e-HR was important to the organisation and had been established as a building block for wider transformation, those impacted by it still had their normal roles and responsibilities and other programmes that they were involved in. This learning was key to the programme team, as whilst the e-HR programme was their total focus, they recognised that this was not the case with the stakeholder communities and acted accordingly, their target being to move from the programme "pushing" its messages out, to the business "pulling" the programme in.

stage – build and test – as business procedures and training material can be developed from this and the system configuration performed. From an HR transformation programme team perspective this means that the process and technology work streams (see Chapter 5) clearly need to work together closely and sometimes the individuals within those work streams may fulfil roles on both streams.

At the end of detailed design an excellent tool for confirming that the design is effective and for keeping the wider organisation involved in the programme is to perform a series of detailed design walk-throughs. Typically the diagrams produced in Figure 7.1 are linked together and displayed on a wall to show the detailed, end-to-end process. Programme team members then "walk-through" these processes with representatives from HR and the line in order to validate and test their feasibility and of course modify processes where necessary. The walk-throughs should try to capture as wide an audience as possible, but as a minimum should include those who have contributed to the design in the design workshops mentioned earlier.

Finally, the overall detailed design needs to be validated to ensure that the benefits targeted at the beginning of this stage are still valid and that the costs are within the cost envelope agreed during the business case. If this is the case, then it is safe to proceed into build and test. However, if not, then it is usual to seek steering board sanction that the change in costs or benefits has not reduced the cost–benefit analysis below the level that is viable for the programme.

7.4 Build and Test

There are two main alternative approaches to this stage and it is important that you choose the right approach for your circumstances. The first approach is prototyping; that is, the incremental configuration of elements of the systems solution followed by testing with the users followed by further iterations of fine-tuning. This process is repeated for all elements of the systems solution. The second is a full build against a detailed specification or blueprint followed by full system testing.

One advantage with the first approach is that the HR and business users get the opportunity to see and feel e-HR quite early in the build process. This serves to maintain momentum and enthusiasm and helps to match expectations against system delivery. The main disadvantage with this approach is that it can take longer unless it is tightly managed – the temptation can be to continue with minor refinements rather than finish that element of the solution and move on to the next.

In the case of the second approach, the main advantage is that you have better control of the costs and schedule and at the end of the build you have a more complete solution. But there is less possibility of making changes during the build and after it is delivered any changes will be more expensive. There is a heavy reliance on the quality of the detailed specification that the system configurers are using.

During this stage there is a greater distinction between the technology- and the process-related activities than during the detailed design stage. Even with the prototyping approach, the system configurers are primarily focused on the technology build and system test activity. The HR and business users, however, should be primarily focused on: operating procedure definition, training course preparation, development of user security profiles, test script development and user acceptance testing. The methodology and programme plan provide the means of linking the process and technology (and people) streams here. The interdependencies and "touch points" are closely aligned through this even though the team members may be working on their own specific tasks.

The change management theme of course continues. The change leaders mobilised during detailed design perform the next iteration of impact and readiness assessments, often at the local functional or site level, and initiate the resulting actions. The change focus should not be restricted to the line areas; HR must be preparing for this change. There is an important link here with the capabilities work (see Chapter 6), as HR needs to get ready to let go of much of the transactional work and begin to focus on what the business partner role really means and how they will equip themselves for this. An excellent way of bringing this to life is the use of "conference room pilots" where the business and HR users of e-HR adopt their new roles in a controlled environment, testing how the new roles, process and system fit together in a simulation of the new environment.

Conference room pilots provide a good example of how wider involvement in the programme activities can be achieved and there is greater opportunity during this stage to use involvement in the programme activities as an action to promote awareness and commitment. Typically, involvement from HR and the business in defining operating procedures, preparing training course material and particularly user acceptance testing, make the programme "come alive" for many. One area that provides excellent opportunity for involvement but is often neglected is that of data cleansing and preparation. This involves checking the validity of existing data, mapping it to the data required in the new system and creating any additional data fields that are not present in the current systems. Involvement in this can be achieved across all employees in the organisation as they are requested to check and validate their own individual employee record data. This is a very powerful approach to moving the perception of the HR transformation programme from concept to reality.

7.5 Cutover and the Transition to Business As Usual

With the system and processes now tested and accepted by the HR and business user communities, the attention turns to the planning and execution of the cutover to the new system and processes. Whilst there are distinct technology and process facets to this stage, they are more closely interdependent than those in the build and test stage. Indeed, the interdependency with the capabilities work (see Chapter 6) is also critical as these streams of work need to cutover as a coordinated whole rather than as separate entities. Clearly, the technology and processes need to be in place for the transactional responsibility to shift but the new capabilities within the HR function must also be in place if HR is to vacate its transactional role.

From a technology perspective the main activities are:

- To ensure that the live technical environment (hardware, software and network) is ready for the e-HR system.
- To ensure that the data is ready to be loaded and the mechanism for performing the load, often a combination of automated and manual approaches, is also ready.
- To ensure all users have the means to access the new system.
- To develop the technical cutover plans.

From a process perspective the main activities are:

- The scheduling and delivery of the system and process training. Often the change leaders take a role in this either as trainers themselves or in a "train the trainer" role.
- Business cutover planning, including planning data reconciliations, system downtime and any parallel running of the old system and new.

Before the live cutover is performed, many programmes opt for an integrated cutover rehearsal that coordinates the whole technology and process cutover and determines how long and in what precise order each element is addressed.

Throughout this stage and towards the latter part of the build and test stage, the hub of the change shifts from something that the programme is "pushing out" to the organisation to something that the organisation is embracing and "pulling in". The increased involvement of the line areas and HR in the programme is a major catalyst in this. This is then consolidated during this stage, as the transition from the programme team to those responsible for supporting the new system and processes is effected. This is an important symbol in the transition to the new "business as usual" and begins to draw to a close the "implement and embed the change" phase of the change cycle model (see Figure 1.3).

7.6 Benefits Realisation

Whilst we cover benefits realisation as a topic in this chapter about implementation it should be very evident that we believe business benefit is a key driver of HR transformation and as such is inherent at every stage. However, the major benefits from HR transformation are not actually realised until implementation has been completed and the transition to business as usual is in place.

There are three main areas to consider:

1. Measurement and evaluation.
2. Avoiding benefits loss.
3. Sustaining benefits.

Measurement and evaluation

In order for measurement to be a worthwhile activity, you need to know where you are starting from – to have a baseline measurement showing how HR is performing at the moment. It is important to capture this during the work on the business case, because the baseline will change as soon as any elements are implemented.

Those who "own" the areas impacted by HR transformation should take ownership for the production of the baseline data and the subsequent measurement of the effect of the changes. As HR transformation starts to be delivered, these owners are in the best place to view this in the context of other things happening elsewhere in the organisation, both "business as usual" and other programmes or initiatives, and determining what is attributable to HR transformation and what is not.

Measures are usually at both a macro and detailed level. Macro measures can include the cost of HR to the business expressed in terms of total budget or in the unit cost of HR per employee. The ratio of HR staff to staff within the rest of the organisation is also a popular measure at this level. If using these measures to compare performance to other organisations, it is important to ensure that the basis for the measures is the same, that is, you are comparing "apples with apples". If not, the comparisons will be misleading, potentially resulting in inappropriate decisions. However, using a consistent base and then looking at the trends in these measures as the programme is implemented can provide real evidence of its success.

In breaking down the measures to a more detailed level, it is common to measure across the HR scope of services (see Figure 4.1). For example, detailed measures for employee information and reporting, recruitment and selection, and training and development may include:

- The quantity of online training versus classroom training.
- The quantity of candidates sourced through the Intranet versus traditional routes.
- The volume of automated processes and administration versus manual transactions.
- The volume of input to systems at source (i.e. by managers and employees) versus back office administration input.
- Recruitment directly sourced versus agency sourcing.

The important point with measures of HR service is not to have so many that you "cannot see the wood for the trees"; rather, that the key service measures affecting the overall macro measures are monitored and decisions taken accordingly.

In the world of e-HR there is a further set of measures that organisations find useful; these are *system measures*. These measures provide information on the usage trends of the e-HR applications. Examples include:

- e-HR Intranet page hits compared to other Intranet applications.
- Measures of managers' and employees' use of self-service functionality.
- e-HR functionality measures, for example numbers of e-appraisals delivered versus planned.

These measures can help to identify groups or communities that are finding the e-HR technology either particularly easy or difficult to use and driving action as a result of that. For those who are finding the technology difficult to come to terms with, additional targeted training or support may be required. For those who are coming to terms with it quickly there are usually lessons that the rest of the organisation can learn. As the organisation becomes more sophisticated in its use of these measures, individual managers can be supported by HR business partners armed with the knowledge of how each manager uses the information from the e-HR applications and how they can improve its use, that is, take more effective decisions based on it.

The measures discussed so far provide the mechanism for measuring the ongoing performance of HR (and the line areas) post HR transformation.

Often these measures are consolidated into an HR balanced scorecard enabling trends to be analysed and actioned over time.

The second area of measurement that needs to be considered is the achievement of the individual benefits cited in the business case. The mechanism that we have found most effective here is the benefits realisation plan which lists what benefit levels are expected, at what point in the implementation they are expected and the measure that will identify this. Figure 7.2 gives an example of a benefits realisation plan showing potential benefits for e-recruitment administration. The key points to note are that benefits will be delivered over a significant period of time; a baseline initial value has been established; there are usually different types of units of measure in operation, and the distinction between accountability for delivering a benefit and the responsibility for measuring it is drawn.

Having defined the benefits realisation plan, the actual levels of benefit achieved are compared against the plan. As a result of this, gaps may emerge in what was expected to be delivered compared with what has actually been delivered, potentially requiring the solution to be refined in order to address the gaps. Conversely, there will often be unexpected benefits identified that were not in the original business case. Finally, this process also acts as a catalyst for developing ideas of areas where additional benefits may be sought (see Chapter 8).

Avoiding Benefits Loss

There are three areas where benefits can start to "leak" away from the transformation programme: people, process and technology. The risk of this increases as implementation draws nearer, as often compromises are made and decisions taken that affect the delivery of benefit.

People

Without HR and the line demonstrating that they are ready for the new way of working, HR transformation will be heading for failure. Close monitoring through the change management tools described in this book will provide an assessment of how far the changes are being embraced and the actions to promote further adoption. The change leaders on the ground are a critical resource in this both in terms of the actions they take and the feedback that they are able to give.

Figure 7.2 Example of a benefits realisation plan

Expected benefits	How is it measured?	Current level	Breakdown of benefits delivery by year (post implementation)			Who is accountable for delivery?	Who is responsible for monitoring?
Recruitment administration			Year 1	Year 2	Year 3		
Media cost	£	£100K	£30K	£50K	£50K	Manager A	Manager A
Cost of preparing and processing application packs	£	£30K	£5K	£7K	£10K	Manager B	Manager C
Transition processing of hiring requisitions	Admin time FTE	25	3	7	10	Manager C	Manager C

Processes

Check carefully for gradual moves away from the design blueprint, especially anything that looks as though it will lessen the emphasis on the transformation. Simply refining a few processes to speed things up, basic e-enablement, is all very well, but true HR transformation sees the HR function demonstrating its real value to the wider business.

Technology

The quality of the data in the new system is the main risk. If the data is flawed then the whole reputation of the HR transformation programme is affected and usage and adoption reduced. Data cleansing and preparation, as discussed earlier in this chapter, are critical in reducing this risk.

Sustaining Benefits

In terms of locking in benefits, the key is what you do immediately post go-live to embed and sustain the change. We have found the following four areas to be highly effective in this.

Continue training after go-live

It is often after people begin to use the new systems that they realise what they needed to learn during system and process training! Therefore it is worth planning and budgeting for "refresher" training in the post go-live period. Having this available will promote usage of the new system and reduce the "fear of the new".

Demonstrate leadership from the top

If you can demonstrate leadership from the highest levels within the organisation, then this will cascade through the organisation, encouraging acceptance of the new ways of working. For instance, the new HR systems will have the capability to produce organisation charts from the information contained within the system. Previously managers would have produced organisation charts using standard desktop tools rather than being able to generate them directly from the HR system. However, now that this capability is in place, if the senior manager insists that only organisation charts produced by the HR system will be accepted for use in presentations, then the new way of working will have a very strong and clear sponsorship.

Remove the old way of doing things

If old systems or ways of working remain, there is always a risk that people will revert to using them rather than the new processes and systems. For example, if you are trying to implement an online approach to changing employee details through employee self-service, but the service centre still accepts the faxed forms that were used before, the change will not stick. The old mechanism needs to be removed and not accepted anymore.

Using an incremental approach, you can also remove the old processes in a systematic and planned, not reactive way, which is a powerful demonstration that something has changed permanently.

Make measurement an ongoing activity

Having taken these actions and others post go-live, you should continue to measure benefits and changes post implementation, so that doing so becomes part of how the "new" HR function evaluates itself and demonstrates increased value going forward. As you will be assessing actual delivery against benefits, you will need to be ready to take action when there is any shortfall, not only up to implementation but also beyond.

Summary

The first part of this chapter shows that the approach to technology and process implementation moves through a series of clear stages from detailed design to build and test and finally cutover. The linkage between technology and process is such that activities within the stages are often iterative.

Within each stage the focus on change management continues. Work at the detail level to first define the change and then to take actions to effect it is key. Involvement in the programme across the organisation is an important mechanism for promoting commitment.

The second part of this chapter considers benefits realisation. The focus on benefit delivery begins at the business case stage and continues post implementation. The benefits realisation plan is the mechanism by which you can monitor and drive through benefit delivery at the detail level. This plan gives the timing, size, measures and owners of benefits. It is important that benefits do not "leak" away from the programme through inappropriate decisions around the design and implementation from a people, process and technology perspective.

Finally, the need remains to continue to focus on benefits delivery after go-live in order both to deliver and sustain benefits. Paying attention to this will significantly increase the likelihood of success, whereas not doing so places the benefit delivery at considerable risk.

8

Taking Stock and Moving Forward

This chapter has two main aims. Firstly, it takes us into the final phase of the change cycle (embed and evaluate the change), setting out approaches to help you assess whether your transformation has *really* delivered across each element of the HR delivery model. Secondly, it presents our thoughts on the future direction of HR and addresses what HR leaders should be considering post-transformation. In doing so, our intention is not to provide the answers, but instead to share trends we are observing and to pose questions to guide you to your own conclusions and actions.

Chapter Structure

Key Themes

■ HR's proximity to and interaction with the business are key indicators both of the success of transformation and as a guide to the "post-transformation" future. The ubiquitous "seat at the table", HR as change leaders, the relative focus and balance of specialists and business partners, and the reputation of the HR function within the business are all relevant indicators of progress.

■ Measurement of what you have achieved and knowledge of what others have done will guide the consolidation of your transformation and the realisation of further benefits. This is the classic "continuous improvement" that typically follows radical change and transformation.

■ It is a truism that global and local markets are driving innovation in the way HR service is sourced and delivered. Even 5 years ago, the range of options here was far more limited than it is today. The next paradigm shift for HR begins with recognition of these options and their potential in enabling HR to redefine its role.

8.1 Context

This final chapter has two broad sections. The first section continues and closes on the themes that run throughout this book, offering a practical guide through the final stages of the HR transformation journey. This section is illustrated by interviews with people who are on the journey and also draws on our own observations made during a wide variety of engagements in different sectors. It is written to enable our reader to understand and reassess where their organisation is on its particular journey of transformation: to take stock, mark progress and assess the options for moving forward from a position of strength.

The second section is more discursive and asks a series of open-ended questions around a core question: "You have taken significant steps to transform HR – so what's next?"

If you are a reader who immediately turns to the end of a book to see what the "answer" is, please be reassured that this is not one of those books that send readers back to the introduction with firm instructions to read and put every word into practice before getting to the end. You are welcome here to join in the emerging debate about the future of HR that we are contributing to. But please understand that this final section does not contain the one right "answer" to the above question. That is for you and others to comment on in time. Our aim is to share our perspectives, and we hope that our contribution will be received as positive and constructive.

8.2 Practitioner Perspectives

Given the context and objectives set out above, what do senior HR practitioners believe that the future challenges for HR will be? Our discussions have highlighted a number of important themes, which we present below.

- *HR must embed its transformation and build on that to improve performance*

Philip Barr subscribes fully to this view. "I do not see any really big themes: more change and restructuring; more hiring and exiting; and a greater focus on performance. HR needs to improve across the whole offering."

Richard Brady reinforces the views about greater focus on performance and the capabilities of the HR function. "Going forward, there is huge opportunity for HR to simplify its message and focus on core competence and measure the impact of its efforts either to communicate or to roll out business enablement through people management to its client base."

"I think this is happening to a certain degree as well because people do gravitate to the things that they are best at hopefully, and may be thought best at. Sometimes they need some guidance and clarity – I think we need to be more explicit about the expectations and the support that's given to HR and use some greater insights into matching people to human resources roles. So, take the business partner role. Essentially the word 'partner' implies a relationship, so the best business partners are those who establish close relationships; they communicate well, they are aligned to, they understand how the business is shifting, moving, and attempt to adapt their deliverables to meet the needs of a changing business world, without being expedient and giving in. So there's a need for assertiveness and for the capability to influence and persuade their customers to make a wise decision, and there are attributes of personality and behaviour that support this."

- *HR will get still closer to the business*

Philip Barr is emphatic on this point. "HR will be smaller and focused on value-add. This means being closer to the business and working in ways that will help the business deliver ongoing performance improvements. Aligned with and attuned to the business is the key to HR's future success."

Helen Corey expands on this. "I would like to see HR mimicking the role of line managers, spending time with the line and really getting to understand the issues that concern them around profit and loss performance, motivation issues and so on. If HR can do this, and be seen progressively as a genuine business support and development function, its credibility will rise."

Kath Lowey focuses on the support that HR senior management should provide to senior business management. "I get a lot of personal enjoyment out of that and I've had a lot of success in working with our MD in doing whatever we need to do to help lift morale. It's noticeable, and that's very rewarding. I understand my guys who think that if they're not with the business it's not as fulfilling, because when you are, and if you can affect that change and you are relied on as a consultant and as a confidant, it's very gratifying."

■ *HR must take up the mantle of change enabler across the organisation*
If HR has got close enough to the business, then the trust and respect needed to become a true change agent within the organisation may be conferred. Both Tony Williams and Claudia Hall believe that having led HR transformational change, HR is ready to support the business in its change programmes. Tony states, "It's fair to say that on the back of integration we've learned a hell of a lot about change management across the group, and we have therefore tried to capitalise on those learnings by packaging up another set of projects that generally do the same thing but in different ways and new ways. So that is to an extent a galvanising force, and to an extent it is the new context by which the HR business partners can add value."

Similarly, Claudia comments that, "Moving forward, we need to learn from the lessons of the past couple of years to ensure that we maintain a relentless focus on improving the 'One HR' model, through judicious investment in human capability, process refinements and enabling technology. In particular, we must be appreciative of the impacts on the HR and business communities of major transformation projects and look to factor in effective change management strategies to secure buy-in on all sides."

■ *HR must build strong relationships with employees and develop a clear employment proposition*
So far, our practitioners have focused on the "classic" transformational areas of HR performance, business partnering and HR in its change

agent role. We now turn to an equally important area, but one that typically receives less "air-time" than others – that is, HR's future relationship with employees.

Kath Lowey highlights the role of HR in raising morale and the linkage to overall business performance. "It's important to look at how we engage our employees more widely and lift their morale. We've got people running functions and I say, 'Let them do that, because that's their job. We need to improve morale, grow the business.'"

Randy Harris compares the facets of the employee with those of customers, and hence the link between customer relationship management and employee relationship management. "I talked about being in line with the customers. Our Chief Services Officer wants us to develop and refine our 'customer life cycle' and 'customer touch point strategy'. On the customer side, we understand our customers very well; we understand why they buy from us, we understand why they stay with us, and if they leave us we understand why they leave us, and we've got a lot of passion around that. Well, I believe that employee behaviour and customer behaviour are very similar. I believe employees buy from the company or join the company for a very similar reason to our customers. They have an expectation when they become a part of Nextel that we're going to do certain things with them, to them, for them. I believe that the reason a customer stays with you is because you meet their expectation, you see their expectation, you continue to add value and they buy more from you and they grow in value. I believe employees do the same thing. If you meet their expectations more days than not, they will grow in value, they'll learn new skills, their productivity will increase and their value to the company becomes greater."

"I believe that when you fail to meet a customer's expectations, they leave. I also believe that when you fail to meet an employee's expectations, they do too. So we have calculated the lifetime value of the customer in very specific terms. We're developing our model to understand the lifetime value of an employee, and we're getting more specific than some of the softer models I've seen the consulting firms develop. Well, that becomes the landscape for everything we do within HR, because the customer side has been so compelling that we figured out if we can reduce a percentage of customer attrition – e.g. one tenth of one percent – we know the exact number of dollars saved by the company. We're not just doing it for the quantitative side on the attrition number; we're also

217

doing it for the qualitative side. We love all our customers, but there are some customers that contribute more profitably to us than others. So it's critically important when we look at customer turnover that we understand not only how many we are losing, but also who we are losing. The same thing's true on the employee side. I have a goal of a voluntary attrition rate by function and by level of the company. If, say, we lose 12% of our retail people voluntarily at the manager level, I'm more interested in who we lose. Did we lose high-performing managers, or did we lose people who were outrunning termination? So we're putting a qualitative bent on those metrics as well as a quantitative."

"All the metrics, all the reporting, all the plans are beginning to become more understood, and every time we put something out there, I try to position it as part of what we're doing as related to the life cycle. The reason the customer life cycle strategy has received so much attention is because the senior leadership group from customer care were on the road themselves, told the story repeatedly, began to show impact and equate the impact back to actions taken as part of the life cycle, and that's exactly what we're doing within HR."

■ *HR must invest appropriately in technology*

The future role of technology in supporting HR transformation depends, of course, on your starting point. For Tony Williams, the focus has been more on structural and service delivery change through the use of shared services. This has left further demand for the use of HR technology, but from where should this be obtained? "Unfortunately, because we haven't got a lot of e-HR in place and progress is relatively slow, it's quite frustrating for the business guys because they want to push us much quicker. However, there have been undoubted advantages in some areas by introducing tactical e-HR 'by stealth', through the introduction of things like flexible benefits. It has been a slow process, but at the same time has demonstrated to people sufficiently that it is worth doing."

Andy Field highlights the relationship between HR technology and how HR and external organisations gear up to deliver service to the business. In doing so, Andy starts to pose some of the bigger questions that we need to consider in the future for HR. "I'm interested in what e-HR really is. Is it a big back office or small back office? Is it point solutions or large integrated systems that knit processes together? This is more solution than strategy, and needs to be explored."

"I think in future small companies will be far greater users of e-HR. At the moment, most products are focused on large- or medium-sized companies or public sector organisations that can afford the development costs and people. In the future, could you have a do-it-yourself portal, one that does not require you to be a programmer to reskin and rebrand? I see something like an offering for 20 to 30 companies to use the same resource, such as a big company, to increase buying power – this is exactly how a portal approach would work well."

Finally, Kath Lowey warns against seeing technology as a panacea. "Although technology, processes and systems will play a big part in HR service delivery, I don't ever want to lose the human touch, because that's what we're about and we have an important responsibility in this area. For example, in the area of employee welfare, I have a team member who solely focuses on this – he's fantastic at it – and he goes out and deals with people, and that is a very proactive and very well-received service we provide. You can't automate something like that."

■ *HR professionals will continue to hone the focus of their contribution*
Gradually, our practitioners have moved from consolidation and delivering true HR transformation through to what they believe are the next challenges for the function. Andy Field has clear views about this. "The 'HR department' will cease to exist in its current form. What we will move to is a small group of HR professionals who deliver a service to the business – for example, recruitment. Transactions need to go into a service centre and/or be delivered through technology, and so, for that matter, could those of finance and other business functions. Business partners become management teams. Potentially, there is room for a small strategic element looking after group strategy, systems, process change and disseminating new information."

Vance Kearney supports the view of further change and focus for the HR team. "I think that in the future there will be areas that we've yet to really get to. For example, for many years we've talked about organisational development. I don't know any HR department that really does organisational development. They do individual development, they do some teamwork development, but I don't think they truly do organisational development. If they do, I'd like to meet someone who goes to the Chief Executive and says, 'You've got the business divided into these 15 departments rolling up to three divisions that sit within two regions.

Well, really you've got it all wrong and it would be much more effective if you had four divisions and five regions and only five departments.' I don't think it happens very often."

"But overall HR will be trying to set a better understanding of the environment in which people thrive and develop; create that virtuous circle with very well-trained, very well-selected managers, who in themselves will understand that their job is managing people. I would like to think that HR would be recognised as the people who help managers be better managers, as opposed to being associated with the transactions. We shall see."

"But when I've talked about this in the past, people say to me, 'Well, OK, what about all the nasty stuff? This all sounds lovely, but who's going to do the sacking, who's going to do the disciplining?' And my answer to that is that the managers will do that themselves. They'll have the skills to do it and if they are really good, they'll never need to."

Finally, Richard Brady points towards the future analytical role of the function. "The newer capabilities and skills for HR practitioners include measurement, evaluating return on investment, process consulting, communicating and persuading, problem solving, using technology to deliver improved processes, customer service and management and evaluation of contracted services."

- *Line managers develop greater the capability and HR practitioners develop their business skills*
So if HR really does move to the roles above, how does the manager's role change and how does that impact HR? Vance Kearney takes the view that, "In the future people will understand when somebody says, 'I'm a manager' that they're a manager of people, whether those people happen to be in selling, accounting or even in banking or retailing, whatever it is. It will just be understood that when you're a manager, you're somebody who's involved in leadership. Given sufficient freedom, managers will be allowed to hire their employees, they will be allowed to promote them, to decide for themselves many of the things that HR has had an interest in previously. I mean, signing off salary increases is something that HR has traditionally done. I don't know why, because 98% of all proposed salary increases are agreed by HR, so why do we need HR signing off pay rises – because the managers might get 2% wrong? So what? This also implies that the skills of the generalist HR rep or business partner will become part of the business line manager's basic skill set; they'll have generalist

HR skills as part of their managerial profile, supported by the self-service functionality, delivering transactional support. They'll call on HR for high level specialist advice just as many businesses today call on HR consultants when they face particular challenges of growth, acquisition or change."

So Helen Corey's focus on getting underneath the role of line managers is taken full circle, where HR managers become part of the cadre of line managers.

But does this mean that HR will become the "function of choice" for the next generation of top management? Richard Brady believes that there is still some way to go here. "There are very few examples where HR directors have made it to the top job in an organisation – maybe it's because in other business functions they are better at covering the breadth of capability that they need in order to deliver a consistent service to their internal customers. The key change needed, in my view, is to simplify the interrelationship between different HR functions so that there is less of a 'silo mentality' and more of an interconnectivity between the core approaches of people management and how these impact on business performance."

In conclusion, the practitioner views coincide with the broad themes of this chapter, underlining the need to:

- *Ensure that HR transformation has really delivered*: HR transformation is no different from other radical change agendas: once the programme has delivered, ensure that the benefits have *really* been achieved and look for ways to realise further benefits from the baseline that you have delivered. When our practitioners discuss embedding transformation to improve performance, HR's role with the business, leading change, HR's role with employees and the use of technology are all areas that HR needs to "get right" if transformation is deemed to have been a success.
- *Guide HR to the next stage of transformation*: The role of HR in a "post-transformation" world debates the balance between specialism and generalism with the conclusion that as managers become true "people" managers, HR professionals will need to demonstrate value add through their knowledge base e.g. in organisational development.

Like the practitioners, we believe that these two areas provide the key to the future of HR. Firstly, taking stock of what you have actually delivered and what you need to do to consolidate this and fully realise the value of this in your organisation. Secondly, where do you need to focus post-transformation – what is next for you and your organisation? Having introduced these concepts earlier in the chapter and having seen the practitioners' views, we now address each of them in Sections 8.3 and 8.4.

8.3 Taking Stock of Where You Are and the Immediate Future

Before you look forward, it is worth ensuring that you know where you are in order to confirm the benefits that you have delivered and to be clear on the baseline from which you are developing your future plans.

Of course, in the real world, programmes and projects do not come to a neat and ordered end. What usually ensues is a period of continuous improvement or further realisation of benefits where the delivery of the transformation is completed and then built on.

So what can you do practically to take stock of where you are? We suggest the following four activities:

1. *Use the organisational levers model to review progress*
Go back to the documentation you have produced through the course of the transformation programme to confirm your vision and baseline. This will have been refined and redefined as the programme has been undertaken, but this will provide a definition of "where we were" (the "as-is") and "where we wanted to get to" (the "to-be"). You may have used the organisational levers model (see Figure 1.2) to help you with this, and using that model again here provides an excellent foundation for assessing the extent to which you have reached what you set out to achieve. Appendix 1 provides a real example of how the organisational levers model has been used by a global Internet technology business to review progress after a significant phase in their HR transformation journey.

2. *Review scope delivered against the original scope of transformation*
Review needs to take account of two main factors. The first is the original scope of the programme compared to the delivered scope.

The second is to describe the benefit of what has been delivered. It is inevitable that through the course of the transformation programme the detailed scope will have been refined and redefined. There are a number of reasons for this, including the cost of delivery versus anticipated benefit; other dependencies required before a particular area can be delivered; running out of time and/or budget; prioritisation and/or phasing of delivery. At this stage, it is important to consider the areas of scope that have not been delivered and to assess whether there is a case for delivering that now in order to realise further benefit on top of the base that has already been implemented. The financial argument could be strong; you may decide that the costs needed to close the gap outweigh the benefit, or it could be the other way round, in that a small additional outlay will mean that the benefits give disproportionately greater value. Figure 8.1 illustrates this point.

Of course, you will find that some of the decisions to leave something out of scope remain justified, in which case close that issue and move on.

3. *Measure progress made*

Having considered delivery against scope, you need to move on to look at the measures you put in place that were designed to tell you how you were doing and where further benefits may be realised – see Chapter 7

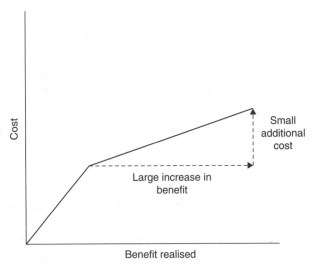

Figure 8.1 The value of continuous improvement

for a full description of this. For each element of the organisational levers model, challenge yourself and ask, "Have we really achieved that, and what is the evidence for this?" For example, look at the process area: you may have said that you wanted to move from a model where HR did a lot of the transactional work to one where the business took responsibility. Has that been achieved? If so, consider how to communicate success to the various different audiences. If not, what plans do you put in place to make that happen? Effectively what you will begin to do is to work through a process of "post-implementation benefits realisation", which is more than picking up the last version of the business case and marking things delivered/not delivered.

4. Gather stakeholder perceptions

As well as revisiting the vision, scope and measures, you should also talk to some of the stakeholders who were affected by your journey. We suggest that you undertake a formal review, as it will send out the signal that the transformation has delivered, in much the same way as you used the business case development process to engage people with the current deficit in HR provision. Asking for feedback on particular areas will remind people of the changes that they have been through and in some cases helped to implement – and in some cases may not have noticed. Either way, this is part of the process of reinforcing and sustaining the change.

The reviews suggested so far assess the transformation and the potential for further benefits realisation and continuous improvement from the perspective of what was defined in the business case and the HR delivery model for your specific transformation. Whilst this is an important element of "taking stock and moving forward", there is the risk that this limits it to an internally focused perspective rather than widening this out to consider further "what could be". There are two areas that you should consider in particular.

The first area is the advance that e-HR technology has made since you embarked upon your transformation. Changes in technology move at a fast pace, and whilst not all advances may be appropriate or mature enough to implement, there are often opportunities for a relatively small incremental investment to yield further benefits in a similar way to that illustrated in Figure 8.1.

The second area is to look at HR roles. We have discussed these in Chapter 2 (see Figure 2.4) in the context of the work presented by Dave Ulrich, and in Chapter 6 in the context of implementation. We discuss how roles in delivering HR may evolve further in Section 8.4. At the review stage, key questions to address will be as follows:

- Are HR professionals contributing purposefully to the development of business strategy?
- Is the organisation benefitting from HR's contribution to strategy execution/change management?
- Does HR operate more efficiently?
- Are there higher levels of employee engagement?
- Is HR more able to measure and articulate its value proposition?

Change is, of course, cyclical, and the end of one phase of change marks the beginning of another. It is important, therefore, that the improvements and initiatives that you identify through this process to define the next steps for HR transformation have a business case and a plan. As such, we return to the need to make a compelling business case for change, and much of what you did for the original transformation will be required again, although this is on a smaller scale, in the form of continuous improvement as opposed to transformational change.

8.4 The Next Paradigm Shift for HR?

Recent research published by Lawler and Mohrman (2003) suggests that anticipated change in the way HR contributes to organisational life has not really taken place. Change has occurred, but not as quickly and dramatically as they had earlier envisaged.

We share these observations, and counsel caution around talking up the size of change that has been achieved through HR transformation to date. So, from our own work with a wide range of organisations, the first point we feel we ought to make about the future is that HR still has work to do to deliver and embed the current paradigm shift, let alone move on to the next agenda. However, let us try to evaluate progress to date.

If it is possible to capture in one sentence what HR has moved through in the last business cycle, it might read something like this: "HR has moved from a broadly administrative and transaction function to one that adds more tangible value to the wider business." Some of the reasons for this statement have been made earlier in this book (see Chapter 2). Here are some additional reasons why we make this statement:

The HR function is actively addressing the transactional aspects of its work. If the quality of HR information had been world-class in the past, then the case for change would have been difficult to argue. However, this has not been the case. HR administration is often deficient and HR information unreliable. Whilst not the glamour end of HR, good HR administration consistently features highly on manager lists of their expectations of HR. Transactional HR needs to be done well – but it is not the be-all and end-all of HR management. Fortunately, transactional HR is standardising and alternative options to the old, fragmented, labour-intensive, expensive in-house model now exist. Shared service centres (whether in-house or outsourced) are now present in many organisations, and there is increasing uptake of e-HR. The challenges for HR remain justifying organisational capex on e-HR and then delivering the full benefits of that capital investment. Ultimately, these solutions must deliver better service to managers so that HR professionals are truly freed to contribute to higher value issues.

There is greater appetite amongst HR professionals to move into the value-adding space. Whilst the horizons of many HR professionals are still focused on "case work" around sickness management, grievance and disciplinary handling, the role of HR professional as business partner has really caught the imagination of the profession. Although there have always been high value-adding HR professionals closely aligned to their line management colleagues, the years since the publication of Ulrich's *HR Champions* (1997) have given people a vocabulary and focus for the HR role. The challenges remain those of building the capability of HR professionals to move onto the ground of strategic business partnership, and changing the attitudes of line managers who still see HR as an administrative/advisory function.

The business drivers that are pulling a stronger contribution from HR are still present and arguably stronger now than ever before. These business drivers are set out in Chapter 2. People costs remain one of the largest elements (if not the largest element) of organisational fixed costs, and we are hearing much more in recent years about the need to value human capital. There is now a high level of interest in finding ways of measuring the contribution of people other than as costs. Work undertaken by Lev (2001) and others around the measurement of intangibles is enabling HR to engage with the business more purposefully. Additionally, the research cited in Chapter 1 linking progressive HR to superior business performance is slowly beginning to register on the minds of senior business leaders.

However, although at a general level there may well have been change in the way HR contributes to organisational life, there is still some way to go for HR to be truly operating as a strategic business partner. So let us turn to the future and to the specifics of your own HR transformation journey.

For those who are nearing the end of their transformation journey, or consider that they have completed it, now is the time to look ahead. The remainder of this section poses some of the wider questions and examines some of the issues that naturally emerge from HR transformation.

We have already stated that it is not our intention to provide definitive answers to these questions and issues, but rather to discuss some of the potential implications. We would like to encourage the reader to think about possible future paradigm shifts in the way that HR operates and delivers services and benefits to the organisation. This is, of course, a great opportunity to engage in some fresh envisioning as a HR team and with the line. In this way, you will start to co-create a vision for HR that will become your next paradigm shift.

We propose to present this discussion about the next paradigm shift for HR through three lenses, namely:

- Presenting a small number of "big ticket" questions for organisations to address.
- Setting out three scenarios of how HR may look in the future.
- Reflecting on issues and challenges currently faced by the function.

We must emphasise and reiterate that we believe there is no one single organisational solution for HR. We are strong advocates of contingent thinking and, whilst there are broad trends that influence the direction the function will take, each organisation will need to find a way that best fits with its unique situation.

We turn now to each of the three lenses.

Big ticket questions

In thinking through what you want from HR post-transformation, you will need to engage in addressing the following "big ticket" questions:

- What role does the business need the HR function to play when moving beyond the current phase of HR transformation?
- What will HR professionals do that will bring most value to the wider organisation beyond the current phase of HR transformation?

Then comes a number of *supplementary* questions:

- Should HR continue to exist in anything like its present form?
- How should we measure the value that people contribute, and what is the role of the HR function in defining that value?
- Do we want the reputation of HR as a contributor to the business to grow, remain stable or diminish?

These are deliberately broad questions and are written to stimulate a wide contribution of input from different HR stakeholders.

Three scenarios

A second lens through which to engage in debate about the future role of HR is to consider the following scenarios that present possible ways the HR function might evolve:

Scenario 1: This scenario assumes that there will be no HR function as we know it now. Perhaps you can imagine a world where all transactions take place via the organisation Intranet. There are no more service centres. Managers and employees use e-HR to its transactional maximum. They see the value of controlling things themselves; there is a self-renewing capability of managers, which has been developed to such a degree that they naturally consider the value of people in the organisation. The vital importance of human capital is managed and nurtured.

In this scenario, the line manager role is taken to its logical limit, as both the transactional and the strategic aspects of HR service delivery are completed without the need for a traditional HR function to facilitate or provide the "conscience" to ensure that these things are done. Technological development is driven through the strategic information system function and, when other web-based tools have been exhausted, external consultants provide specialist skills to support specific project work or organisational development initiatives.

This is an ultimate scenario for HR transformation, where transactional activity is moved out of HR to a point where transactions happen automatically and where there is a high level of people management and strategic capability amongst line managers.

We will revisit this scenario after we have discussed another view:

Scenario 2: Another scenario, and in many ways perhaps not a million miles away from some current HR models, is a possibility that line managers resist attempts to take on what they see as additional administrative tasks, and focus instead on what they see as their core contribution to the organisation. (We are not talking about resistance in terms of some form of industrial action, but rather about a HR transformation that gradually goes into a reverse gear with continued dependency on HR to do personnel administration, provide policy advice and handle case work.)

In this scenario, the HR service centre (which could be in-house or outsourced) staffed with HR administrators will be the norm, along with HR advisers on the ground who will take up case work and provide direct, person-to-person advice on the full range of HR policies and practices. In this instance, a new role could emerge from the current HR adviser: someone with the technical ability and influence to encourage the line manager to use, say, the e-HR system, but also equipped to step in and get involved with some of the more complex people issues, without being a full (and therefore expensive) business partner. A small number of strategic business partners will be present, but only at the most senior levels of the organisation.

In this scenario, there will continue to be a high level of in-house HR capability, focused mainly on generalist and administrative support. Here the balance of HR headcount would remain in transactional and advisory areas.

Scenario 3: This scenario presents an organisational environment where there is reasonable take-up of e-HR, with managers and employees actively engaged in self-service. As a consequence, managers and employees are comfortable in looking up policy information on the Intranet or in contacting a small outsourced HR shared service centre that runs e-HR and provides generalist HR advice and support on more complex HR matters.

In-house HR expertise is specialist, focusing on critical areas such as strategic resourcing, employee development and organisational development. It is through specialists that line managers receive support from HR in addressing strategic people issues. External consultants are brought in on a project-by-project basis to supplement internal resources.

Engaging your organisation in a discussion around these scenarios will reap significant benefits in defining HR's value proposition. Whilst the future HR model is likely to contain elements of each scenario set out above, from the manager's point of view this could get confusing – what should be done on screen, and what should be done in collaboration with someone on the phone? Where does the conversation I am having with my business partner end and the one with someone in a shared service centre begin? What issue can I expect my business partner to address and when might I need to involve a specialist? There may be some room for overlapping, with e-HR straying into complex areas and service centre staff advising or doing simple transactional, administrative roles. Yes, there is a danger of some doubling up of expenditure, or even some confusion in a manager's mind over who does what. Although confusion is clearly unhelpful, if some overlap makes the engine run smoothly, even if a little on the rich side, it is probably a price worth paying – *if* that overlap is seen to add value by managers and is set up to cope with the unexpected.

Issues and challenges

This third lens deals with some specific issues about the future shape of HR. Whilst the other two lenses provide different ways to engage in broad debate about the future of the HR function, this lens focuses in on seven specific issues. These issues are related, of course, but an exploration of each should enable organisations to build a clearer picture of future priorities in taking HR transformation to its next step.

Issue 1: HR professionals and line managers

A common mantra in recent years is that line managers should manage and HR professionals should support them. Yet effective HR management depends on a strong partnership between HR professionals and line managers, where there is mutual recognition and respect and where both sides are working towards a common goal. This kind of relationship does not come easy and will not happen through wishful thinking. An honest review of current relationships needs to be held and the expectations of both sides aired. Some issues that we encounter are around the following:

- lack of manager time to build sufficient expertise in HR policies;
- the HR business partners being a one-stop shop – up to a point;
- lack of accountability concerning the way managers manage people.

These points are interrelated. Managers are under enormous pressure to deliver the technical/business aspects of their role, and they feel that they do not have the time to navigate the Intranet and/or attend training to build sufficient expertise to deal with people issues that a good HR professional should be able to help them with. Similarly, there is frustration when managers hear a great deal about the business partner being able to support managers on the full range of HR issues, but when they need advice being told to contact a service centre or look things up on the Intranet. At that point in time, they do not feel that HR is adding value. Finally, organisations often pay lip service to the people management aspects of a manager's role – how many line managers are rated as poorer performers if they deliver on the technical aspects of their job but are not good people managers? There are too few, in our experience. Organisations need to face up to these issues in an honest way if an effective HR delivery model is to be implemented.

Issue 2: The role of shared service centres

Service centres are now a part of all our lives. We deal with them when we contact our banks, utility companies, order supplies for our offices and places of work, even our domestic goods. We are used to using them and they can be relatively inexpensive – which is a major factor in support of their existence. The first organisations to use them had an advantage over their competitors, but now they are more "business as usual" with many companies. Costs per transaction can be so low that in some cases they are approaching the cost benefits of fully e-enabled systems, with their attendant development and operating costs. But e-HR costs should, in theory, continue to fall in the future. So where should organisations be making their investments?

Some larger organisations will develop "global" service centres, handling all the transactional needs of many divisions and even corporations. Finance, procurement and information technology can all be handled remotely, with information provided on top as all transactions are performed within them.

Consider taking this to the logical extreme. Why not scrap the fancy e-HR system and go down the service centre route? e-HR then simply becomes a message-bearing conduit and storage/enquiry system.

If you believe that this is the future (e.g. you are one of those reading this book in a bookshop and have flicked to the last chapter, but have a lot of people writing a business case back at the ranch), then consider this possibility. There will still be costs and a need for a business case, but why invest in technology, if economies of scale barely work? Why not invest instead in a service centre, outsourcing tasks and people to those who can provide those services to managers?

Another development could be that e-HR systems become more intelligent, with the result that there are no service centres. What are the implications? You do not incur the costs or have the complexity of outsourcing and/or setting up service centres. But it means that your systems need to be excellent and that they must be used. There is no backup. What happens in a shared-service-centre-free world is that managers and employees have no choice but to do all HR transactions online. In working online, for less frequent and more complex tasks, people will need an expert systems approach that is business scenario based and that will lead people through to the solution. Also, there is an underlying presumption that it is worth managers spending their time completing these more complex transactions, even if the system is well-designed and even infrequent transactions are made easy to undertake.

Some considerations are:

- How realistic is a predominantly e-HR world without the need for a shared service centre(s)?
- If you need a shared service centre(s), where can you get efficiencies of scale, either within the boundaries of HR or through merging back office activities?
- How do you maintain/improve service levels, creating a better customer experience?

- How do you get that balance right between technology and person interfaces with line customers?
- How far do you want to manage transactional activity through relationships or by contracts/service level agreements?

Whether provided in-house or outsourced, there are clearly opportunities to realise efficiencies and improve service levels by merging the activities of HR, IT finance, procurement – all the so-called "support" functions. Although superficially attractive, some organisations that have tried this route have found that the lack of functional control has resulted in a significant dip in service and quality levels, leading to the shared service centres being returned to functional control and functional specialisation. This experience underlines the need to think through carefully what kind of service you need as a business and the trade-offs you need to make in working through the issues above.

Issue 3: The role of the HR generalist

Organisations need to settle on the place of the HR generalist in the HR delivery model. Should the role be assumed by line managers, shared service centres, expert systems, external vendors or in-house strategic business partners?

If there is an in-house generalist presence, there is also a secondary issue to address concerning the level at which the generalist operates. Linked to some of the debate set out above there is, in our view, an emerging need for an HR role that sits between strategic business partner and the HR administrator. Driven by manager demand (and a preparedness to pay for this support), organisations need to consider whether there is a role for a cheaper and more effective local partner who does "HR stuff" one level above the routine transaction processing that individuals and line managers do. In these instances, what organisations may need is access to someone to provide a sounding board "on the ground" – where managers are based. What we have already noted is a relatively low-level (compared to the potential) exploitation and use of the wealth of information that is gathered and stored by e-HR systems. Some of this, of course, is relatively easy to report on and use. But there is other information, particularly around forecasting, planning and trends, that managers will look at infrequently or not at all. So the new role is potentially about making the most of the information that is present. It is about proactively looking at the information and taking the analysis of that information to line managers and suggesting ways to deal with it, or asking them what they want to do with it.

This is subtly different from the role of a strategic change agent. What we are suggesting here is that there is someone within the business (not placed in a service centre or down a phone line) available to work with middle management to help them to get far more out of their people. What we are also suggesting is that while a modern manager should be competent at looking after and managing their people, there is a debate to be had concerning whether they should in fact concentrate on their core strengths and what they can do to enhance the health and success of that business.

Taking this suggestion forward, this is explicitly *not* about trying to bring everyone up to the same standard, trying to iron out weaknesses in management and therefore potentially harming the core business activity. This is about concentrating on strengths. This model recognises that managers are not necessarily appointed as a result of their people management abilities, but more for other attributes and capabilities, such as thought leadership in their fields. The role of this junior HR generalist role should be to proactively mine the e-HR system for relevant data, equipped with a mandate to reach line managers and be the credible, value-adding face of HR.

This, we suggest, is a "grey area" between strategic level work (senior business partners within the organisation who look after people strategy and overall change) and the transactional level, which makes the employee champion role very real and works with the business to get the best out of teams at a lower level. Another added benefit from the line manager's point of view is that there is now a credible face of HR that middle managers can relate to, rather than a faceless service centre or outsourced function that may seem remote from the business.

Similarly, organisations need to explore how a strategic business partner approach should work in practice. In particular, there is the issue of proximity to the business that needs to be resolved: is the HR strategic business partner an integral part of the management team, or is the role played out as a partnership along the same lines as a strategic alliance with an external vendor might be?

If HR evolves to a position where the HR function focuses on strategic change, working primarily on significant projects (addressing the implications of new software and legislation and providing support on specific organisational changes), this indicates a move to a professional services type role – that of an internal consultant. Internal consultancy services may not be new, but having HR play a leading role as an internal consultant is. Taking this a step further, how beneficial would it be for similar-minded experts from other functions to join together to offer a combined set of services to bring solutions that cut *across* those functions – where relationship managers would work with the business to bring those solutions to the customers in an effective and focused way. This is a model that is very similar to professional service firms.

There may be benefits in this approach, particularly linked to clarifying the value proposition of internal support functions and being able to make better like-for-like comparisons with external providers. There are also significant downsides, not least the inefficiencies of internal charging and the different dynamic between internal and external support. Having said that, in exploring the generalist role of HR and in particular HR's value proposition, it is worthwhile presenting an internal consultancy model so that the organisation can work out the value it gains through day-to-day contact and involvement in the life of the business, and how much it is prepared to pay for this less tangible value.

Issue 4: The reputation of HR

When considering the evolving reputation of HR, one of the things to bear in mind are the questions around transactional versus strategic roles, and whether the organisation should only see HR in a strategic role, and not as a "transactor" at all. This builds on and complements some of the arguments above. If users/customers/clients experience poor transactional execution, the reputation of HR will be tarnished.

This argument suggests that transactions should be divorced from strategic HR roles. There are arguments for that around the reputation area, but if you think about how HR gains respect in organisations, it is about doing the transactional stuff well in order to get permission to go on to other strategic things. So if transactional things go badly, then developing a role that is more strategic will not get a look-in. But one of the issues that will remain is that if HR is divorced from knowledge and data, then information on the strategic roles will be diminished.

So you need to identify which areas are building and destroying HR's reputation; the activities managers put a value on and how effectively these are delivered. There are implications for HR measurement (see below) and for HR's ability to market itself and its capabilities to the business.

Issue 5: HR performance

The use of benchmarking in HR has improved greatly in recent years, and it is now commonplace in most HR functions. Benchmarking, though, has its limitations: ensuring that there is like-for-like comparison and focusing on lag performance indicators being two of them. But we recognise that there is an important place for benchmarking metrics, and expect them to be used into the future.

A bigger challenge for the HR function is to measure more clearly the value it contributes to each respective business. This involves talking to line managers more about the performance expectations of HR, and taking more time to link work to these expectations.

So, in considering your next steps in HR transformation, you need to address:

- how HR currently measures its performance;
- how managers measure HR's contribution (whether formally or informally);
- what set of measures is appropriate as a framework for the future.

Linked to issue 4 – the reputation of HR – there is also a fruitful debate to be had concerning how managers want to engage with HR's performance. Annual reports on HR, surveys of HR value delivery, regular management reporting and HR operating plans can all be effective ways of building partnership between the line and HR.

Issue 6: Organisational boundaries

As explored in Chapter 6, organising to deliver HR is becoming more complex, involving the HR function (which is likely to include generalists, specialists and possibly shared service centres), line managers, employees and external vendors of various types. Where you land organisationally will depend on the outcome of the debate around the issues raised in this section. Some of the broader issues to be addressed will concern the following:

- balance of resource between HR business partner (generalist) roles and in-house specialist roles;
- types of generalist needed (see above debate on the HR generalist);
- role of the line manager in managing people;
- need for a shared service centre (transactional) and where it is located (in HR, in-house but external to HR, or outsourced);
- level of involvement of external vendors.

Wherever the organisational lines are drawn, the challenges will be in managing the interfaces between the different organisational areas. The more complex the organisation, the greater will be the effort invested in managing these interfaces. As you develop the next step in your organisational model, you should think through these boundary issues: how you integrate the different elements of HR delivery and the investment you will need to make in ensuring a coherent and seamless service delivery.

Issue 7: HR capabilities

Chapters 1 and 6 address this issue in some detail, and we recommend that you draw on the resources in these chapters to take the debate forward in the business. It remains our contention that HR professionals need to build new capabilities above and beyond the traditional areas of HR. Specifically, they need to build a sound theoretical basis in the areas of organisational behaviour, business economics and psychology in order to support organisational development and change. Above all else, HR professionals must be recognised first and foremost for their contribution as business people – they must know their business and appreciate the drivers of value in their business. It is from this position that HR professionals will become influencers in their business.

The issues you may need to confront in thinking about your next steps in HR transformation are likely to include:

- what kind of capabilities you need to develop in your HR professionals;
- how your current HR professionals benchmark against these new capabilities;

- what investment you are prepared to make to develop these capabilities;
- what alternatives you have if your current HR professionals cannot step up.

There is a larger issue about HR capability touched on earlier in this book, which is this: if people are the greatest asset of a business, why is it so difficult to get the most able people into HR? This is not to say that there are no able people in HR – there are, and we have worked with and encountered many. But it is true to say that the profession has a talent deficit, and the demands that should be placed on HR in the future mean that we need to create an environment where people know that they will have an opportunity to work on some of the organisation's most difficult issues. Perhaps this too is an issue that might be explored in your business.

In writing this section on the future paradigm shift for HR we have, we hope, offered you a number of tools to explore these issues in your organisation. As we have stated from the outset, we make no apology for not providing the answer. There is no single answer. But we do hope that we have given you the tools to find the right next step for your organisation.

8.5 Conclusion

The transformation of HR to create value through people has a range of facets that have been debated and examined in this book. Key questions have been posed about the face of the HR function of tomorrow, and it is evident that numerous possibilities emerge as credible contenders. The crux of the matter appears to revolve around the perception of the quality of HR services, irrespective of how they are delivered, and when you unpack the features that contribute towards perception, you expose the main themes of cost, the relative capabilities of self-service, shared services, outsourcing and, crucially, the quality of the people in the HR function.

All too often – and the published literature is a testament to this – the *measurement* of perception of the quality of HR services is skewed towards methods designed and operated by HR itself. In other words, the process of data capture and analysis is often heavily influenced and filtered by HR so that the results fail to reflect the views of management and employee populations.

Looking ahead, therefore, one of the principles underpinning any new HR paradigm will be a robust and credible process for demonstrating ongoing value contribution that manifests itself as genuine perceived quality by the whole business, and not simply a vested interest group within the HR function. To achieve this outcome will demand HR to deploy appropriate disciplines in the creation, development and delivery of its services in such a way that its business becomes intimately and effectively interwoven with the broader business – and, more importantly, is perceived to be so.

The practical advice offered in the book wrestles with the opportunities and challenges associated in delivering such an important outcome, and is intended to contribute to the richness of debate so critical to the future of HR. Perhaps the ultimate determinant of the success of HR will be its own ability to source and develop human talent with the capability to shape and lead HR into a pre-eminent position within the business, where its own value is then truly perceived to be creating value through people.

9

Summary of Key Points and Actions

We thought that it would be helpful to hold in one place a summary of key actions associated with each chapter. So here it is …

Chapter 1 Getting Started

- Take some time to understand the tools and techniques presented here so that you feel confident to use them to support change and transformation.
- If you are involved with HR transformation, you need to consider the broader organisational system within which you need to bring about change – so across technology, work processes, people/culture, structure and performance outcomes.
- Recognise that change is a process and that you will need to work through its various stages step by step – building a compelling business case, planning, implementing and reviewing (which you will learn later in this book).
- Understand that stakeholder commitment to HR transformation needs to be secured and sustained throughout the transformation journey.
- Be able to demonstrate that the perceived costs of change are outweighed by a combination of clarity on the reasons for change, knowledge of how to make the next step to bring about change and a commitment to see things through.

Chapter 2 Envisioning the New World of HR

- Identify the main business drivers for change in your organisation.
- Engage key stakeholders with the "irresistible forces" to frame the context for HR transformation discussion.
- Decide which of the envisioning tools will be most appropriate to use in your organisation.
- Use the appropriate envisioning tools to develop a shared view on the current position of HR and the new world of HR.

Chapter 3 Service Delivery Approaches

The HR service model and its implementation must contain the following:

- Reflect the business requirements.
- Focus on delivering business benefit.
- Take full account of the impact of the service delivery approaches within the context of your own business environment.
- Recognise the importance of relationships as well as technical expertise, price and reputation in supplier selection.
- Manage the inherent tensions between cost savings and human interaction.
- Ensure that the management organisation is set up to succeed.
- Recognise and mitigate risks.
- Enable quality contracts to be negotiated, giving good value for all parties.

Chapter 4 Making the Business Case for Transformation

- Define benefits, ensuring that owners for benefits are in place and have taken responsibility for their delivery.
- Define and attribute ownership of costs.
- Work up the first draft of a business case engaging HR and the line areas.
- Develop your roadmap for implementation.

- Refine your business case as you clarify your plan, costs and benefits.
- Pay attention to both the "hard" and "soft" side of business case development.

Chapter 5 Stakeholder Engagement and Programme Management

- Invest time and effort segmenting/measuring the stakeholder community.
- Remember that the people you will be gathering data from or about have ongoing roles and responsibilities to do – be sensitive to this.
- Incorporate stakeholder engagement as a defined activity from day one.
- Deploy appropriate methods to determine their disposition towards the change process.
- Plan stakeholder campaigns to address issues and concerns, and invest most time and effort in securing the commitment of the stakeholders you have defined as highly important.
- Plan for regular measurement so that you can track movement on the resistance to commitment continuum.
- Act immediately on anyone identified as a "secret subversive".
- Ensure that you and the programme sponsor agree who will direct the programme and also ensure that that person has the capability and resources to do so.
- Ensure from the start that you monitor costs, benefits and key delivery milestones.
- Make sure throughout the programme implementation that appropriate stakeholder management is conducted, including an unwavering commitment from senior management.
- Never be afraid to admit to problems before they reach a serious and disruptive level.
- Make sure that the conditions of success of the programme remain clearly articulated and understood.
- Think about how the members of the programme team are going to be rehabilitated into the business when the programme is over.

Chapter 6 Implementation: Structure, Culture and Capability

- Identify the main channels used to deliver HR management in your organisation.
- Use the "straw man" scope of services to map *current* and *future* delivery of each aspect of HR management onto delivery channels.
- Use the above to assess the impact of HR transformation and to develop structural implications/options and impact on skills, capabilities and culture.
- Help HR professionals and line managers to understand what has changed, and use the straw man capability framework to help you achieve this.
- Invest heavily in developing the HR team and working through organisational boundary issues/integrating the work of HR.
- Make specific interventions to build the change leadership of the HR leaders.

Chapter 7 Implementation: Process, Technology and Benefits Realisation

- Define the e-HR solution in detail, ensuring that the interaction between people, process and technology is clearly articulated and the impact understood.
- Confirm that the process and technology solution will deliver the vision and the tangible and intangible benefits that were defined in the business case.
- Plan for resistance to change and develop mechanisms for assessing and addressing resistance.
- Build a benefits realisation plan to ensure that you can track and deliver the benefits contained in the business case.
- Ensure that you know and define your starting points in order to measure the progress of benefit delivery against the benefits realisation plan.
- Pay attention to moving from an HR transformation programme to "business as usual" by making measurement an ongoing activity, removing the old ways of doing things and continuing education and training after go-live.

Chapter 8 Taking Stock and Moving Forward

- Key questions have been posed about the face of the HR function of tomorrow, and it is evident that numerous possibilities emerge as credible contenders.
- Use the tools and frameworks described in this book to help you decide where you are on your transformation journey and what the most appropriate next steps will be.
- The crux of the matter appears to revolve around the perception of the quality of HR services, irrespective of how they are delivered, and when you unpack the features that contribute towards perception, you expose the main themes of cost, the relative capabilities of self-service, shared services, outsourcing and, crucially, the quality of the people in the HR function.
- All too often in reality – and the published literature is a testament to this – the *measurement* of perception of the quality of HR services is often heavily influenced and filtered by HR so that the results fail to reflect the views of management and employee populations.
- Looking ahead, one of the central tenets underpinning any new HR paradigm will be a robust and credible process for demonstrating ongoing value contribution that manifests itself as genuine perceived quality by the whole business and not simply a vested interest group within the HR function.
- HR needs to deploy appropriate disciplines in the creation, development and delivery of its services in such a way that its business becomes intimately and effectively interwoven with the broader business and, more importantly, is perceived to be so.
- Perhaps the ultimate determinant of the success of HR will be its own ability to source and develop human talent with the capability to shape and lead HR into a pre-eminent position within the business, where its own value is then truly perceived as creating value through people.

Appendix 1: Organisational Levers Output

Chapter Structure

In this appendix we have shown an example of how a client has used the organisational levers model to develop a set of "as is" and "to be" statements. We have shown just two of the levers: "Technology" and "People and culture", to illustrate its use.

As you will see, the descriptors are succinct, but specific enough to enable the next steps in the process to take place: gap analysis and project planning.

The example shown was actually produced 1 year after the initial envisioning exercise. By this stage, the HR transformation process was well under way, and this review point enabled the HR leadership group to take stock of where they were and to energise for the next 12 months.

A1.1 "As is"/"To be" Descriptors for Technology

As is	*To be*
■ SAP chosen as the global HR back office system; blueprint for development still being defined/outsourcing options still being considered ■ Areas for workflow have been identified, for example, recruitment and learning, but not yet implemented ■ e-HR implementation route map defined, limited functionality available and speed of implementation now critical for HR to realise greater efficiencies ■ Integration with non-HR systems planned but not yet implemented ■ Good progress has been made in defining common data standards and definitions ■ There is still some way to go before HR reporting is robust; ownership and accountability for business headcount is still an issue	■ Global HR back office system fully implemented, whether in-house or outsourced ■ e-tools implemented for all areas in e-HR business case ■ e-learning is embedded throughout the organisation ■ HR systems integrated with non-HR systems ■ Common data standards and definitions ■ Common HR reporting and enhanced HR decision support capability ■ HR knowledge databases implemented ■ HR has a high level of web enablement ■ High levels of IT literacy in the use of HR and office systems ■ Acquisitions and disposals cause no systems problems to HR or to the business ■ HR has stopped doing lots of transactional work following technology and culture/capability change

A1.2 "As is"/"To be" Descriptors for People and Culture

As is	*To be*
■ A smaller HR function is now mainly comprised of HR business partners and specialists	■ HR delivers to a high standard on the basics, mainly through e-HR and outsourcing
■ HR performance levels have been agreed and capability has been assessed at a high level, although much more communication is needed	■ The use of capability workshops, learning groups and knowledge management online will be the primary ways used to share knowledge, build capability and shape culture
■ A programme to build HR capability has been agreed but not yet implemented	■ The programme to build HR capabilities will have been delivered successfully
■ The function has still a way to go in changing the way it works with the line	■ Business partners and specialists will be influencing at a strategic level
■ The vision for manager and employee self-service has still to be fully communicated to the business	■ A high proportion of work will be delivered as a project with clear deliverables and scope
■ The HR conference touched on HR transformation, but there is still work to be done to engage the HR community with the HR transformation challenge and to develop the skills needed to deliver the task	■ Business partners are aligned with key business stakeholders
	■ HR professionals are valued by line managers as much for their business skills as their technical capability in HR matters
	■ Knowledge and capability is valued within the HR team more than seniority and length of service
	■ HR is considered by the line to be a valued consulting resource

Appendix 2: Management Perception Survey

This kind of survey would be deployed before the implementation of e-HR, and is designed to provide a broad baseline of perception towards the introduction of the new functionality. The results would inform the rollout phase; for example, if there were negative perception towards communication and support, this would be an area that would need more careful attention going forward.

During or post implementation, the survey could be more detailed and specific around particular aspects of e-HR functionality, and again the approach would be to understand the positive and negative drivers, to allow more focused effort in respect of any issues or concerns, and to celebrate success where appropriate.

It may then be helpful, particularly with the significant stakeholders, to probe these issues in more detail. This is usually best done in the form of focus groups or one-to-one interviews.

In this example, the Likert scale would be used for each question, and participants would select the most appropriate option from: Strongly Agree, Agree, Partly Agree/Disagree, Disagree, Strongly Disagree, Do Not Know, Not Applicable. The responses would then be mapped onto the scale below.

| Satisfactory/ favourable | Apathy/neutrality | Unsatisfactory/ unfavourable |

Pre-implementation Illustration

Demographics
Name: [Optional]
Age:
Less than 25
25–29
30–34
35–39
40–44
45–49
50–59
60 or above

Business function: [Title]

Management band: [Title/Grade]

Years employed:
Less than one year
between 1 and 2 years
between 2 and 5 years
between 5 and 10 years
between 10 and 20 years
20 years or more

Introduction to e-enabled Technology

1. e-enabling HR processes in the organisation is a positive step to the overall operation of the organisation.
2. Managers should be able to take more direct control of people issues using e-enabled technology.
3. Employees should be responsible for the management and correctness of their own personal data.

Data Quality and Integrity

1. I am confident that the data held within e-HR that I am personally responsible for will be accurate.

2. I will be able to rely on the data for management purposes.
3. Staff at all levels recognise the importance of the data held within e-HR in order to drive other online systems in the organisation.

System Flexibility

1. e-HR is a flexible system that will meet the needs of all employees who have access to it.
2. It will be easy to obtain management information from e-HR.

HR Support

1. The implementation of e-HR will improve the total quality of HR support available to me.
2. The implementation of e-HR will reduce my people management workload.
3. In general, HR business partners will provide the support I need as a manager.

Communication, Support and Training

1. The communication about e-HR has been informative and useful.
2. I understand my role as a manager when using e-HR.
3. I have received sufficient training to be able to use e-HR.

Further Comments

■ Please add any further comments you may have regarding any aspect of e-HR.

Appendix 3: Scope of HR Services

This appendix shows a scope of HR services template that we have found useful. It should be remembered that this template should be used in conjunction with the delivery channels, as many services will be delivered through multiple channels.

Service area	Scope
People development and performance management	■ Organisational values and culture ■ Organisational and role design ■ Change management ■ Organisational learning ■ Team development ■ Leadership development ■ Individual development ■ Technical/product training ■ Talent management and succession planning ■ Reward and retention strategy ■ Skills training ■ Employee opinion surveys ■ Performance management process
Resource management	■ Workforce planning ■ Recruitment and selection ■ Induction ■ Staff development ■ Assessment of potential ■ Employee release ■ Non-core and temporary employee management ■ International placements

(contd)

Service area	Scope
Employee relations and communication	<ul><li>Employer brand</li><li>Internal communication</li><li>Internal publications</li><li>Counselling/welfare</li><li>Compliance</li><li>Grievance/disciplinary</li><li>Consultation and negotiation</li><li>Diversity</li><li>Health and safety</li><li>Employment policies</li></ul>
Retention and reward	<ul><li>Compensation framework</li><li>Role evaluation</li><li>Performance related pay schemes</li><li>Commission schemes</li><li>Incentive plans</li><li>Share schemes</li><li>Retention strategies</li></ul>
HR information	<ul><li>Maintain employee data</li><li>Maintain organisational data</li><li>Employee reporting and information</li><li>Payroll</li><li>Pensions</li><li>Benefits and other payment administration</li></ul>

Appendix 4: Extract from an Accountabilities Workshop

Chapter Structure

This appendix shows an example output from an accountabilities workshop, in particular, the use of the scope of services document and delivery channels to record the changes in the role of line manager.

We also show the impact on the employee, another outcome of an accountabilities workshop.

A4.1 The Role of the Line Manager in People Management

Activity	*Expectations*
Strategy and organisation	*Stronger*
■ Business planning and budgeting	■ Engages with the HR business
■ HR strategy, planning and budgeting	partner early to ensure that
■ HR structure and work processes	the people issues are captured
■ External benchmarking	into the thinking

(contd)

Activity	Expectations
	■ Works with the HR business partner to influence budget decisions, particularly in presenting the case for investments in building human capital ■ Signs off and executes the people (HR) strategy ■ Defines acceptable HR performance standards and ensures they are met ■ Involves the HR business partner in mergers and acquisitions due diligence *Neutral* ■ Responsible for driving the business strategy and operational plans in their area ■ Responsible for setting the budgets in their area, and for working within the constraints placed upon them ■ Reviews regularly the effectiveness of the strategy and employees' understanding ■ Communicates the strategy to direct reports and to peers ■ Works with other people's strategies *e-HR impacted* ■ Availability of management information to development of strategy and plans
People development and performance management ■ Organisational values and culture ■ Organisational and role design ■ Business change management ■ Organisational learning ■ Team development	*Stronger* ■ Plays a leading role in making effective change happen in their area and is expected to use appropriate change management, tools and techniques

(*contd*)

Activity	Expectations
■ Individual development ■ Technical/product training ■ Talent management and succession planning ■ Reward and retention strategy ■ Skills training	■ Works in ways to shape the target culture and sets an example ■ Responsible for writing role definitions ■ Coaches individuals to help them raise their performance ■ Selects and builds high performing teams ■ Identifies and nurtures talent in their area, and acts as an advocate for the team ■ Employs appropriate retention strategies ■ Evaluates the effectiveness of learning and formalises feedback with HR *Neutral* ■ Responsible for the design of their department/area ■ Helps employees to shape their personal development plans ■ Supports employees to keep their knowledge and skills up to date ■ Ensures that direct reports are developed to perform effectively in their current role and for the future ■ Supports people through change ■ Sets and reviews performance against objectives ■ Acts as a mentor, for example, graduates and new joiners *e-HR impacted* ■ E-authorises development/ learning opportunities ■ Participates in the design and implementation of e-learning solutions ■ Performance management

(contd)

Activity	Expectations
Resource management ■ Workforce planning ■ Recruitment and selection ■ Induction ■ Staff development ■ Assessment of potential ■ Employee release ■ Temporary employee management ■ Global assignees	*Stronger* ■ Prepares the job/person specification and role requirements ■ Operates the recruitment process – which means picking up most (workflow generated) recruitment admin ■ Involved in pre-selection, interviewing and other assessment activities ■ Involved in attracting candidates via chat rooms, fairs, networking, etc. ■ For direct reports, holds first induction meeting and determines local induction requirements ■ Works with approved external suppliers ■ Handles most candidate queries *Neutral* ■ Initiates the recruitment need ■ Takes the recruitment decision ■ Defines the contract offer ■ Recruits internal staff in ways consistent with policy ■ Provides feedback on external suppliers *e-HR impacted* ■ Uses e-HR to capture learning around recruitment ■ E-recruitment process ■ Internal vacancy to employee profile matching ■ Automated employment contracts
Employee relations and communication ■ Employer brand ■ Internal publications	*Stronger* ■ Works in ways to promote a positive employee relations climate

(contd)

Activity	*Expectations*
■ Counselling/welfare ■ Compliance ■ Grievance/disciplinary ■ Consultation and negotiation ■ Diversity/equal opportunities ■ Communication of reward levels ■ Role evaluation	■ When required, handles grievance, disciplinary and poor performance issues in a timely and compliant manner ■ Ensures compliance with policy and procedures ■ Consults team on proposed changes to working practices (especially important in EU countries in the light of Works Council Directive) ■ Understands and uses market data on rewards to inform decisions ■ Culturally sensitive, and promotes this sensitivity in the team ■ Able to work in different employment/legal environments ■ Involved in company consultative bodies (wherever appropriate) ■ Responsible for communicating with their teams ■ Manages in a fair way, without reference to race, gender, disability, etc. *Neutral* ■ Provides first instance counselling and welfare support ■ Responsible for health and safety in their area ■ Sets expectations on reward levels and recommends individual compensation awards ■ Recommends people for promotion *e-HR impacted* ■ Pay review process
HR information ■ Maintain employee data ■ Maintain organisational data	*Stronger* ■ Maintains organisational data (e-HR related)

(contd)

Activity	Expectations
■ Employee reporting and information ■ Payroll ■ Pensions ■ Benefits and payment admin	■ Gives feedback on the effectiveness of e-HR/ participates in systems improvements *e-HR impacted* ■ Maintains organisational data – information on their staff ■ Authorises a whole range of amendments via e-HR, where financial changes are involved; contractual changes; absence; awards; health tests; learning; company equipment; carry-over of leave ■ Self-service reports

The workshop considered the likely tension between line pull (e.g. wanting more flexible compensation arrangements) and HR push (e.g. making time to run assessment centres will lead to more effective recruitment decisions). People thought that this tension was inevitable and desirable. They did not believe that this tension detracted from the aim of making the line more accountable for people management and HR more accountable for providing a unique contribution to improve performance.

A4.2 Line Manager: Priority Knowledge and Skills

If the line manager is to meet the HR management requirements of their role as defined in the section above, the largest capability gaps that need to be closed are:

Teams

■ selecting excellent people, who will not only perform well individually but also as part of a team (real or virtual);
■ building high-performing teams, which includes the skills and activities that underpin this, such as coaching.

There was an issue raised under the label of delegation that relates to "team". The underlying issue was that too much manager time is spent on technical problem-solving and not on managing. The need is to redress this imbalance, for managers to develop capability in their team to deliver on the technical side while they focus on the task of management. Part of the reason for this imbalance is that people are promoted to the position of manager usually because of their excellent technical skills.

Operating as a Global Manager

- working across geographies;
- working across different national cultures;
- understanding different legal employment frameworks;
- working in virtual teams.

Change Management and Change Readiness

- using appropriate tools and techniques to prepare for change;
- using appropriate tools and techniques to bring about effective change in their area.

Communication

- specific communication skills such as using video conferencing, speaking in other national cultures, and public speaking;
- broader communication skills such as identifying stakeholders, and communicating in a matrix organisation.

Other skills identified that were not considered quite so high a priority were:

- IT literacy;
- managing conflict;
- diversity;
- decision-making;
- how the line can use different elements of the reward tool kit;
- leadership, the ability to motivate the organisation;
- commercial awareness, where they fit into the overall strategy.

A4.3 The Role of Employees in Delivering HR Management

Activity	Expectations
Strategy and organisation	*Neutral* ■ Should be engaged in the business planning process for their area ■ Provides feedback to inform business and HR planning through surveys, such as employee opinion surveys ■ Should be able to articulate the basic principles of the strategy
People development and performance management	*Stronger* ■ Provides feedback on manager (and peer) performance ■ Shares knowledge with colleagues ■ Recommends improvements in work ■ Demonstrates the values and culture *Neutral* ■ Works with their line manager to shape their personal development plan ■ Works with their line manager to keep their skills and knowledge up to date ■ Attends booked training/learning ■ Implements agreed change *e-HR impacted* ■ Self-service e-learning opportunities ■ Places learning bookings online ■ Registers/enrols on learning events ■ Provides feedback on training received ■ Maintains training records
Resource management	*Stronger* ■ Refers vacancies to friends *Neutral* ■ Provide personal information for records and payroll in time specified *e-HR impacted* ■ Candidate application online ■ Candidate accept/decline online

(contd)

Activity	*Expectations*
	■ Make use of available e-induction ■ Use e-recruitment for internal applications ■ Candidate chat rooms ■ Provide personal information for records and payroll in time specified
Employee relations and communication	*Stronger* ■ Represents company and promotes the employment brand ■ Demonstrates cultural awareness and sensitivity *Neutral* ■ Understand and follow grievance procedure ■ Participation in communication/ consultation activities ■ Provides feedback on employee satisfaction surveys ■ Maintains high safety standards *e-HR impacted* ■ Intranet delivered communication ■ e-delivered employee surveys ■ HR policies delivered through e-HR
HR information	*Stronger* ■ Self-service update of personal details as defined by the system (e-HR impacted) *Neutral* ■ Initiates changes in personal details, whether manually or electronically ■ Initiates recording of absence, vacation, sickness, etc. *e-HR impacted* ■ Self-service update of personal details as defined by the system ■ Makes changes to benefits

References and Further Reading

References

Becker, B.E. and Huselid, M.A., *High Performance Work Systems and Firm Performance: A Synthesis of Research and Managerial Implications*, Research in Personnel and Human Resources Management, 1998

Beckhard, R. and Harris, R.T., *Organisational Transitions*, Addison-Wesley, 1987

Bridges, W., *Managing Transitions: Making the Most of Change*, Perseus Books, 1993

Connor, D.L., *Managing at the Speed of Change*, New York: Wiley, 1998 www.getcommitment.com

Lawler, E.E. and Mohrman, S.A., *Creating a Strategic Human Resources Organisation*, Stanford University Press, 2003

Lev, B., *Intangibles*, The Brookings Institution, 2001

O'Farrell, B. and Furnham, A., *2002 European e-HR Survey*, University of London and IHRIM Europe, October 2002

Schein, E., *Process Consulting Revisited*, Addison-Wesley, 1998

Thew, B., *Dramatic Changes in Store for HR in Outsourced Future*, paper published by Ceridian, April 2004

Towers Perrin, *HR BPO Comes of Age: From Expectation to Reality*, 2004

Ulrich, D., *Human Resource Champions*, Boston: Harvard Business School, 1997

eHR™: *Getting Results Along the Journey – 2002 Survey Report*, Watson Wyatt, 2002

Further Reading

Becker, B.E. and Huselid, M.A., *Overview: Strategic Human Resource Management in Five Leading Firms*, Human Resource Management, 1999

Becker, B.E., Huselid, M.A. and Ulrich, D., *The HR Scorecard: Linking People, Strategy and Performance*, Boston: Harvard Business School, 2001

Coetsee, L., From resistance to commitment, *Public Administration Quarterly*, 23, 1999

Dyson, J.R., *Accounting for Non-Accounting Students*, 3rd edition, Pitman Publishing, 1994

Kettley, P. and Reilly, P., *e-HR: An Introduction*, IES Report 398, 2003

Reddington, M., Williamson, M. and Withers, M., *Delivering Value from HR Transformation*, Roffey Park Institute, 2003

Reddington, M., Williamson, M. and Withers, M., Shared vision, *Personnel Today*, 23 March 2004; 26

Reddington, M., Williamson, M. and Withers, M., Secure the stakeholder's commitment, *Personnel Today*, 30 March 2004; 24

Reddington, M., Williamson, M. and Withers, M., Realising the benefits, *Personnel Today*, 06 April 2004; 22

Reilly, P. and Williams, T., *How to Get Best Value from HR – The Shared Services Option*, Gower, 2003

Richardson, R. and Thompson, M., *Issues in People Management: The Impact of People Management Practices on Business Performance*, The Chartered Institute of Personnel and Development, 1999

Index

Index